THE WOMEN WHO RAISED ME

VICTORIA ROWELL

THE WOMEN WHO RAISED ME

— A MEMOIR —

WM

WILLIAM MORROW
An Imprint of HarperCollins*Publishers*

THE WOMEN WHO RAISED ME. Copyright © 2007 by Victoria Rowell. All rights reserved. Printed in the United States of America. No part of this book may be used or reproduced in any manner whatsoever without written permission except in the case of brief quotations embodied in critical articles and reviews. For information address HarperCollins Publishers, 10 East 53rd Street, New York, NY 10022.

HarperCollins books may be purchased for educational, business, or sales promotional use. For information please write: Special Markets Department, HarperCollins Publishers, 10 East 53rd Street, New York, NY 10022.

FIRST EDITION

Designed by Susan Yang

Library of Congress Cataloging-in-Publication Data has been applied for.

ISBN: 978-0-06-124659-3
ISBN-10: 0-06-124659-X

07   08   09   10   11 WBC/RRD 10   9   8   7   6   5

I WISH TO DEDICATE MY BOOK TO
foster and adoptive parents and their families,
caregivers, neighbors, communities, charities, social workers,
justices, and legislators who fight for and feed orphans,
and orphans of the living, domestically and globally . . .

and to my children, Maya and Jasper,
who have given me unconditional love.

Do not look around to discover other people's ruling principles, but look straight to this, to what nature leads you, both the universal nature through which things happen to you, and your own nature through the acts which must be done by you.

—THE MEDITATIONS OF MARCUS AURELIUS

Dorothy Mabel Bevan Sawyer Collins Rowell
Bertha Taylor
Laura Sawyer
Retha Dunn
Agatha C. Wooten Armstead
Esther "Bird" Doliber
Marion Wooten Williams
Theodora Wooten Roberts
Ruth Wooten Williams
Kathleen Armstead Kimber
Sylvia Armstead Robinson
Valentina Pereyslavec
Millie Spencer
Paulina Ruvinska Dichter

CONTENTS

THE VIEWING

For anyone who has spent any portion of their childhood as a ward of the state, the notion of emancipation has multiple meanings. Though I was legally and financially emancipated at the requisite age of eighteen and had always been fiercely independent, it wasn't until I was forty-three years old and a working mother of two that I finally set myself free.

The turning of the wheels that led to my true emancipation began some time in mid-2002 when I did the unthinkable, something that (at least where I come from and where I live, work, and drive in L.A.'s fast lane) has always been taboo: I became still.

Into a cave of introspection I crept while a tidal wave of memories and feelings crashed upon me all at once. Overwhelmed by primal rip currents that I had supposedly outdanced, outrun, outswum, and outloved, I reached out to all that was tangible, real, and known about my early life—facts, documents, records, chronologies, even maps.

Of particular interest was a medical report of an event that took place in 1968 in Portland, Maine, that had gone unreported by the press. It involved a middle-aged Caucasian woman by the name of Dorothy Mabel Collins who was severely injured when—in order to escape an unidentified pursuer—she leapt from the third-floor balcony of her apartment.

Barely breathing, she was rushed by ambulance to the local emergency room. A descendant of bona fide Yankee blood, Dorothy called on the survival skills of her Howland-Collins forebears. They had come from the rocky shores of rugged Anglo-Saxon England, settling into similar straits in Castine, Cape Jellison in Stockton Springs, and Searsport, Maine, as well as various points in Massachusetts in the early 1800s. Before that, an early ancestor, John Howland, made the voyage to America aboard the *Mayflower*. It was never made clear if he had jumped ship or fell overboard, but one thing was certain, Howland survived. This history was documented by Dorothy's sister, Elizabeth Collins Babineau, a former member of the Mayflower Society. Dorothy was a twelfth-generation descendant of John Howland. As her daughter, I am a member of the thirteenth generation.

The Collins clan scattered itself across American history: My great-grandfather, Joseph Collins, was born in 1848 and lied about his age so that he could serve in the Civil War, first a member of the Thirty-first Maine Infantry, then a drummer boy for the Sixteenth Regiment, from 1864 to his discharge on July 17. He had the great honor of meeting President Abraham Lincoln and commented on how soft the president's hands were. Joseph married Sarah Pressey, whose first husband was lost at sea. Two of their sons, Willard and Warren Collins, became famed doctors of Roxbury, Boston, and Framingham, Massachusetts, and Castine, Maine, in the late 1800s. Warren E. Collins of the Warren E. Collins Company, Boston, Massachussetts, manufactured medical instruments as well as the Collins-Dinker tank respirator, also known as the iron lung, which saved countless people stricken with bulbar polio. According to my aunt Elizabeth, these were the more "toney" Collinses. My grandfather Harry S. Collins, decided not to go into a medical profession; instead, he became a fisherman, working on the weirs in Castine Harbor, Searsport, and Stockton Springs. The Collins family was of good pedigree and strong marriages and the family name would not be tarnished even if Warren Collins Jr.'s wife, Helen, hung herself. My great-aunt Zillah loved to paint as much as she might have loved other women but was prohibited to do so. They were a hardy stock throughout New England. The *Mayflower,* the iron lung, the famed Collins–Sawyer doctors of Massachusetts—Dorothy was descended from all of this.

And despite her fall from three floors, and the dire predictions about her ability to survive this ordeal, Dorothy escaped death this time, at least as it was measured in mortal terms. But she was never able to escape her insidious predator: schizophrenia, a debilitating hereditary disease.

During that period in mid-2002, I tried to disentangle my own history from the few remnants of information I had managed to salvage about Dorothy.

Over the years, my mother and I met in person no more than three times. Following her actual death from lung cancer in September 1983, I had made unsuccessful attempts to reclaim her for posterity, if for no one but myself. That was what I told my daughter, Maya Elizabeth, during a 2004 Fourth of July Rowell-Collins family reunion and barn raising in Paris, Maine. We rented a fishing boat in Camden; the captain navigated the waters, docking safely in Castine Harbor. On foot, I returned with my daughter, walking past palatial summer camps built by wealthy cotton, lumber, and shoe industrialists, formally known as the "Rusticators," who vacationed there in the 1800s, calling it "The Summer Playground of the Nation." We arrived at Dorothy's burial site, high on a knoll where she was laid to rest in the family plot amid untold numbers of ancestors. Scattered throughout the cemetery were the Bevans, the Sawyers, and the Collinses. On our knees, Maya and I cleared the weeds around my mother's stone, no wider than twenty inches across, flush with the earth. I often wondered if her family had sunk her stone into the earth deliberately, amid all the illustrious ancestral headstones in the cemetery, out of view and perhaps out of mind.

I looked across the vista, imagining the battles fought between the French, British, Dutch, and Americans—from the Breda Treaty in 1667 deeding the land to Jean Vincent d'Abbadie de Saint-Castin, to the British evacuation in 1815, when Castine finally became an American town. This history was important to me as my own personal history. I could not forget Dorothy, no matter how circuitous our journey had been; I knew she loved me.

> *Life counts not hours by joy or pains,*
> *But just by duties done.*
> *And when I lie on the green kirkyard*
> *With the mould upon my breast,*
> *Say not that she did well or ill,*
> *Only she did her best.*
> —Dorothea L. Dix, 1802–1887

My dear friend Dura Winder took a picture of Maya and me after we placed fresh-cut wildflowers around Dorothy's stone. I sat on the grass next to my mother in death and hoped that my fifteen-year-old daughter, Maya, in life, would continue to make this pilgrimage in my absence to sing this poem to her grandmother.

In 1999 I made a trip alone to Maine to visit the aging Hallowell granite-and-brick asylum where my mother had spent portions of her adult life. It is one of the oldest psychiatric hospitals in the nation, which opened in October 1840 under the direction of Dr. Cyrus Knapp and world famous Dr. Isaac Ray as the Maine Insane Hospital ten years after Governor Jonathan Hunton urged in his annual address to the legislature the need for a mental institution. It was later known as the Augusta Mental Health Institute, once treating as many as eighteen hundred patients at a time. I became a human camera, snapping and freezing images in rapid succession over the course of my drive there by rental car. At first glimpse, the nineteenth-century sprawling Victorian estate was the ghostly manor I had expected, guarded by wrought-iron gates through which I drove tentatively. Later, I learned that a number of buildings on the grounds had been used for ammunitions storage during the Civil War. Hopeful, afraid, and determined, I forged on.

After parking, I slowly climbed the steps past an administrator, too preoccupied to notice me, and brazenly ascended the fine mahogany staircase. I soon became unnerved and went back downstairs to the reception area to explain myself. Behind a glass window, the receptionist's face showed classic, weathered Maine lines and silver hair as she invited me to go upstairs, where I was shown into a parlor. There, I was introduced to the director of the asylum; his face and voice personified kindness. He bore no remarkable traits of age or accent and was of such striking Cary Grant good looks that I wondered what he was doing there. I asked if he remembered my earlier calls.

"Yes," he said, and nodded his agreement, remembering my phone call and to let me go to where Dorothy had once slept.

With my heart pounding wildly, I could see the ends of my curls vibrating as we approached her door. Then it opened.

Although it was a gray day, light streamed in through a gable. I felt the atomic fragments of Dorothy's faded presence and, I daresay, her anguish. In the background were patients, languishing in a medicinal haze, perhaps holding on to the hope that someday a loved one might come to rescue them. But this day, I had come to rescue and resurrect my mother.

Of course, my mother, Dorothy, wasn't there at all. She remained there as I had frozen her in my imagination in this cold, yet strangely serene place. A place she so desperately wanted to escape from. A place from where she had written so many letters to me, never describing where she was—only where she wasn't.

I asked to see every room, every corner. I went to the morgue, to the rooftop, to the industrial-size laundry room where Dorothy had worked, to the vast exterior where sun peeked through clouds sending pools of light on fields once farmed by my mother as a kind of occupational therapy. I continued to walk to the river bank overlooking the state capitol separated by the Kennebec. I remembered reading that in 1840 Governor John Fairfield believed the site was chosen so that future legislatures and governors would see it out their windows and never forget this hospital that housed "one hundred lunatic persons, furiously mad." Slowly I walked back to the buildings and was escorted to the basement where there had once been holding cages, the wrought iron gates now removed from the granite. I poked my index finger into one of the holes, crossed the threshold, sat down, and cried with my mother's anguished tears.

I had felt something for Dorothy from the moment we first met, even though her visit was unannounced to Forest Edge, the farm in West Lebanon, Maine, an almsfarm township in the 1800s, where I spent my early childhood.

No one, not even Agatha, the woman I called "Ma," explained who this outsider was. We were black. She was not. For me, at seven years old, the world broke down simply that way. Still, she was more than a stranger. In her pink gingham food-stained dress, hair swept up into a messy French twist. Compromised beauty. All tortured.

As an adult I acquired a photograph of a much different Dorothy Mabel Collins Rowell, taken in the 1950s. She had Elizabeth Taylor good looks. Creamy white skin, thick black hair, laughing eyes. An abandon. Maybe a wild side. She didn't drink or smoke, I was told, but she loved music, dancing, and strong black military men.

Dorothy bore six children. First there were two boys, then three girls—of whom I was the youngest—and then another boy. We were each of different paternity but all given the last name of Dorothy's first and only husband, Norman Rowell Sr.—a motorcycle-riding, trailer-inhabiting white man from Bath whose heart was permanently broken when she left him. Eventually Dorothy's family and the law interceded, deeming Dorothy unfit to raise her four younger children, all born out of wedlock. Whether this had mainly to do with the different fathers being Hispanic and African American was never admitted. Nonetheless, court correspondence does support this conclusion.

Who was my birth mother? How did her mental illness first manifest? The answers were not in a second photograph of Dorothy, on a dark, barren landscape alongside her three storklike, old-crone-looking Collins sisters, whose expressions appear much more disturbed than hers.

My childhood memories were just as cryptic. Though her visit to Forest Edge when I was seven years old had been unexplained at first, I later found out that her three-day stay had been carefully planned in trademark Agatha Armstead fashion—meaning that it was done for a reason, to gently introduce Dorothy to me, paving the way for an understanding of what that word *foster* meant. It was a word that went before everything, like a prefix, whenever I was introduced to the world. Such explanations had never mattered before at Forest Edge, where residents and regular visitors were all treated as family.

Despite Dorothy's violent Tardive, Dyskinesia tremors, a type of Parkinson's caused by years of prescribed Thorazine, chemotherapy, Prolixin, Serentil, Navane, Akineton, Mellaril, Tofranil, Valium, Coqentin, Enanthate, Permitil, and Quide, her unkempt state, the pink gingham dress that was too girlish for a woman who was too young to have hair turned prematurely white, and though I was confused and afraid, there was a gravitational pull between us. It wasn't a recognition, because I couldn't see my face in hers. But as she came into first view in the evening twilight, standing awkwardly on the unpaved Barley Road at the foot of the path leading up to the house, I experienced the same farm girl's response that I had to discarded robin hatchlings that had fallen from their nests. Compassion. I had never seen a woman in such a weakened state. Agatha, "Ma" to everyone, was the epitome of strength, young looking in her midsixties, a black Bostonian born in the Carolinas, with a mix of Kickapoo Indian in her background.

"Come in and take a load off," Ma sang out, beckoning Dorothy inside the house, telling her that supper was ready and waiting for her, leading her to the seat of honor at the head of our royal blue painted dining room table, and communicating to me with her eyes as if to say: "Sit closer, she won't bite." Still a little scared, I smiled politely and bowed my head as Agatha led us in saying grace.

Dorothy rocked back and forth, eating ravenously. Food was barely in her mouth before she pierced the next forkful. From where I sat, it was possible to see her foot shaking uncontrollably. This ravaged person could not be my mother. But that was what Agatha said at this dinner, in front of Dorothy, as honestly, courageously, and plainly as possible.

In time, the simple humanity that had played out in front of my eyes would hang like a jewel in my memory: the unselfishness of two women from two entirely different backgrounds coming together with the sole concern of the child they had in common. But I would have to get past the idea that I was Dorothy's daughter, born in sin, unable to be absolved no matter how many confessions I made or how many Hail Marys I said.

Ultimately, what mattered most was that I would have to absolve myself for the shame I had felt about Dorothy, for the unintended flashes of feeling that stick in the windpipe of self-forgiveness.

One flash: the horrendous sound of vomiting I hear at age seven from the cot in the dining room where I sleep when company comes. It's in the middle of the night after dinner, after Dorothy had gorged herself, when she rose to go to the bathroom and woke the house.

Ma's footsteps followed the thunder of Dorothy vomiting into the bathroom sink.

Ma's spirited reprimand came next. "Dorothy, what on earth are you doing? You will not leave all that mess in the sink." I listened as Ma explained that the children would have to use the bathroom for washing up in the morning before school. Dorothy whimpered in apology as Agatha helped her clean it up.

Why, I wondered, had Dorothy thrown up in the sink and not the toilet?

My world was in jeopardy. Scrunching down into the bedding on the cot, I can think only of how badly I wanted her to leave.

When Monday morning finally came, all I wanted was for the school bus to whisk me away to West Lebanon Elementary. When at last it came, I ran to meet it; my next prayer was that Dorothy wouldn't follow me anywhere close to where anyone on the bus could see her.

But she did. Not discreetly. Dorothy stood in plain view, there for everyone and God to see, dressed in that same stained pink gingham dress, a prideful mother taking center stage, waving good-bye right at me.

Numb by now, I stumbled to a green leather seat and fixed my eyes straight ahead.

The little girl sitting next to me asked, "Who is that?"

"I don't know."

I remember my heart beating at an alarming rate—out of embarrassment but also because I had denied Dorothy as my mother. When I came home later that day from school, I found Agatha pruning her prized Double Syringa shrub. As I walked toward her, Agatha turned to me unprovoked and answered the question in my eyes: "She's gone."

I was fifteen years old the next time I laid eyes on Dorothy. I had been living in and around Boston for much of the previous seven years, with various foster families, while studying at the Cambridge School of Ballet. Again, Agatha met an unannounced Dorothy at the Trailways bus station in downtown Boston and lovingly arranged a meeting for us at an adjacent Howard Johnson's, lending support by her presence. Nothing of note happened during this brief encounter until it was time to leave, and I excused myself to use the bathroom. I couldn't help but notice Dorothy following me, several steps behind. Once inside, without warning, she grabbed me, sobbing and involuntarily trembling. I'm not sure why I stood there, immobile, in the face of what seemed hideous. But I did.

Helplessly, Dorothy gave me a last embrace, mumbling something incoherent. Mother to child. Her cries became louder and more desperate. Grief-stricken and guilty. In my periphery were other women passing this spectacle in the Howard Johnson's bathroom, stealing glances. I pried Dorothy's arms from around my fifteen-year-old waist and said, "I can't be late for ballet class."

Her wet face just looked up at me.

But my last image of her from that meeting came a short while later, as I marched up the cobblestone street to catch my train, when I turned to witness a sight that bound together all the scattered moments of my first fifteen years of life, sending me off into a looming future. There they were, Dorothy and Agatha, arm in arm, linked together in such a way that it was impossible to tell who was supporting whom, both waving, both solemn.

On that day, I waved once and never looked back because I couldn't bear to do so.

A number of years later, during a period in my early twenties, I was ready to look back but it was too late. By this time I had done an exhaustive search and had found my three brothers, not all of them wanting to be found. However, my main ally was my half-brother David Rowell, second-born in our lineage, another motorcycle-riding, guitar-strumming vintage car enthusiast, who had responded to my initial effort to make contact by climbing on his Harley and roaring all the way down from Maine to Manhattan to meet me. David was the one who called me in the spring of 1983 to tell me that our mother, Dorothy, was dying of lung cancer. Grateful for the information, I tried to get in touch with her, but I was kept at bay by Dorothy's gatekeeper, her spinster sister Lillian, who wanted nothing to do with me.

Pickled by the vinegar of her meanness, well preserved and energetic for her advanced years, Lillian had no qualms about referring to me as one of the "nigger children" in a letter she had written to Agatha years earlier. Agatha sat me down one evening after Girl Scouts and read it aloud, unedited, so that I could further understand my circumstances and the hard cold truth about the world I lived in. I was seven

years old. Lillian's insufferable bigotry warned that I should never en-
tertain the idea of visiting Dorothy in Maine, stating that I would be an
embarrassment. I almost never crossed that line.

To her only credit, Lillian took care of my mother in the last years of
her tortured life. It was there, in Bath, Maine, that my brother David,
who was white and lived in a neighboring township, drove me in freezing temperatures in his 1935 Ford pickup so that I could see Dorothy one
last time. We stood outside, tossing pebbles at Lillian's window, calling
for our mother, who lay bedridden. Even with the shouted demands of
my brother, whom Lillian adored, she remained defiant as we yelled out,
"Lillian, let us in!" She refused, answering with a sealed door.

In September 1983, David phoned me in Boston to say our mother
had died. He mentioned that a funeral service was being planned but left
the decision of whether to go and the logistics for attending up to me. I
immediately realized that although David had accepted me as his sister
and his kindness had led him to inform me of our mother's passing, he
would not impose his decisions on the rest of the Collins-Rowell family.

Calling the funeral director at the Mayo Funeral Home proved to
be unsuccessful. "The funeral is private at the request of the Collins
family," he said.

"But I'm one of Dorothy Collins Rowell's children."

"I'm sorry, but you're not on the guest list." He added, "Mrs. Rowell
only had three sons."

"That's not correct," I said as I shook with anger. "She also had
three daughters."

Apologizing that there was nothing more that he could do, the funeral director hung up.

With barely enough money for bus fare to travel from Boston to
Maine and no money for lodging, I hesitantly called an ex-boyfriend
and convinced him to use his credit card to book a room for me at the
only motel in the area. I packed a garment bag with my blue-and-white
polka-dot dress and my ubiquitous white gloves for my mother's
funeral and I headed out.

The bus, I soon learned, had a final stop some thirty miles away from the funeral home, but dropped me within walking distance to the motel. As I set off, the starless night sky reminded me that by mid-September, temperatures in coastal Maine can be notoriously unpredictable, often plunging to below freezing, with sudden snow flurries—just like the ones that had begun to fall. Though I was not dressed for the onslaught of early winter, I was too focused on reaching my destination to feel the cutting air.

I arrived at the motel, which turned out to be a very low frills truck stop. And worse, the woman at the desk had no reservation for me. Obviously, my ex had failed to make the reservation.

Cold and with no place to sleep, I dug in and curled up on a lobby couch until the night clerk offered, "Hey, Miss, I've got a used room that a trucker just checked out of. Do you want it?" I said, "Yes."

The next morning I awoke to a long trek before me. I headed up the ramp on to the highway, in the same clothes that I slept in, with my garment bag slung over my left arm. I had a peace of no understanding as I stuck out my thumb, knowing that my Saint Christopher's medal would protect me.

I walked backward on the shoulder of the highway, and it wasn't long before a pickup truck pulled over. We shared few words but the driver was good-natured.

He dropped me off at the edge of town, blocks away from the funeral home, and so I trudged through the melting snow, passing a diner with a small floral shop. A single bell rang above the door as I entered, causing some customers to turn and stare. With my last dollar, I purchased a single red rose.

Finally, I reached the door of the Mayo Funeral Home, a 1920s white clapboard structure on a knoll. I knocked, and from behind a lace-curtained window, the funeral director peered out at me, then opened the door in silence. We did not exchange any words except:

"I'm Vicki Rowell, Dorothy's daughter."

Noticing my garment bag, he said, "Please use my room upstairs to change. You are the first to arrive." I thanked him and signed the guest book.

I began to head upstairs but stopped. To my left was Dorothy, lying ever so peacefully, her delicate profile still evident. With all the grace that I could muster, I gently approached, not fearing her lifeless body but rather feeling, even in death, our indisputable bond. We were finally having our visit. I placed the solitary rose in the crease of the cream-tufted casket, to represent her daughters, two of whom were not present, and went upstairs. I looked around the stark bedroom; everything was neatly placed: comb, brush, and other toiletries. I laid my garment bag across the bed and unzipped it, removing my unwrinkled dress. I looked at myself in a small vanity mirror atop a chest of drawers before sliding on the gloves I wore for reasons I kept so secret, I hadn't even come into a full understanding of their mystery. I reassured myself and headed downstairs.

The Collins family had begun to arrive. Their expressions changed from indignant stares to mild-mannered nods, and even smiles. Some whispered comments, like "Oh, she's not that bad" and "Can we take a picture of you with your mother?"

The Collinses asked in a matter-of-fact manner as though Dorothy was still alive. I realized this would be the only photograph of my mother and me together, so I obliged with the stipulation that they send me copies. And they did.

I stood in front of Dorothy's casket and looked defiantly into the Collinses' collective lens. *Flash* went their cameras. At some point, I was joined by my three older brothers. The look on Lillian's face when she saw me standing with them was one of disgust and disbelief. She sat by herself on the opposite side of the chapel, staring out a stained-glass window. In my mind, Dorothy was having the last say. And so was I.

Following the service, members of the Collins family invited me to attend the burial. In that moment, I remembered Agatha's amazing grace, how if it were not for her, I never would have had any relationship with my natural mother. So I simply smiled and said, "No, thank you."

David gave me a ride back to the bus station, and I solemnly returned to Boston feeling fulfilled, at least for now. After a lifetime of exclusion and denial, I had found the courage to show up. It was the courage to reveal a family's secret that I was the human stain on the blue-blood pedigree: Dorothy's daughter, a thirteenth direct descendant of John Howland, a daughter of Maine. I confronted a part of my family in a funeral home, in Maine, on September 11, 1983. That was the viewing that had truly taken place.

But maybe there was another reason I didn't attend her burial. Maybe I wasn't ready to let her go. In the days and years that followed, I tried to know the mother who had evaded me all that time, not only with visits to her gravesite, and later to the mental asylum in Augusta, but by obtaining her records from the state hospital, and by poring over every hard-won photograph, the first of which I waited ten years to acquire after a request from a family member, or every scrap of a clue I could locate, all of this done in an effort to decode her illness, to rescue her finally.

In 2002, almost twenty years after her death, it occurred to me in the midst of my self-imposed seclusion that it was time to come out from Dorothy's shadow, to release myself from the search to know who she was. It was time to truly emancipate, to search for Vicki, and to do so by turning my attention to the gifts I had been given, not only from Agatha Armstead, but from the many surrogate mothers, grandmothers, aunts, fosterers, mentors, grande dames, and sisters who were as much in my blood as was my own blood—the women who raised me.

It was time to tell their story—and mine.

PART ONE

GRANDMOTHERS, MOTHERS, AUNTS

(1959–1968)

I do but say what she is. So delicate with her needle:
an admirable musician! O, she will sing the savageness out of a bear.
Of so high and plenteous wit and invention!
OTHELLO
—WILLIAM SHAKESPEARE

BERTHA C. TAYLOR

What comes first, before conscious memory, before recorded images, and before the oral accounts that later helped me understand what happened during my first two and a half years of life, is a melody. It's the sound of a lullaby sung by a woman who loves me infinitely, in a full voice that is untrained but on-key, perhaps with a frill here and there that she would never dare use at choir practice or in church, but allows herself just for me. The melody is accompanied in my primal senses by the sensation of motion, as I am held to her bosom and rocked.

Fittingly, my life begins with a dance—a waltz!

Out of this music and movement, other impressions remain of my first foster mother, Bertha Taylor, who received me from the Holy Innocents Home, the orphanage connected to Mercy Hospital in Portland, Maine. When I was three weeks old, Bertha took me to her home, fifteen miles away in the small town of Gray, Maine, with the absolute conviction that she would raise me to adulthood as her own. I know in my cells that this was her maternal plan, just as I know how generously and tenderly every day she kissed my forehead, the nape of my neck, and all my fingers and toes. I know that with her husband at her side and helping, too, she bathed me and changed my diapers for two and a half years, and that with her two best friends, Laura Sawyer and Retha Dunn, and their husbands, created a foundation of love and community that would live on in my self-esteem even when I couldn't name its origin. I know that Bertha was my mother who bundled me up and took me outside as winter approached to introduce me to my first falling snow, the same mother who encouraged me to take my first steps.

Here in Gray, Maine, population 2,100 or so, approximately 99.9 percent Caucasian in the early 1960s, in the Taylor home on Greenleaf Street—formerly an old redbrick railroad station that Bertha converted into a ten-room residence—joy was born in my life. This imprinted happiness was a lasting gift that my first foster mother bestowed upon me.

What I also know, however, is that it was in this same place where I first heard a grown woman crying. That sound of anguish after a prolonged but failed effort to adopt me left a confusing shadow over my childhood—a dark mystery rooted not only in the circumstances of my birth, but in the very history of Maine.

Perched in the shape of a large ear, as if listening to the secrets of the vast Atlantic Ocean, situated at the most northeastern corner of the American Northeast, the state of Maine is not only the soil from which I sprang, but it ultimately represents my only legal parent. I was literally a daughter of Maine, influenced to an important degree by commonly held, decent values. Mainers on the whole are hardworking, down-to-earth people, devoted to family and community, austere, practical, faithful. Lives depend on survival of the elements and demand a respect for nature. Seasons mattered. We farmed, trapped, shoveled, tapped trees. Some fished, others cut timber and hunted, raised crops, milked cows, slopped pigs, and cleaned coops. We farmers took care of one another and what we had because life depended on it. We had long ago learned to recognize the consequences of failing to do so. We learned how to make things by hand and how to fix them when they were broken.

Of course, when I was growing up, there were noticeable regional and class differences. Northern or coastal Mainers, like members of the Collins family of Castine or lineages from places like Kennebunkport, Camden, and Booth Bay Harbor, tended to be wealthier, more educated, more connected to our nation's founding families; the smaller rural or industrial towns of the south and interior—like Berwick, Gray, and West Lebanon—tended to be poorer and more working class, with lesser known but still long ago planted family names like Lord, Quimby, James, and Shapleigh of Lebanon, Maine. Ahead of their time, establishing early welfare in the United States, before and after the Civil War, these farmers bought and sold farms to aid the sick, the poor, and children, thus creating almsfarms (charity farms). Aside from other distinctions determined by social status, money, education level, and religious affiliation, differences were strong between the part-timers who summered in state and the year-round Mainers. Nonetheless, between most groups of people, a tradition of civility—if not actual tolerance—prevailed.

So you might conclude that the ills of racial discrimination would never have come to roost in a state known for its political independence and its historically significant antislavery role. In 1820, when Maine was granted statehood as the twenty-third state, it was in fact thanks to the terms of the Missouri Compromise—allowing Maine to separate from ownership by Massachusetts and to join the Union as a "free state" while Missouri was to be admitted as a "slave state," thus maintaining a numerical balance between states that forbade human bondage and those that permitted it. Abolitionist societies soon flourished in Maine, in an atmosphere that empowered Harriet Beecher Stowe, then a resident of Brunswick, to write *Uncle Tom's Cabin*—the antislavery rallying cry heard in the years leading up to the Civil War. In some regards, Maine led the way over the next century when it came to laws protecting the rights of its African American citizens. But unfortunately there were exceptions to this tradition—as evidenced by one of Maine's most shameful chapters, otherwise known as Malaga Island.

From the time that I was in my twenties and first heard about the tragic history of this obscure island, one among several inhabitable isles dotting Casco Bay near Phippsburg, I was haunted by it. Whether or not what happened on Malaga Island in 1912 has any direct connection to my story, I can't say, but it helps to expose some of the social and legal contradictions that Bertha Taylor had to battle on my behalf.

There are different versions of how the founder of Malaga Island, Benjamin Darling, a young, strong, and enterprising man of African descent who had been born into slavery in North Carolina, first arrived in the vicinity of Casco Bay in the 1790s. The version I've gleaned from research begins with a nightmarish storm aboard a ship, in which Darling, though shackled, risks his life to save the captain—his actual father and slave master—holding on to the mast throughout the terrifying night. After the shipwreck onto the rocky coast near Phippsburg, the captain rewarded Darling, his own flesh and blood, after all, by giving him his freedom.

Legend has it that nearby Bear Island got its name after Benjamin Darling next went there and single-handedly fought off a bear attack. Soon after that, records indicate, the heroic Darling married a white Mainer, Sarah Proverbs, purchased what was then Horse Island, and fathered two sons.

By 1847, many Darling descendants had put down stakes in various mainland cities, while Benjamin and other family members had relocated to nearby Malaga Island. In these years, many of the area islands had been settled unofficially by a variety of ethnic groups, including Africans fleeing slavery and persecution—which was why as many as five different isles in the area were each officially named Negro Island—Native Americans avoiding government interference in their lives, and seafarers and fishermen of European descent. Some islanders built dwellings for temporary use, to stash gear and goods; others waited out bad weather in the island caves; still others looked for refuge where they could evade authorities, taxes, census takers, and other contact from the mainland. Sometimes languages and customs of origin were preserved; sometimes they commingled. Medical care, education, religion, and burial were frequently handled in homes or communally.

On Malaga Island, by the turn of the century, marriage between different races had resulted in something of an Afro-centered culture with a range of white, black, and biracial citizens, what was then termed a "maroon society." Initially this was not a complete taboo, since mixed-race marriages had been legalized in Maine long before many other states. Moreover, the community of Malaga Island had kept contact with mainland towns, procuring work as masons and carpenters, traveling back and forth by boat for supplies and commerce and to attend church as regularly as the weather allowed—yet still keeping a separate identity. But in 1903, when a series of dismal harvests led to rampant malnutrition, the people of Malaga Island appealed to the town of Phippsburg to adopt the island and its inhabitants, especially their children.

In Phippsburg, the nouveau riche, enjoying the town's new acclaim as a favored vacation spot, raised their eyebrows, worrying that the specter of poverty and so-called illegitimate breeding might taint their upward mobility. Town officials pointed fingers at Harpswell, suggesting that the coastal city on the other side was better suited to adopt Malaga Island. When the state of Maine went ahead and granted ownership to Phippsburg, the summer people complained and the decision was reversed. Malaga Island, unclaimed, became the proverbial no-man's-land, in essence a ward of the state.

Concerned citizens from across Maine tried to intervene. One philanthropist began the construction of a school. After visiting Malaga Island with his wife, Maine's governor urged compassion and assistance. But newspapers like the *Casco Bay Breeze* in 1905, egged on by the land barons, fixated on the Benjamin Darling story and ran head-lines calling the island the home of "Southern Negro blood" that marred a "spot of natural beauty in Casco Bay." Most of the blacks on the island were already fourth-generation Mainers but the public was persuaded that a migration of African Americans from down South had turned it into a "salt water skid row" and that the "Scandal Island" that had diluted pure Anglo-Saxon blood could threaten "respectable" Maine communities. As always, rumors that managed to combine race and sex—like one old tale that local ship captains had returned with black Caribbean mistresses and had stashed them on the island for love trysts—were all the Puritan sensibilities needed to be pushed over the edge.

The solution, proposed by the moneyed interests and not stopped by the state, was eviction. On a terrible night in 1912, without warn-ing, a mob reputedly descended in boats upon the rockweed and poison ivy–covered beach of Malaga Island. Bearing torches, they broke through doors at every dwelling they found and dragged out all the islanders, estimated to be around sixty Malagaites, including men, women, and children, except for those untold few who managed to get away. Several island citizens were examined by a doctor who lacked legitimate credentials but who determined them to be mentally ill and incompetent. Without advocates or means of appeal, they were imme-diately committed to the Maine School for the Feeble Minded. The rest of the community was dispersed, sent to a handful of towns in Maine, but not offered any compensation or help. Their estrangement from the only family, language, and customs they had ever known was made worse by the Malaga stigma that followed them.

The schoolhouse was rescued, and it is believed that a couple of escaped Malaga Island families were able to float their cabins on rafts to another island in the vicinity, but all other remaining buildings and artifacts were destroyed by officials during the eviction. Even their cemetery was dug up, with the remains of generations of island ances-tors exhumed, then moved to the grounds of the Maine School for the

Feeble Minded and buried in unmarked graves. In one fell swoop, all traces of their unique history, their civilization, their very existence were obliterated.

A hundred years later, Maine has come a long way from the true scandal of Malaga Island, not only by acknowledging the wrongs that were done but by making sure that the wrongdoing is not forgotten or ever repeated. But during some of the interim, many of the attitudes stigmatizing mixed-race unions remained. Many antiquated and overtly racist laws on the books that would have otherwise been overturned were kept on, including those laws that forbade the adoption of African American or mixed-race children into white families.

These laws were still in effect on May 10, 1959, when Dorothy Mabel Collins Rowell, unquestionably of 100 percent white Anglo-Saxon Protestant descent, arrived at Portland's Mercy Hospital in the advanced stages of labor. The unidentified black man who accompanied Dorothy and attended my subsequent birth—making his only recorded appearance in my life as my father—set off a required hunt for prospective African American foster parents in the area. Besides the fact that there were not many black families in the state of Maine, then or later, there were further concerns that complicated the state's attempt to place me in a home of color.

Before returning to Gray, these particulars deserve their own mention.

⁓

The reason the child welfare authorities sought a foster family in the first place comes from Dorothy's history.

Dorothy, Dottie, Dot, Dee Dee, Dorothy Mabel Collins. Of the five siblings, she was the family beauty, athletic, the adventurous one. Earthy, funny, rebellious, troublesome. Born on September 19, 1923, in Searsport, Maine—on the coast across the water from Castine, up near Bar Harbor—the daughter of Harry S. Collins and Mabel Bevan, Dorothy may not have exhibited any signs of mental illness until adolescence, and if it was noticed by her parents, it would have been handled clandestinely. I imagine if her parents had considered sending her away, they would have sought treatment at a private sanitarium, from which she would have been welcomed back into a loving home by her parents, her sisters Elizabeth, Edith, and Lillian, and her brother, Harry. Safe. Secure. But soon: boring and then stifling and finally oppressive.

I could speculate that Elizabeth and Edith Collins each married to escape confinement in the stern, proper but chaotic household brought on by alcoholism, where eighteen-year-old Dorothy shied away from talk of money and status—themes that would dominate her own conversation in later years.

World War II was on. Handsome, valiant men in uniform marched off to serve their country, strutting down sidewalks of small Maine towns toward Bath, where ironworks and shipyards supported a navy base and a major military installation for shipping out and returning from overseas. Soldiers on liberty congregated at local entertainment establishments, an intoxicating world for a pretty, vivacious young girl. But before anyone else could make their play for the New England beauty, Norman Rowell, a soft-spoken, good-natured man from a working-class background, turned her head and proposed marriage.

By 1943, Dorothy became a new mother to a son, Norman Rowell Jr. Her baby was precious, healthy, perfect; her husband was devoted to her, and though they had little on which to get by, it seemed she was free of the conscripts of the past and free of the earlier disturbances. All was well: Family and home. Safe. Secure. But soon: boring, then stifling and even oppressive.

In the nine years that followed, Dorothy stepped out, perhaps, then returned to the unconditionally loving arms of Norman. By 1952, she was pregnant again, this time with David. When he arrived, however, it was apparent by his darker coloring and curly hair (later assumed to be of South American origins) that Norman Sr. may not be the father, although the question of paternity did not dim his love for Dorothy and did not deter him from wanting to raise David as his own.

Norman Rowell Sr. begged Dorothy not to leave him after she asked for a divorce. She stayed on, trying to be the best mother that she could, loving both her sons, but again she became uneasy, fearful, distrustful. Soon she was gone.

Norman was inconsolable. He would not understand until much later that his wife's behavior had nothing to do with him.

Dorothy received custody of Norman Jr. and David and then made her way to Brunswick, putting together enough money, by working at Bill's Restaurant, Averbach Shoe Factory, and Bath Laundry, for an apartment, which was situated over a bar where soldiers on leave from the Korean War congregated. As it happened, Maine became home to many black soldiers. Enjoying their liberty while in Bath and Portsmouth, New Hampshire, the men were dazzled by Dorothy's pinup looks and quick wit. From time to time, she invited a number of the soldiers to her privately hosted after-hours soirees at her apartment, where a swinging time was to be had. The parties were interracial, inclusive, less about the drinking and smoking, more about the camaraderie and showing off moves to the music of Bobby Darin and Peggy Lee.

Two more children followed—a daughter, Sheree, in 1956, whose father was Puerto Rican, and another daughter, Lori, in 1957, whose father was African American. Sheree and Lori were given the surname Rowell and raised in this lively atmosphere by Dorothy, much to the horror of onlookers and, no doubt, family members. Things were said. Warnings. In tight-jawed, flat-voweled Yankee undertones. "Carrying on with a child and two babies under the same roof, for shame!" The neighborhood whispered about the three colored children, passersby stared at the scarlet woman, or turned away, shaking their heads, clucking their tongues, and Dorothy could imagine what they were saying—"Why, it's another Malaga Island, right here in Bath!"

Maybe this was what tipped the scales with her schizophrenia, her paranoid beliefs, based on actual painful gossip, all starting to compete for control of her psyche. Maybe she needed the sex, that physical release to escape her voices, like an alcoholic needing to drink or a drug addict needing a fix to numb out the pain, with vast quantities of whatever. Dorothy needed to feel that click in her brain that let her feel peace, or nothingness.

Another theory was that maybe Dorothy's chemical imbalances were temporarily cured by the hormones of pregnancy, so that for nine months she was given a reprieve, a sense of joy and serenity, such that her drive to conceive and carry babies to term was innate, a function of her will to survive. To live.

With this kind of drive, none of the warnings mattered, none of the gossip, not the fact that she was divorced without visible means of support, not even that local social welfare workers had been to see her on a landlady's observation that she stayed inside for weeks to months at a time, not bathing herself or her children. Some had reported that the older child was a girl, based on how long his hair was. Learning of this state of affairs, Norman Rowell Sr. petitioned the court for custody, which Dorothy insisted she would fight. None of these particulars, nor her age of thirty-five, would prevent her from having another affair in the summer of 1958 with a dashing young black sailor.

I want to believe that this man and Dorothy Collins Rowell had more than a passing lust for each other. Having been denied the experience of ever knowing my biological father—or any father for that matter—I feel that I am due the license to believe that I was conceived in love, that perhaps my mother and father listened to Lady Day sing "Moonlight in Vermont" as they embraced. If permitted to imagine myself present at the moment of my conception, hovering as a soul awaiting invitation into human form, I could say without a question that something greater than physical attraction between strangers is what summoned my being into this life. My proof was nothing more than a birth certificate acknowledging a man as *father unknown*. Why else would he have shown up at the hospital if there wasn't more between them, some sort of relationship? Dorothy planned on marrying my father, just as she undoubtedly planned to marry the four daddies before mine. And maybe that could have happened, were it not for a bad sequence of events tied to my untimely arrival on Sunday, May 10, 1959.

Dorothy had made no advance arrangements for going to the hospital, nor had she received prenatal care while carrying me. When her water broke, with no phone in the apartment, which she had not left for days, she struggled downstairs to the bar and used the pay phone to call a taxi to get her to the hospital. Dorothy didn't ask a soul to watch her children, because there was nobody to ask to look after seven-year-old David, three-year-old Sheree, and two-year-old Lori. Besides, no one was trustworthy. There were no family members or friends she could count on. She didn't want to risk her children getting hurt, molested, or stolen as children were every day by perfectly normal-looking people. She believed it was better to leave her children safely at home, get to the hospital, have me, and hurry back.

Outside, a taxi arrived, its engine idling and horn honking, loud enough to interrupt the otherwise quiet Sunday afternoon.

A few neighbors were drawn to watch the spectacle below as a frighteningly unkempt Dorothy struggled out of the building, wobbling on high heels, holding her swollen stomach with me inside while getting into the cab. This was when, significantly, the landlady wondered who was looking after the screaming children upstairs and decided to investigate.

When Child Welfare Services arrived and found three hungry, unbathed, frightened children in a "deplorably filthy, cluttered home," that was all it took for the wheels to be set into motion for Dorothy Collins Rowell to be prosecuted and ultimately found to be an unfit mother. The hospital report noted that Dorothy herself appeared so dirty and ill that the emergency ward put her into quarantine for my delivery. Norman Rowell Sr. was notified and came to rescue David at once, while Sheree and Lori were taken into custody by Child Welfare

Services and transferred to an orphanage until a suitable *Negro* foster or adoptive family could be found for them. As for me, Dorothy's newborn baby girl, there was to my knowledge never a chance that I would be allowed to go home with my mother. I lived for five days at Mercy Hospital, run by nuns, and was then transferred to the Holy Innocents Home orphanage on Mellen Street until an appropriate placement could be arranged for me.

There was never a time when Dorothy stopped believing that she would have her girls back with her. It was now her driving force, her reason to live, and when she became pregnant again, with my younger brother, she did her mightiest to raise him on her own, despite some interruptions. But we three Rowell daughters were another story.

Clearly, there weren't easy answers in May 1959. The social service agencies serving the state of Maine recognized that they were going to be hard-pressed to find a Negro foster family willing to take in two toddlers and later a newborn. But they understood that it was likely to be just as difficult to find more than one African American home looking to foster or adopt. Perhaps this was why, after two weeks of searching, a social worker was forced to listen when a grandmotherly fifty-four-year-old married white woman from Gray, named Bertha C. Taylor, stood before her and said she was ideally suited as a prospective foster mother and strongly asserted that no justification on earth should stand in the way of an infant being placed in a loving, safe home.

"But Mrs. Taylor . . ."

In her unassuming manner, with her plain clothes and graying nononsense hairdo, Bertha stared out from behind her functional wire-rim spectacles with a steely-eyed intensity. She leaned forward in her sensible shoes, tapping the caseworker's desk, and promised politely to drive to Augusta and speak to the governor himself. The social worker tried again to explain but to no avail.

Bertha just didn't see color; she saw only a baby in need of mothering. It was as simple as that.

A series of rotary-dialed phone calls were launched that criss-crossed the counties, not producing any answers for the very insistent prospective foster mother from Gray, until finally someone close to Governor Clinton A. Clauson, one of the four governors who served office in 1959, did indeed agree that as a temporary solution, the State of Maine would basically look the other way.

Against this backdrop and these many machinations, Bertha C. Taylor was granted her wish to take me home on June 8, 1959. On September of that same year, my caseworker, Ms. Small, noted that administrative permission was being requested

> to place this little girl in adoption, as we believe that this particular child's welfare can best be served by adoption in a negro or part-negro family. The mother, who is white, is willing to sign the courtesy consent but wants long-time boarding care in a negro foster home for this child. . . . It was suggested that she (Mrs. Rowell) seek legal advice which she did.

> Attorney I. Edward Cohen phoned me of his decision not to represent Mrs. Rowell as he believed our agency understood the situation and was making the best plan possible for this child. He seemed sympathetic of Mrs. Rowell's problem but did believe it was our responsibility to make as good a plan as possible for these part-negro children of Mrs. Rowell's.

> Mrs. Rowell is of the Protestant faith and Vicki should be placed in a Protestant adoptive home.

Mr. Collins Taylor must have known that he was a lucky man to have married Miss Bertha C. Wing, originally of Montville, a small burg not far from Belfast, but he may not have known what to say on that day in the early 1940s when she asked him to come with her to see a piece of property in Gray that she had purchased with her savings and the remainder of her family inheritance.

Bertha, every bit a Mainer, totally practical, with a keen eye for the inherent usefulness of otherwise overlooked things and individuals, had that quintessentially feminine ability to look at something or someone and not see what it was, but, rather, what it could be.

Collins stood on the property in the overgrown grass on the last of what had once been railroad tracks and saw in front of him a turn-of-the-century two-story redbrick railroad station, closed long ago, like so many whistlestop station houses now slated for extinction.

Bertha saw their future home. With a total of ten rooms, the building could be remodeled without too much trouble to accommodate as many as five foster children, with bedrooms left over for the three Taylor children, Collen, Kathy, and Roy, already growing up in their household.

It wouldn't have mattered if Collins did have misgivings about the work involved in transforming the stationhouse into her vision, or whether he was ready to foster what would amount in the coming decades to as many as sixty foster children, ranging in age from newborn to four years old. As any man who marries a woman like Bertha—that is, someone for whom foster parenting is a true calling, a destiny—he would have known better than to object. People were going to talk, because that's what they did. They'd think her eccentric. Well, maybe she was. Just a little.

This was, after all, the same gal who had previously left Montville and gotten a job in a shoe factory in Belfast, when most of the jobs went to men. With the Depression on, it had been better to be eccentric and have food on the table than to go hungry. When the two married and struck on the possibility of moving to Gray, more than a hundred miles southwest, practically a world away, instead of being worried about how locals would take to her, she cared more about how she'd take to them. Bertha's two best friends, Laura Sawyer and Retha Dunn, were not only independent-minded like her but would share in her undertakings.

Collins Taylor went along with whatever his wife set her sights on doing, the same reaction he must have had when she arrived home with me, sixteen years later. In a town where everybody knew everybody and no person of color had ever lived—at least to anyone's knowledge—there had to have been an initial wave of gossip, some of it probably titillating, but less about me than about quirky Bertha Taylor's hardheadedness. At the same time, the city of Gray would never have come to be had it not been for its quirky, hardheaded founders. One of them, a man by the name of Samuel Mayall, who in 1791 had built the first water-powered wool mill in North America, right there in Gray, had defied the British woolen guilds by smuggling out designs for the machinery—a crime punishable by death. Seeking revenge, one of the English guild lords sent him a hat in which poison pins were hidden, while another lord sent him a package containing pistols set to fire when he opened the box. Being a man of his wits, Mayall saw through these ruses and lived long enough to see his mills became a foundation of America's industrial revolution, thriving in and around Gray until the 1900s.

Had Bertha Taylor been forced to fend off poison and exploding packages on my behalf, she would have done so. She was that wholly focused on securing me in her home and in Gray.

True to New England tradition, Bertha was neither prideful nor overly modest (both considered forms of self-centeredness) and was never prone to showing off, but she apparently couldn't help herself when it came to me and—I am told—dressed me up in an array of baby girl clothes, then took me everywhere she went, bristling when anyone dared suggest I was not her own. Obviously, she was nearing the age of a grandmother, with graying board-straight hair that was originally blond, and I was a baby of mixed race, with brown skin and a head full of dark loose tiny curls that formed early on. Nonetheless, Bertha made me hers from the word go, allowing herself the most unabashed maternal pride, holding me up and presenting me as her little Vicki to neighbors and strangers alike.

Between Bertha, Laura, and Retha, and additional members of the three families, I could not have wanted for more attention, to be more cherished or doted upon. Laura Sawyer's two teenagers, Pam and Dennis, actually competed for babysitting time. Dennis even missed baseball practice to rock me to sleep. How this special extended family came to be and came to take me into their hearts and lives—so much so that when we reunited in my adulthood, they were able to rattle off stories from my earliest years right from the tips of their tongues—remains the mystery of love.

Bertha was absolute in her conviction that she would prevail in her quest to prove the law wrong. She was determined to show the powers that be that I was not merely being fed and housed—as required by the weekly $7.00 check that the state paid per child—but that I had been embraced as a member of a family and of a community. Social workers assigned to my case had to have been amazed to see that instead of emotional or physical delays that can occur with displaced babies and toddlers, this abundance of love, nurturing, and early education seemed to be responsible for advanced development in every area.

The effervescent, outgoing Laura Sawyer—younger by some years than Bertha and Retha, and the most talkative of the three—loved to invent games to engage and cultivate my abilities. The "duck" game was developed by accident one morning when she asked me to help her find a missing keepsake. Laura was the first of a long line of collectors who would inspire my own passion for holding on to pieces of the past. Her jewelry collection contained a vast assortment of pins and brooches, and her other big thing was frogs—in whatever keepsake version she could obtain.

Laura asked me to help find her missing frog, under Bertha's couch. With the Taylors, Laura's husband, Lawrence, her two children, Dennis and Pam, and the Dunns collectively egging me on, I bent over to search, and the white ruffles on the back of my underwear fluffed up, like the tail of a duck.

When I located the frog that had been strategically hidden for me to find, I received a hearty round of applause. If performing was in my blood, as the threesome believed, they did everything imaginable to reinforce that natural inclination.

No concrete images have stayed with me from those gatherings, but in my senses I remember this trio of women, can-do Mainers, like female elders of a tribe, hovering around me, pleased with my every gesture and every utterance. They combined the roles of grandmother, mother, and aunt, and each went on to prove over time—no matter how many children they ultimately raised, fostered, adopted, or mentored—that their capacity to give love was limitless, a well that never ran dry.

Together with their genuine love for children, these three were also natural-born teachers, recognizing well ahead of their time what sociologists of later years liked to point out—that the object of early education is to build the infrastructure for lifelong learning. That was certainly their legacy to me in creating an improvised school setting in their midst. Bertha was unquestionably the no-nonsense headmistress, embodying Maine's motto—"I lead"—as she took me purposefully under her wing. It was Laura's role, with her hand-holding and cheerleading, to make every learning opportunity fun, and Retha, perhaps most of all, left her mark by teaching me how to overcome my fear when facing unfamiliar situations. These were lessons that had come from her own turbulent childhood.

Retha—or Grammy Dunn, as she was later known by everyone in the county—had a disarmingly dry wit and infectiously warm smile that she must have used to great effect in helping Bertha navigate the state bureaucracy on my behalf. Though there wasn't anything remarkable in her looks, something about Retha's inner beauty was so striking that people of all ages were drawn to her. Devoted to what would become four generations of offspring that she and her husband, Archie, would personally raise—including four children, thirteen grandchildren, twenty-six great-grandchildren, and four great-great-grandchildren, together with thirty-one foster grandchildren—Retha honestly came by her frequent comparison to the Little Ole Lady Who

Lived in a Shoe. She was really Gray's own version of Mother Teresa, spending her extracurricular hours volunteering at the local schools, well into her nineties, and making the most of her time by driving fast in a series of small, sporty cars she had a weakness for, and, as a terrific fan of sports, somehow managing never to miss any of her grandchildren's or students' games.

Though she was known widely in many public and private quarters for her good works, only her closest friends and family knew that Retha had once been in an orphanage and had been raised as a foster child in her native Kingfield, Maine, eighty miles north of Gray. Knowing from firsthand experience what kinds of fundamental fears can afflict a foster child, she worked doubly hard not just to help Bertha overcome the obstacles to my adoption, but also to instill that sense of courage and self-protection in me—in the event that their efforts failed.

From the end of May 1959 until the end of 1961, families Taylor, Sawyer, and Dunn were relentless, filing petitions in court, driving back and forth to Augusta to meet with legislators and child welfare workers, pressing for answers and asking for a change in a law that served no one. Bertha, Laura, and Retha were of a generation and a culture in which women were not encouraged to embrace their womanly powers, but rather to employ them subtly, through men, or behind the scenes. At some point, it may have been discreetly communicated to them that they had rocked the boat, kicked up too much dust, caused much more of a commotion than was flattering for women of their station. They might have been warned. There may have been a social worker willing to risk her or his job to help them, but the more they pressed for the State to permit the adoption, the more scrutiny they drew. Finally an answer came back, but it wasn't the one they wanted. A plan was in the works to move me.

Apparently, the official reason for the decision was that Bertha was too old to adopt me, and so, too, was Retha. Laura Sawyer then stepped in, suggesting that she could be the adoptive parent of record, and that all three families would continue to raise me. "Dear Mrs. Hurley," she began an earnest letter to my social worker on February 25, 1961, "I am writing concerning our neighborhood angel, Vicki . . ." and went on to attest that there was not a community in the world that could love me more, or adoptive parents who could care for me as much, regardless of faith, color, or age.

Since the issue of race had been raised, Child Welfare was now in the position of explaining that though the decision had been difficult, it was made carefully:

> It would be easy for us to leave Vicki in a home where we know she is loved and well cared for and to close our eyes and minds to what life would hold for her in ten and fifteen years hence. But in thinking of the future we must remember that being brought up in a foster home is difficult enough without aiding the problems of racial difference and separation from what little "own family" is left. . . . We must face the fact that the same people who love her at age two might feel differently when she is in her teens. We also know that Vicki herself is going to be aware of the "differences" as the years pass, and she will have problems to work out living in a totally white community.

(Decades later, I received a letter from Retha Dunn that would reunite me with her, Laura Sawyer, and Bertha Taylor's family. Laura Sawyer would be the first former mother I would encounter. When we met in Dresden, Maine, she burst into tears recalling the heartache they had all suffered. "I wanted you," she said very loudly, fingering her whimsical frog pin on her lapel. "I wanted you, I loved you like my own! But they wouldn't let me have you!" Laura fell into my arms and we both wept together.)

For the pending move, the Maine Division of Child Welfare had its eye on a young Negro couple in Portland, a town that had a larger community of Negroes than other locations. This couple seemed perfect but was ultimately denied due to an important puzzle piece in the decision-making process by the State. Dorothy, who relentlessly visited the Welfare workers' office, had tried in vain to give them one dollar a week for a fund to reunite me with my sisters, who were in the same Negro foster home. Three things mattered to her—that I be raised with Sheree and Lori, that I be in a home where the adults were Negro, but, most of all, that it was a foster home and not with adoptive parents. Her point was that this way she would be able to visit all three of us on occasion and one day reclaim her girls. Dorothy's appeal as my birth mother prevailed.

Not knowing any of this, Laura Sawyer and her husband, Lawrence, arranged for a meeting with the Child Welfare district supervisor who merely repeated their reasoning as stated in an earlier letter. The supervisor went on to report to the director of the division in Augusta:

> The Sawyers became very angry, could see no reason why we should disturb the placement of a child who was getting along beautifully, quoted the Bible, indicated that love could overcome all obstacles, and finally, as always, stated that we could not know anything about parental love anyway since were not parents.

The supervisor described how illogical and hysterical the Sawyers were, especially in blaming the state for having allowed me to come to Gray in the first place, if only to remove me later. She went on:

> The Sawyers are also talking of starting a petition. They had much to say about Gray being a "Christian" town and therefore, there isn't all this horrid prejudice there. . . . In their opinion the decision is a totally wicked one and we are not at all concerned with anyone's "welfare" as a welfare agency should be. As a nation, we are supposedly workings towards integration, yet when we have it we destroy it.

The supervisor did ask the Sawyers why Bertha and Collins Taylor hadn't raised these same objections, and Laura's answer was a choked-out response, "They would have, but didn't have the courage." By the end, Laura had collapsed into a fit of hysterical sobs, and Lawrence could only try to comfort her. Such drama was extremely out of the ordinary, but it had dawned on the Sawyers that my removal was now imminent. The traumatic separation not only affected me but also my foster parents. Bertha and Collins Taylor could never bring themselves to foster another child.

Retha Dunn followed my life and career, further dedicating herself to children in every walk of life and to quietly having a hand in changing the system that had taken me from their community. Emphasizing education, Grammy Dunn had quite an influence on her son, Burchard E. Dunn, when he pursued a path in public service and was elected to the Maine state senate. Among the many pieces of legislation Burchard helped author and the projects he undertook to help kids was on the advice of Retha—the purchase of a defunct hospital that was remade into a school, later named for him. Upon Retha's death in 2004 at the age of ninety-five, in addition to volunteer awards that were established in her name, the U.S. representative from the district recognized her on the floor of the House—for the ripple effect that her years of fostering and mentoring had contributed to Maine.

Bertha and Collins Taylor, along with their daughters, maintained some contact with me, including a few visits, letters, and gifts at Forest Edge, but I was told that their grief was such that it was better to allow for a distance, so that they had time to heal and allow me time to bond with my new family. Parting was always traumatic, so much so that I, too, couldn't allow it to register in my conscious memory, and associated it abstractly through Agatha telling me of an unforeseen winter storm that occurred in April 1961, which shattered my foundation of family and safety, when I was one month shy of my second birthday.

In my early thirties, I made the trip to visit Bertha in a nursing home in Gray, to thank her in person for what she had given me early in life and for taking me into her heart, home, and community. Eighty-seven, very frail, and suffering from Alzheimer's, my second mother still had a dim light in her eyes, and she looked at me in a way as though she might have remembered me, then she dozed off. I lay down on the bed next to her and put my arm across her chest. There were no words, only hearts. It was here that our embrace brought back that which the senses best document; as I held her while she slept, I thought of the lullaby she must have sung to me, the way she had tenderly rocked me in her arms, and a permanent ache caused by our final separation. As I prepared to sit up, Bertha let out an uncensored wail, probably one of the rare times in her life she had allowed herself to howl like that, as an attendant tried to explain to a disoriented Bertha why I was leaving. Her wail resounded in the deep recesses of my memory. A feeling was triggered, reclaiming me in that moment. Now I was all grown up and Bertha was more like the child, lying there helpless, me not wanting to leave her there alone with strange people.

Bertha C. Taylor, predeceased by her husband, Collins, by several years, passed away four days after my visit.

Aside from a few photographs, she had held on to one keepsake from my time with her, protected in the smallest of plastic ring boxes. At some point, for reasons never revealed, she gave it to Laura Sawyer, who eventually presented it to me in my adulthood, after I gave birth to the first of my two children, as though to make sure I knew what my stay had meant to Bertha, and to the community of Gray—or as proof that Vicki had really been there and really mattered.

Upon receiving it, I closed my eyes, feeling the soft warmth of Laura's hands over mine, and paused before lifting the lid, wondering what it could be. It weighed no more than a feather and had traveled so far and so purposefully to arrive in my hands. Finally, I clicked open the box. Inside, as though it was the entire ocean preserved in the most miniature of seashells, was my earliest childhood, wholly captured in a saved lock of my hair—a single tiny perfect curl.

TWO

Agatha Wooten Armstead

Now I began to remember things. Like awakening from a slow dream, the first involved my being led into a familiar room that contained toys, *my* toys and *my* dolls. A woman and two little girls entered. Questions: why were the girls playing with *my* dolls? Why did the woman, a stranger, seem familiar? At *my* table, she set up a tea party, and I couldn't take my eyes off how she delicately grasped my play teacups and poured the imaginary tea, then held the cup between her fingers so carefully, with her pinky pointed toward heaven, explaining that we had to let it cool before drinking it, then blew into the empty cup. Her voice was warm, sparkling, kind. I tried hard not to trust her, yet I did.

Next: another day, now a trip in a car. In the front seat, this same woman sat next to another strange woman who drove, as both turned around every now and then to say comforting things to me. I don't remember hearing anything. Later, I learned that this car trip had taken place on April 17, 1961, a two-hour unbearable drive through nasty weather and my crying. According to the social worker who drove us and my recently appointed foster mother, Agatha Armstead, I cried the entire way from Gray, farther north up near Portland, down to West Lebanon in the more southern part, just on the New Hampshire state line.

These remembered fragments culminate in a full memory that finds me sitting on the knee of Robert Armstead, aka Grandpa, the two of us seated at the red Formica table in the kitchen of the two-hundred-year-old farmhouse at Forest Edge, bathed in autumn morning sunshine that streamed through freshly pressed curtains. We provided a captive audience for Agatha Catherine Wooten Armstead, who presided here over hearth, home, and field, a kingdom, or queendom, rather, of her own making. Agatha, Ma, Granny, or Kit—as Grandpa called her—was the dazzling superstar of this universe. She was my mother, grandmother, teacher, guru, inspiration, best friend. She would become my everything.

Ma towered over every memory of the next six years, not imperiously, but with genuine amazing grace. Lovingly, magnificently, immortally. For anyone fortunate enough to have been part of her extended family, blood related or not, a chance to be in her sphere—for however long was granted—was not luck. Divine intervention was at work, and so, too, from behind the scenes, was Dorothy; through her debilitating Thorazine haze, pulling strings, as she had all along, by insisting that she have some say in who the State determined were suitable foster parents for her daughters. To have that, she gave another dollar.

Unlike my first caretaker, Bertha, Agatha did not make a conscious decision to become a foster mother. To the contrary, these were the years she had set aside for her well-earned, glorious retirement. But a confluence of circumstances that had brought her and her husband to Mercy Hospital in 1959 changed those plans.

When agents from Child Welfare came to Dorothy's home and discovered the conditions in which my sisters, who were ages two and three, were living, they were taken immediately to Mercy Hospital. During this time a devastated Dorothy was trying without success to reclaim us. This was before Agatha and Robert Armstead came to my sisters' rescue and became their foster parents—the result of an all-points bulletin looking for a foster family of color.

The anguish of the situation must have been felt by all concerned. Here were two beautiful girls, still traumatized, and no suitable home could be found because of their race. Upset at the arcane, cruel law, social workers at Mercy Hospital were desperate to find a foster home for the Rowell girls, so much so that a meeting was convened, and one of the staff recalled an incident earlier when a black couple in their late fifties had been spotted as they traversed the lobby—and how word had traveled faster than Western Union that possibly, just possibly, potential foster parents were on the premises.

Much to the amazement of the Armsteads, before they had a chance to explain what they were actually doing at the hospital, a group of administrators swooped out of their offices to greet them as if they were visiting royalty, ushering them into a comfortable, confidential meeting. No one had the temerity in 1959 to come right out and say, "We are in desperate need of colored parents for two colored children who need to be adopted or placed in foster care. Would you consider opening up your home?" That would not be the Maine approach. Instead, what followed was a query into their biographical background, as would normally be conducted for a job interview—which, unbeknownst to the hospital staff, was precisely the reason that the Armsteads were there.

Naturally, they were forthcoming, with Ma taking the lead in providing only the highlights of the events that had brought the two of them to Mercy Hospital that day. It was a story that really went back to her earliest days.

Agatha had been born in North Carolina in 1903, the second eldest of the four phenomenal Wooten sisters—entrepreneurial black Bostonians renowned for their intelligence, talent, good looks, and fine upbringing. Their mother, Mary Jane King Wooten, was one of twenty freeborn children. Her mother had been forced into slavery on the King Plantation of Charleston, South Carolina. In the wake of the

Civil War, the slave master's son, Joseph P. King, fell in love with her and they married—an act of defiance for which he was harshly punished and disinherited. The twenty mixed-race offspring went on to scatter their roots, spreading some of the King lineage up and around the Boston area; some chose to pass for white at a time when Jim Crow was taking hold after the failed era of Reconstruction, with many accruing considerable wealth and property. In the meantime, other King branches settled in rural Southern towns where Native American and African American communities found common ground. In New Bern, North Carolina, in such a setting, one of the daughters of Mr. and Mrs. Joseph P. King, Mary Jane, married John Wooten, whose roots were African American intertwined on paternal and maternal sides with both the Kickapoo and Blackfoot Indian tribes.

Born there in the South but raised in the North, Agatha was an old soul with ancient folk wisdom from Africa commingling with her Native American ancestors. On the surface, that mix of genes gave her an aristocratic appearance—making her petite five-foot frame seem almost tall, except when she was standing next to her six-foot-three strapping, barrel-chested husband, Robert. Agatha's glowing complexion hid how old she really was and helped detract from the Paget's disease, phlebitis, and cancer she suffered from. Her high cheekbones and almond-shaped eyes epitomized her wise being and good nature. In short, Agatha was a beauty. Moreover, she saw the beauty in everyone and everything.

Every day that unfolded around her was Ma's personal celebration of life, nature, art, music, language, family, and work. Not necessarily in that order. A gifted jazz pianist and singer with an encyclopedia's worth of knowledge of every flower, every genus, every hybrid, she was masterful at everything she pursued and did nothing halfway. She could cook with a capital "C," and she could bake even better. She could cane, paint, knit, sew, hook a rug, crochet, till, plant, harvest, design, build, fix, and teach. She was a top-notch amateur photographer and movie documentarian, with her handy Brownie always holstered to record and document her adventures. She would say, "Now everybody wait right there," and with that she was gone. We all knew how important photography was to Agatha. We would just stay there, poised in the front room in the positions she placed us in, as still as if posing for a daguerreotype. In my seated position, I could hear Agatha rummaging through her metal closet in her bedroom—through bags and bags of nondescript possessions. Finally, she would emerge, her wig slightly askew, clenching flashbulbs. She loved all that was elegant and beautiful—crystal, silver, hats, anything with *style*. If she couldn't afford it, she made it with her pedal-operated Singer sewing machine, black with gold lettering. She also loved her Steinway, the baby grand piano that traveled with her everywhere.

Agatha Armstead revered and practiced the art of letter writing, just as she respected the English language, correct spelling, grammar, enunciation, and perfect penmanship, and she spoke Spanish and Latin. She preferred an authentic turn of the phrase to an overused cliché. Due to an unfortunate altercation with her problematic son Raymond, she later wrote, "He carried on something terrible; he laid my soul low." Poetic, yet pointed.

Ma had her priorities, too. She placed education in school second only to education as a devout Catholic. She lived by her faith.

The pianist, the painter, the writer, the gardener, the entrepreneur— she was who she was, distinguished in who she was, living her very own life, regardless of the opinions, gossip, or condescension of others. This had been true from childhood on and was definitely the case when—much to the chagrin of some of the upwardly mobile Wootens—Agatha married Robert Armstead, an orphaned black child.

To some, Agatha may have already seemed to have broken high society rules when she put aside the training she had received at the New England Conservatory of Music to pursue an opportunity to work alongside The Jenkins Band. The bandleader invited Agatha to accompany his band to New York City to perform in clubs up and down Harlem. Her head spun thinking about The Lafayette and The Harlem Opera House where Bill "Bojangles" Robinson performed and the even more scandalous hope of passing through a revolving bookcase into the secret world of a speakeasy. She breathlessly had hoped to work with some of the most famous names in ragtime, blues, and vaudeville. Agatha had heard and learned as much of Scott Joplin, Jelly Roll Morton, and Count Basie's music as she could possibly get her hands on. She was inspired by Hazel Scott, Bessie Smith, Ethel Waters, and the Alma Long Scott's All Girl Band, believing that women could hold their own in New York's tough entertainment circles. Agatha wanted to be a part of the Harlem Renaissance. But, alas, in the midst of pursuing her dream in the late 1900s and the early 1920s, concern for her aging mother, she said, made her decide to switch gears, staying closer to home and to begin to raise a family. But why she chose to marry someone who had not met with much of her mother's approval remained a lifelong mystery. Maybe this was her way of choosing her own path, for better and for worse.

Robert, on whose knee I sat in my earliest real memory, was born in 1900 when his mother, Sylvia Armstead, arrived from Virginia for yet another summer of work, per the request of Mrs. Chapman at her New Hampshire estate. An unmarried Sylvia went into labor and died giving birth to Robert Armstead that August. Mrs. Chapman, who had lost her own son in a tragic accident, kept Robert and took care of him. Having come of age back in the mid-1800s, Mrs. Chapman told Robert little more about his history other than his mother's first and last name and that she hailed from Virginia. Following Agatha and Robert's elaborate 1920s wedding, they were invited to honeymoon at Mrs. Chapman's estate.

In later years, it occurred to me that he and I had a special bond because we both arrived in life without known histories—one of the reasons I have always been magnetically drawn to the histories of others and even history itself. But to some of Agatha's family, the fact that Robert was not from any known background and had not yet put forth a plan for any known future meant only that she was marrying below herself. There were other objections. He was a hard-drinking man, susceptible to all the temptations that came along with the bottle. Some of the family even called him a rogue. He had his weaknesses, no doubt, but his Kit, his endearment for Agatha, loved him unconditionally and refused to let a word of her family's skepticism take away from her devotion to him.

In Dorchester, Massachusetts, Agatha and Robert went forward and were fruitful, creating a multitude, a total of ten children born to them between the 1920s and 1940s: Kathleen, Robert Ronald Jr., identical twins Richard and Ralphie, Barbara, Joan, Sylvia, and Raymond. The ultimate working man, Robert Sr. never erred in supporting his growing dynasty, laboring throughout the years for the railroads and as a custodian, managing at times to hold down three jobs simultaneously in and around Boston, even at the height of the Great Depression. Ma, meanwhile, did it all: raised the children and did her part to supplement the family income. She was a saleswoman at high-end department stores, where her flair for style won her a devoted clientele; had a small, separate income from property investments; and was an in-demand professional in the art of pressing and tailoring. With all that, she still maneuvered brilliantly to keep Robert from drinking away his earnings by doing things like just happening to pick up his paychecks before he did.

At the height of the Depression, five-month-old Ralphie, one of the twins, was stricken with pneumonia and died in Agatha's arms. I once asked her, as a teenager, when she had stopped mourning for her son, and she softly replied, "Never." This was not the first or the last test of Agatha's ability to contend with excruciating pain, emotional or physical. As it was already, her body was a memorial battlefield proving that neither injury nor disease could triumph over her sheer will to survive. But the loss of a child—combined with medical concerns that caused doctors to declare, "Mrs. Armstead, carrying one more baby to full term will kill you"—well, this was something else.

Agatha, a practical New Englander by this era, was not so naïve as to shrug off the doctors' advice. Yet, after taking their counsel under advisement, she conferred finally with her Higher Power, a priest, and the Virgin Mary. Agatha was determined that she would live to bring more lives into the world—five more, in fact. And she went on to be a doting grandmother to another twentysomething grandchildren and more than a dozen great-grandchildren. Along the way, she withstood the ravages of breast cancer, incurring a radical mastectomy, losing her right breast, along with most of her armpit and part of her ribs. As a result of the surgery, her right arm was permanently swollen to twice the size of her left arm. The phlebitis she suffered also enlarged her right hand, adding to the impairments that left the right side of her body constricted and concave, all of which she took in stride. Her burdens never impeded her needle and crochet work; she still knit some three dozen new pairs of mittens for each and every grand and great-grand each fall. Navy blue wool mittens with a red Charlie Brown stripe at the cuff. Year in and year out. Agatha was nothing if not consistent.

As her long-ago dream of a musical career dimmed into the past, another dream must have begun to burn brightly in its place at some point in the 1940s after her last child was born. Where it came from exactly, no one could say, except that once she hit upon the idea of owning a farm in rural Maine that she could transform into her own personal Garden of Eden and where she could spend her retirement without the constraints of children to raise, she pursued that vision with a fervor.

At this juncture, Agatha was reborn in her dream. From her work as a Rosie the Riveter during World War II at the Charlestown Shipyard, she had saved two thousand dollars to bring her reverie to fruition. A masterful negotiator, she continued to lobby Robert that a farm would be in his best interest, a wise investment. Having grown up in New Hampshire, most likely having to work from sunup to sundown, Robert had no desire to revisit the country. Comfortable in his familiar urban neighborhood of Boston, he would not back down and Agatha didn't want a fight. She'd already had plenty of those. He put his head-of-the-household foot down by saying in his booming voice, "No, Kit, uh-uh." Robert knew that Agatha could talk a wolf off a meat truck and let her know in no uncertain terms that he'd rather die before moving to the "wilderness." Horrified by the mere suggestion of his mortality, Ma quieted him, and promised that he'd feel differently in ten years or so.

Before long, Agatha found a "For Sale" listing for Forest Edge, a sixty-acre homestead and working farm that bordered an apple orchard and a wooded hillside, situated at the end of Barley Road in West Lebanon, Maine. The moment she read the description, she fell in love, purchased a ticket on the Boston & Maine Railroad, and took the train up from Boston to see the place. It didn't matter that everything was in need of a great deal of work, and that the two-hundred-year-old farmhouse had no indoor plumbing or phone lines and required extensive time and resources to become inhabitable. She only saw her dream unfolding here. Nor did it occur to Agatha that there was not one other person of color in the township, probably not in the entire county or the county next to it.

The question of race did not cross her mind when she traveled to West Lebanon to have a meeting with the man who was selling Forest Edge. He looked out of the window and saw Agatha. It was after several minutes of knocking and waiting, and singing out her signature "Yoohoo, anyone home?" with no response, that she realized she would have to administer some persuading to overcome his prejudice. Undaunted, she later returned, taking the B&M Railroad from Boston with unflappable confidence—always dressed impeccably, with a stylish hat and gloves, her chapeau tipped just at the right angle to identify that she was a woman, and 100 percent determined to do business.

On her third visit, the door was opened by a young woman who turned out to be the man's daughter; she was instantly won over by Agatha's demeanor and invited her in.

The wheels were set in motion. Even though Ma didn't leave with the deed to the property that same day and even though there were still several more hurdles to overcome, the end result was that Agatha C. Wooten Armstead became the owner of Forest Edge. She tended her dream, with the concerted effort of her children, patching up the farmhouse, barn, sheds, pens, and outhouse and working the land. For extra income she sold her pine, hay, and extra vegetables. Then in the mid to late 1950s, she prepared for the big and permanent move. There was only one problem yet to be resolved: Robert Armstead.

Grandpa's thinking hadn't changed from the time he voiced his first objections. To live in the "wilderness," away from where he could find gainful employment, that alone would kill him. He was a workingman. What was a man without work? No man at all, according to Robert. Besides, he might have been thinking that with all those dry counties, he would have to drive fifty miles for a taste of liquor.

Agatha countered that he would find better jobs in Maine. Less competition. Robert countered Agatha and said, "If you learn how to make beer, I'll stay." She assured her husband that she would brew him the most mouthwatering, thirst-quenching homemade beer that he had ever tasted.

True to her word, Ma studied up on the art of brewing and proceeded to master the ideal measurements of hops and yeast—soon yielding a brew that was said to get better every season. While she was at it, Ma learned to make root beer for all the kids.

Agatha's brewery up in the attic of the white clapboard two-story farmhouse at Forest Edge thus became a sight to behold: orderly rows of two-toned brown-glazed earthenware jugs that no human dared touch until fermentation had fully captured the rising summer heat. As soon as Ma could hear the corks popping, she knew the beer had reached its robust potential—and it was time for the army of jugs to be moved down to the cold stone cellar, ready for Grandpa to sample, consume, and enjoy year-round.

The beer in and of itself almost wooed him. He drank it straight from the cream and dark brown jugs that we later used for doorstops. Resting the jug on his shoulder, Grandpa would let the beer pour into his mouth. Nobody said a word. His children and grandchildren understood without being told what Ma figured, that Grandpa was mellowing, ripening like the bounty in her garden and in her orchard, like the grapes on her Concord vines. That part of him that had commanded respect but had also been fearsome in the past now peeled away and he found a peace he had never known, as everybody experienced in the enchantment that was Forest Edge. Eventually he discovered the rhythm of the days, weeks, and seasons, the rewards of his prized squash garden that he planted in front of the barn, the enjoyment he gleaned from hunting for pheasant and wild turkey. Robert had made his own rifle range for target practice, set back in the woods in an open patch, near a towering sawdust pile created by loggers who purchased Agatha's lumber. Content, he swore never to return to the city again.

Robert Sr. had only one complaint; namely, that no job was to be found anywhere close to West Lebanon, or even far from it for that matter.

In early 1959, almost exhausted of ideas, Agatha came up with a last-ditch suggestion that she proposed to Grandpa that went something along the lines of: "Why don't we pay a visit to Mercy Hospital in Portland? I'm sure they've got an opening."

By this time, Grandpa had laid down the law about Ma's driving. She had many talents, but the steering and operation of a two-ton hulk of fuel-powered machinery was not her area of expertise. Or at least that's what she led her husband to believe. Everyone knew that Agatha could drive her red Farmall tractor like the best of them, but wanting to please her husband, she abided. Robert would not let Agatha drive, causing her to be dependent on him or others for transportation—including regular errands and emergencies. Nonetheless, there was no doubt about who was actually steering their course that winter day as Robert reversed the car down the ice- and snow-encrusted driveway and out onto what was then the entirely unpaved Barley Road, on their way to Portland.

Years later when the county finally got around to paving, the stretch in front of Forest Edge would never be paved, which may or may not have had anything to do with the Armsteads being the only African Americans in the area. It was rather starkly obvious every time the winter-battered road was repaved. A superlative job was done all the way down the stone-walled Barley Road, past the meticulous Goth-white homestead, curving past open fields, and uninhabited groves, past the Amadons' dairy farm, through the centuries-old cemetery, past the rolling hills where the Nadeaus' horses blithely grazed, all the way to the end of the property line shared by the Heaths. Then, just at the edge of Agatha's property line, by her open field, and the frog pond, before the string of two-acre parcels she bequeathed to her children—all of which was part of Forest Edge—the pavement suddenly ended.

Nonetheless, snow and ice that January day did not deter the Armsteads from making it to the highway, traveling slowly and carefully, and then on toward Portland and Mercy Hospital, little suspecting what was awaiting them, much less the question they were asked after their abbreviated stories had been told: "Have you two ever thought of becoming foster parents?"

The upshot was that everyone emerged a winner. A very pleased Robert Armstead was referred to a facility nearby where he was hired on as a custodian, based on the hospital's recommendation, and Agatha, having never thought about being a foster parent, filled out an application, feeling perhaps that she was being called to serve. The following May, she received a phone call, and by summer, after falling in love with Sheree and Lori, a new chapter as a foster parent had begun.

Privately, Ma's grown children were bewildered that she would give up the newly conquered freedom she had worked so hard to establish at Forest Edge. But they said only, "Ma, those kids will keep you young," and over the next couple years, as Sheree and Lori were embraced as members of the Armstead family, they did just that.

Less than two years after she brought Sheree and Lori home, almost everyone tried to prevent Ma from even considering taking in a third foster child. That request had been put to her, in person, by Dorothy on September 19 when she paid Agatha and my sisters a visit, desperately explaining to Agatha how she refused a social worker's plans to place me with, "an excellent, young childless Negro family." She told Agatha of how she rejected Ms. Small's plan, saying, "No, I want you to put Vicki with the girls!" Dorothy went on to explain how the social worker had been sympathetic of her feelings, but that they were going ahead with the adoptive placement for Vicki. An exasperated Dorothy continued to say that the Division of Child Welfare believed that Sheree and Lori should also have the security of an adoptive home, but had no definite plans at this time.

Agatha wouldn't hear anything from the naysayers after that visit. Dorothy continued to write to Agatha as one mother to another, thanking her for all she was doing for Sheree and Lori and begging her again and again to do one more heroic act—to reunite Vicki Lynn with her sisters. Due to Dorothy's indefatigable insistence, the adoption with a Negro family never took place. Agatha and Dorothy collaborated tirelessly, even after the objections of another social worker, Ms. Hill, which were noted by Ms. Small, stating,

> It would not be wise to place Vicki with the Armsteads because of the extra physical strain on Mrs. Armstead of caring for and lifting a baby. She is fifty-six years old and has not been used to this kind of work. Mrs. Armstead is not asking that the baby be placed with her though Mrs. Rowell does say that the Armsteads are anxious to have Vicki. We have asked for administrative permission to place Vicki in adoption.

Agatha knew full well that the Taylors didn't want to let me go, and it broke her heart when yet another social worker took her to visit me at Bertha's house, something she'd promised Dorothy she would do.

Agatha wrote to the Taylors, the Sawyers, and the Dunns, letting them know that she saw them as family to me and that they would be welcome to visit me in West Lebanon as often as they wanted.

At Agatha's suggestion, a neutral location was selected so that the Taylors could drop me off and say good-bye in private. A short while later, Agatha and the social worker arrived to take me to Forest Edge. The April snowstorm and my earsplitting cries made Agatha really wonder if the right decision had been made. But Dorothy Rowell and the State of Maine assured her that it was.

I don't know if Robert Sr. objected to taking in a third foster child, because within days of my arrival, the two of us were inseparable. I adored him, and he spoiled me rotten. I was a little older than two and a half years old, and even though there is no explanation for why I have such vivid early memories, I do. Like it was yesterday, I remember sitting on Grandpa's big knee, him giving me a horsey ride at the red Formica kitchen table. I can remember his rhythmic cadence, and, most of all, I can still connect with feeling safe and loved. Agatha later explained that I was the childhood he never had as an orphan and that he was being given a second chance at fatherhood. When Grandpa had to go to work at the hospital, I knew he would return bearing gifts—toys donated and left behind at the children's ward that he loved to bring home to me, especially the dolls.

Agatha's approach to my early education was to give me time to adapt naturally to my new surroundings. I developed attachments to others on my own—not only to Grandpa, but to my sisters and the Armstead grandchildren, whom I learned to call my cousins, as well as Agatha and Robert's children, whom I referred to as aunts and uncles due to our age difference. With strategies befitting a PhD in child psychology, Agatha also saw to it that I felt a sense of continuity with my former foster families, and she continued to arrange for the Taylor, Sawyer, and Dunn families to visit whenever possible. This familial architecture was her way of instilling the idea of heritage in me, encouraging me to honor all my relationships, blood or not, and to maintain contact through correspondence and visits.

My crib sat to the left of a crooked kitchen doorway. One day, just five or six months after I came to Forest Edge, a big white car pulled up and two men dressed in white got out of it. They took my Grandpa and never brought him back. I had lost three fathers in less than three years.

No one told me at age two and a half that death was a consequence of illness. This mountain of a man, an imposing presence, strong and vital at sixty-three years old, a workingman, probably hadn't been sick a day of his life. But as I got older I discovered, in an old bureau, his stainless steel hyperdermic needles and applicators for his diabetes and surgical clamps to tie off syringes, with which I tried in vain to cut out my paper dolls.

The doctors told Ma there was nothing to worry about, but when she was sure that he had come down with pneumonia and showed no improvement, she called for an ambulance. This was not an easy process. For starters, there were no phone lines on Barley Road. One would have to head to the West Lebanon Post Office, twenty miles from the farm, to make a call.

By the time the phone call was placed and the old hearselike ambulance finally roared down the dirt road, it was too late. Grandpa was near death. Although she was a God-fearing woman, I don't know if Ma ever forgave those doctors for not diagnosing her husband properly. From then on, I was not allowed to walk anywhere without something on my feet. If I did attempt to do so, Agatha invariably asked, "Where are your shoes?" and answered before I could, "You're going to catch your death, a cold," reminding me, "Your Grandpa died of pneumonia, walking around barefoot."

Agatha Armstead, widowed at sixty, mourned in her very private way, quietly, led by prayerful meditation and her gardening, until a sufficient time period had passed and she announced to her family that she had a new undertaking to discuss. Instead of grieving for Grandpa's absence, she was going to celebrate his life, every year in August with an elaborate cookout in posthumous honor of his birthday. Armsteads and Wootens and Kings would all come. In-laws and out-laws would all be invited. Better than any holiday or wedding or funeral, there would be food, laughter, softball, cards, good clean fun, music, and, of course, a mass conducted in one of the fields by a priest from our church.

The preparations would be lavish. There was a stone fireplace nestled near a bank of mature pines on the property that would be perfect for grilling. But to properly barbecue, Ma knew she had to have the finest state-of-the-art outdoor rotisserie, something she could only afford if each of us did our part. "Everyone has to tow the line," she stated matter-of-factly, for this dream of hers to come true.

Sheree, Lori, and I nodded sincerely, pledging to help.

During this time, grocery stores rewarded customers with S&H Green Stamps with every purchase. If you collected enough stamps, and pasted them in special books, you could earn gifts and prizes. My sisters and I knew one thing: to get that rotisserie, there were going to be a lot of Green Stamps to lick.

One of my favorite visitors of this early era was the inimitable Mrs. Esther "Bird" Doliber. Once a beauty queen crowned Miss Waltham, Massachusetts, back in the 1920s—"Oh, yes, she was a looker," Agatha told me more than once—Esther "Bird" and her husband, Ross Doliber, shared quite a family history. Mr. Doliber had grown up on our farm, formerly a dairy farm, as a child, insisting that Forest Edge was a slice of Eden. Mr. Doliber was proud of his history and one day told his wife they were taking a summer drive down memory lane, and she was not at all happy about it. Mrs. Doliber was still fuming when her husband recognized Forest Edge, and the two stopped to ask Agatha if she would mind letting them look around. It didn't take long for Ma to invite them in to "take a load off." Nor did it take long for me to introduce myself to this regal lady.

Years later, Mrs. Doliber sent me a letter describing that day. "The car had hardly stopped in the yard when you came right up to me as I was getting out of the car," she wrote. "It made such an impression on me that somehow I felt a kindred spirit with you—the dear little girl that you were." I had the same feeling throughout their visit that spring day. I had a new friend. The only unhappy note was that much too quickly it was time for Mrs. Doliber to leave.

A lifelong aversion to separations, no matter how short they promised to be, had already begun, particularly after what had happened to Grandpa. Just the prospect of saying good-bye filled me with worry, sometimes even making it hard for me to breathe. As though in reverse, on that occasion, rather than acknowledging that it was time for Mrs. Doliber to go, I took off running, not sure where or why, through the woodshed, up the stairs, and into the adjoining kitchen. Perched on my knees at the red Formica table, with paper and crayons, I began to frantically draw, soon producing a series of four images, each in its own square. Perhaps, since it was before I had the ability to write full sentences, I was trying to tell her that I was going to miss her, that she made me feel happy, and that I hoped she would come back soon.

Back outside I ran, dashing through the woodshed, past our artesian well, nearly tripping over myself, and I handed my drawing to Mrs. Doliber. "This is for you," I said breathlessly, and then added, "because I love you."

She gently grasped the drawing, studied it carefully, her eyes widening with interest as was a habit she had, "For me?" she asked, then finally said, "Thank you."

At Christmas, Mrs. Doliber, a published poetess, sent a season's greetings card to Agatha and enclosed a poem she penned describing that day and receiving a drawing from me.

THE GIFT

We drove around to the old farm
Where we used to go in the summer with the children
We were just wondering who lived there now.
We stopped in the yard, and a little child
Came to us from the house, clutching a piece of paper
On which were drawn crude child sketches
And she laid them in my hand and said,
"This is for you because I love you."
She had never seen me before—her skin
Was darker than mine, not of my race,
That little girl—
But the faith and trust that I loved her too
And would cherish her gift shone
In that little face like a precious pearl
Like the Christmas of long ago, God said,
"This is for you, because I love you,"
And He gave us a tiny gift, crudely cradled.
No one had seen Him before, and He had not seen us,
But from that moment all mankind was one people:
And He grew and taught and suffered and died and said:
"This is for you because I love you."
This piece of paper with its crude sketches
From the hand of a little child who said,
"This is for you, because I love you."
I shall cherish to remind me of what Love really is.
(John 13:34—A new commandment I give unto you,
that ye shall love one another as I have loved you).
BY ESTHER BIRD DOLIBER, WALTHAM, MASS.

Agatha was as moved as I was. To prove it, she put the poem on display, atop her baby grand piano, next to a vase of pussy willows she had cut from our pond. Agatha wanted me to understand that it was possible at any age to make an impression on a person, that it was never too late to learn how to love. Mrs. Doliber had given me a taste of the transformational power of art, something that would become a lasting theme in my life. For that gift, I was forever indebted to Mrs. Doliber and stayed in touch with her and her family, namely her grandson, Peter Doliber, from that day forward.

Agatha continued in her determination to find the best education possible for me and my sisters. Following the annual cookout in Maine in August 1963, she insisted that she be granted permission to move my sisters and me to 2 Elm Street in Dorchester, Massachusetts, where she had raised her own nine surviving children, so that I could be enrolled in a local Head Start program at the ages of four and five, with the promise of returning me to Maine each spring. Permission was granted, and so I watched her Steinway roll off of a moving truck and into a new beginning.

Like many children who grapple with instabilities in their home and family lives, I depended on my early observational powers for stability, as a way to give me a desperately needed connection—not just to other human beings but to all that was certain and tangible: things, events, actions, and, most of all, to the ultimate Mother, who became a close personal friend, Nature herself. I became a self-appointed devotee to everything Mother Nature and her protégée, Agatha Armstead, could teach me at the real-life school of Forest Edge.

Forever, I could return to this world and the permanent collage of impressions that became my stability and my happy childhood. I would walk through them blindfolded, knowing in my muscles and cells how long it took to run up the walkway to the front door of the farmhouse from Barley Road, or follow behind Ma through her vegetable garden, row after row, with her eyedropper, squeezing two or three drops of magic oil into the silk of each growing ear of corn. We strolled beyond, to the open field where we gathered to celebrate birthdays and cookouts.

Against the moss-covered stone wall that ran the far border of Forest Edge were wild blueberry bushes, bursting with berries waiting to be picked.

Before I could read and write, I could name flowers, birds, various types of reptiles, and every animal on the farm. Honeysuckle, spirea, forsythia, Japanese irises, roses, gladiolas, poppies, jonquils, peonies, lilacs, phlox, and crocuses all deserved a place of honor and bloomed from spring until our first fall frost.

By scent alone, I followed the delicate fragrance of the Double Serringa blossoms, past our slate-covered well, into our massive barn, which held a museum's worth of other people's lifetimes, including a huge old organ with missing pedals and keys dominating the cavernous space. I would secretly steal away to play it as often as I could, standing on the tops of my toes, swaying back and forth. As I passed the chicken coop, the pig and lamb pens, down a deep gully en route to the frog pond, the soles of my sneakers gripped the tall grass to ascend to the other side. Before me was heaven all over again: an apple orchard.

After climbing a tree and plucking an apple, I headed back, passing our incinerator as it choked and puffed on anything we could turn into ash. As I helped Agatha mix coffee grinds, eggshells, and the ash, she said to me, "This'll put vitamins back into our soil." I watched as she took such care, folding the mixture into the earth, as though preparing to bake a cake.

I befriended every single chick that Sydney Heath, a neighborhood farmer who cut our fields and baled our hay, delivered, only to watch my grown-up pets condemned to die at the hand of Aunt Kay as she swaggered up the road from her trailer, hatchet in hand, like Brecht's Mother Courage. Agatha's firstborn, a tough, full-time factory worker and mother of five, had one thing to say as she hollered to all of us standing around, "You kids stand back!" Obediently, I inched away from the tree stump where the executions were held year in and year out.

The cool and controlled Aunt Kay unleashed her rage by raising the axe high in the air, beheading one chicken after another, spraying blood onto my favorite Capri pants.

Not our place to question the whys of the world or the ways of the farm, we knew what was coming next. My job was to sit there, in dusty pigtails, on the same crate the now dead pets arrived in, plucking their headless bodies. Sheree and I would take turns, striking matches until dusk, running the flame along the naked flesh, removing any remnant of eider, before I sadly carried the lifeless birds in to Agatha.

Farm chores during these years became an extension of myself, like tying my shoelaces. Automatic. Wrapping copper pipes with electrical cord we then plugged into outlets to warm the pipes and keep the water inside from freezing. Securing plastic around windows. Stocking pens and sheds with food. Agatha had the most important job at the end of the day—making sure all the kerosene stoves were turned off.

In an evening ritual, after supper, my sisters and I teamed up or divided duties. Endowed with cleaning tools that Grandpa had brought home from his days at the hospital, we attacked our responsibilities with a sense of purpose. A glorious mustached broom was put to use for sweeping the kitchen's black-and-white speckled linoleum floor. I would jump astride the wooden base and use my fisted hands to nearly choke the life out of its neck while Sheree pulled me around the kitchen, sweeping as we played. Our irrepressible laughter competed with Agatha's TV nightly news.

"Any foolishness and there won't be any dessert tonight" was her melodic warning. This was especially effective on nights when Agatha's homemade strawberry ice cream, apple pie, or both were promised. Continued laughter provoked her to call out to us from the front room with a memorable Agathaism: "Enough is enough and too much is foolish."

Even when she was scolding us, the music of her voice, warm with love, never off-key, was backed by an orchestra of sound that played season in and season out at Forest Edge. It was the musical score of nature and the Rowell girls on the back porch doing renditions of the Supremes and our practiced choreography. It was the percussion of rain and thunder, drumming to accompany Agatha's jazz piano, which she practiced on schedule one hour every day at dusk, sometimes singing standards like "Misty" with a bold, vaguely operatic abandon.

It was the sound of industry, the tapping of Ma's red manicured fingernails against the keys of her dependable vintage Underwood typewriter as she expertly whipped off crisply worded business letters—in duplicate with a carbon between the two pieces of stationery—the contents pertaining no doubt to property and other legal matters or special requests to Child Welfare in Augusta on our behalf.

On warm summer nights, parades of fireflies, mosquitoes, and moths clung to our screened-in porch, where grown-ups congregated to play cards 'til all hours—bid whist, the derivation of which seemed to belong to somebody in this dynasty. Raymond's voice—often threatening—soared above the rest. Grandstanding, making sure that none of the other players ever stood a chance of "making books," the critical component to winning this game, as he slapped his lucky card onto the table, saying to his wife, "We're goin' downtown, Francine!" The sun started to set behind the forest, as rows and rows of cornstalks, reminiscent of a silent audience, faced the porch. Animated voices called for another round of play mixed in with the clinks of cans, bottles, and ashtrays.

Considered a threat due to Sheree's allergies, our cat, Malty, was obliterated by a shotgun blast in the field. Later, my sisters and I buried pieces of Malty, a gravesite I still visit. During hunting season, it was not uncustomary to see deer, eyes bulging, strapped to the roofs of cars or hanging upside down from the pine trees that lined Barely Road, creating tiny rivulets of blood. It also wasn't uncustomary for one of my foster uncles to bring his dead deer back to Lynn, Massachusetts, and hang the carcass from the second floor of his home in the projects and later consume the venison.

And there was the terror my sisters and I felt when a man in a gray paratrooper's jumpsuit, slightly disoriented, walked across our field in broad daylight while we were playing under makeshift picnic tables. With our foster cousin Joanie, we ran screaming into the house, desperate for Agatha's explanation: "He must be from the government; they're always coming around here wanting to talk to me about some foolishness—something about uranium on my property." Needless to say, nobody could force Agatha to do anything.

Acorns, peanuts, cranberries, huckleberries, blackberries, raspberries, teaberries, apples, pears, and grapes all grew in abundance under Agatha's green thumb. Also abundant on the farm were hornets, bees, bats, mice, spiders, and snakes—and that was in the house. Once a mouse I was rescuing bit my finger, drawing blood. In that simple experience, I learned that I could not save everything, and that everything didn't want to be rescued. It would take me many years to apply this lesson to people. During an end of the summer ritual, I, along with five of Agatha's grandchildren, painted our initials on the backs of turtles' shells, using Ma's fire engine red fingernail polish, only to watch our branded turtles disappear into the effluvium of the marshes. Waiting by the edge of the pond the following spring, with great expectation, I jumped up and down when my foster cousin Kevin exclaimed, "There goes Vicki's turtle."

Never to be forgotten on a hot summer day was the cellar. Its distinct, pungent smell emanated from its dirt floor, luring me to carefully step down the uneven, warped stairs, clearing cobwebs along the way to my private cathedral. The natural cooling was lit by a single naked lightbulb and held a bounty that reminded me that we would never starve—eggs in crock dots, canned vegetables, and jarred jellies were everywhere. During harvest season, I would climb into our potato bins and weed out the vegetables with potato rot, before dumping in freshly collected Russets from our burlap bags. I loved everything about farming—earthworms and ladybugs, the powerful freedom of pulling a radish from my Mother's bosom, brushing it against my shorts and popping it into my mouth; the gritty taste of the soil. Agatha always said, "Dirt's good for you—you'll eat a *peck a dirt* a year." I came to understand this meaning in a broader sense later in life. I loved the fertile honesty of moist soil between my hands and under my fingernails. It was life.

Dirt came to mean two things: a source of good, never failing to give back, hence, providing nourishment. For me, later confounded by my rootlessness, destined to be a gypsy, the smell of wet soil would always remind me of home and that dirt was always mine to stand on.

Random images: me busily redecorating the woodshed, arranging the anvil and other tools, staining furniture, bewildered adult onlookers, my first attempts at interior decorating. Ma's Easter egg hunts in the garden amid dead cornstalks and rotten pumpkins. Weeding diminutive carrot plants taught patience, lessons of transformation when green tomatoes, wrapped in newspaper, turned the Big Boys red. Chopping and mixing hay with manure—spreading it across the garden. My bullish stubbornness, wanting to help the family soften brittle linoleum, resulted in me burning my arm badly against our four-foot kerosene stove in the process; Agatha's African folk remedy was in the form of a cooling black salve.

Snow, ice, cold. Frozen pipes. Frozen toilet water. Clean laundry hung out to dry in winter, freezing in shapes like Christmas ornaments hanging on the line. Icicles kissing snowdrifts outside our windows. The wooden fences in the field bent sideways by wrathful winds and storms. Winter nights so black they were blue, pierced by a blanket of stars, then punctuated by the Big and Little Dippers. The resilient emergence of the sun on a Maine winter day, dressing the world in blinding crystallized beauty. En route to the pond after it had been tested for safety, my secondhand skates slung over my shoulder, I avoided sliding on an icy patch of ground before reaching my destination. We all skated on faith, especially Sheree, who was either naturally gifted in this arena or simply unafraid of falling. Me, I looked for assistance in my determination to learn, grabbing onto anything for support—a spray of cat-o'-nine-tails or a jutting branch, anything to avoid hitting the ice. I skated poorly, my ankles rolled in, until I couldn't feel my toes and headed back to the house; Sheree, on the other hand, could skate all day long. As I trekked back, with every step sinking at least one foot into the snow, I thought about Grandpa and his big snowshoes still stored in the woodshed, how vestiges of him were preserved everywhere.

Memories within memories: Expeditions to Fernald Shores for swimming in the lake and skipping rocks; a quarter per person, cars filled to the gills, the chassis scraping against the bumpy path. The way Ma predicted the weather, saying, "Here comes an electrical storm; better unplug the television." The way Ma said, "Shhhhhh, my stories are on." This was her only indulgence, her only distraction from real life. The two lambs I raised since birth escaped death yet again due to an overbooked slaughterhouse. I would burst into the house after school desperately hoping for another day of grace for my lambs. I took a chance and approached Ma, filled with angst. In a controlled whisper, I asked, "Where are Ruth and Joanne?" I had named them after my favorite actresses on the TV show *Laugh-In*. Agatha's eyes stayed hypnotically fixed on the RCA, not blinking a lash, and replied, "Go look in the deep freezer, sugar." Already knowing the answer, tears began to well up as I slowly walked through our house toward the pantry. I took a deep breath before lifting the heavy metal lid of the freezer. A waft of frozen air obscured my view before clearing, then there, all neatly wrapped in white butcher's paper, were my pet lambs. Becoming weak, I let the lid slam shut and ran up to the attic where no one could see or find me. Beneath a window on a chair was Patti Page, exactly as I had left her. Her voice, always dependable, expressed everything I was feeling from our 1940s Crosley record player.

One of Agatha's outlets—which she turned into a kind of meditation—was ironing. She had a professional expertise in laundering and pressing clothes, which she acquired as a young girl when her family took in washing for wealthy clients on Beacon Hill and on the Cape. This meant that laundering at Forest Edge was a major to-do, an art, with conservation of the water supply from our artesian well being of the utmost importance. Mesmerized, I watched the laundry move smoothly through the rollers of our round 1940s-era washing machine that stood on four legs. Everything was hung out on the clothesline to dry. Ma, with a healthy supply of wooden clothespins in her pocket, signaled when it was time for me to haul the cumbersome ironing board from the pantry. A piece of wood four feet in length, wrapped one hundred times in white sheets—with character-building burn stains—held in place by safety pins, it went into position between a makeshift countertop and a kitchen chair. She swung into action, mixing the starch herself, dipping her big hand into the filmy liquid, flicking it from her fingers onto the clothes. Agatha showed me how she wet her index finger and touch it against the face of hot iron with lightning speed, before grasping it and bearing down—committing her whole body into the gentle rhythm of pressing. Blouses, shorts, linens, even my underwear. I could appreciate how Agatha turned something that was labor into an art. She taught me the dance of ironing, as well as the Zen of it.

Images compete for attention in my memory. Trekking into the woods with adults out front, kids in the back, blurring the lines between chores and fun, we were going blueberry picking. Dressed in my striped Capri pants, floral '60s shell, and my red Keds, I took precise, even-paced steps, making sure that I had my necklace—a long piece of twine attached to an empty Chock full o'Nuts coffee can that would hold the blueberries. I treaded in single file, avoiding the oil on the pretty, shiny leaves reaching out to lick my legs—poison ivy—me sniffing the air that was thick with the fragrance of decomposing plants, ripe fruit, and the undeniable scent of dead animal.

Keithie, Agatha's grandson, began to whistle, and the irrepressible beauty of his birdcall echoed throughout the woods. Over our laughter I heard a whip-poor-will singing out its own name and cupped my hands on either side of my mouth to answer back, "Whip-poor-will, whip-poor-will!" Lori, then eight years old with a delicate constitution, rolled her eyes at my birdcall and teased, "You're weird," as she continued on. I wondered why wanting to communicate with nature was weird.

Wishing she could be anywhere else besides picking blueberries in the woods, Sheree shrugged me off, saying, "Don't ask stupid questions." Where one half sister was usually quiet and aloof, the other was a rebel, her anger and hurt simmering just below the surface—normal reactions for a foster child, but made much worse by the harsh punishment she received from Raymond, Agatha's youngest son, a sanctioned and terrifying disciplinarian.

I was eating handfuls of berries at a time, turning my tongue and teeth purple—bugs, stems, and all of nature in my mouth simultaneously. Agatha had promised blueberry pies, provided that everyone came back with a full can. We knew the chiding would be relentless if we didn't oblige. This went for young and old. No exceptions.

Just outside the clearing, tucked behind waxy green leaves, I spotted a solitary Lady's Slipper. She was pink with arresting beauty. I moved closer, transfixed by her long-stemmed neck and translucent bloom, as the group traveled on. My first impulse was to pluck the rare orchid. I refrained only because Agatha had once told me, "It's against the law, sugar, she's a rare flower." Still, I wondered who would see me out there in the middle of the woods alone. I was saved from the temptation by a booming call from one of the adults, "C'mon, let's head back," and off I ran to catch up.

My can was full; the twine cut into the sweaty nape of my neck, and mosquitoes were starting to nip, drawing blood on my ankles and shoulders. I watched the sun begin to fall and imprint a mighty new concept in my being—it was the idea that the appreciation of a thing of beauty like the Lady's Slipper or the rich memory of that day was something that no one could take away from me. What I felt, saw, recognized, and remembered all became part of the true treasures of these years at Forest Edge.

From this revelation I acquired an enduring appreciation for the incredible foliage that changes with the seasons. The different types of trees appeared to be fancy ladies in dress-up clothes, like me going through Ma's closet, thick with the smell of her favorite fragrance, Chantilly, trying on her collection of '40s department store shoes and hats. With her old pedal-driven Singer sewing machine, she managed to create a wardrobe for herself by purchasing patterns and sometimes creating her own, making elegant, tailored dresses, evening wear, suits, costumes, and even coats. A wool skirt she made me for the first grade became a part of my keepsake collection, as would many things I collected from Agatha, including Robert Armstead's rock collection and the hand-painted metal box he had kept them in.

Of course, New England foliage is legendary, but Maine is without rival; in the autumn when the colors were so vibrant, I insisted on saving my favorites by taking each special leaf, placing it between two sheets of wax paper, then using a warm iron to seal it into immortality. Midday walks with Ma down Barley Road into a panorama of bursting oranges, reds, yellows, and browns were stolen moments to hear stories as I kept my eyes on the ground looking for the most vividly colored fallen birch, oak, and maple leaves, understanding that they would soon fade and crumble, eventually becoming one with the soil, bringing new life in another season.

On such a walk one fall day, about a half mile up the road, Agatha paused and pointed at the Amadon farmhouse, recalling how she once had heard someone or something moaning, loud enough to give her cause for concern. She had to investigate.

Enthralled by Ma's bravery, who taught that danger lurks in the unfamiliar, I listened as she described finding Mrs. Amadon, an invalid, collapsed on her toilet, immobile. Ma described how she called on that inexplicable physical strength that appears when women most need it and lifted Mrs. Amadon, washed her, and put her to bed. Ma didn't say how long Mrs. Amadon had been there. What she did say was that when people need help, you help them. Plain and simple.

The pride I felt in Agatha's kindness was immeasurable. Whatever prejudices there might have existed when the Armsteads first moved to West Lebanon were overcome through neighborly gestures like these. To show their appreciation for Ma's kindness, the Amadons sent fresh cream and containers of sweet butter on a regular basis thereafter.

Agatha would see my pride and smile, recognizing that connections were made without her having to give a sermon. In this way, we communicated without words, with me as the student and Agatha as my teacher. This was reinforced later in the evening when Ma gathered her grandchildren around her and spontaneously decided to make ice cream. Ma churned up the Amadons' finest cream with added rock salt, ice, and strawberries I had picked the day before; the tips of my fingers were still stained red. If it weren't for untold numbers of hours spent licking S&H Green Stamps, and placing them into booklets of dotted squares, sometimes in strips and other times individually, which Ma redeemed for our beloved pink ice cream maker, I might never have known the creamy, unrivaled flavor my bowl of heaven offered. Agatha not only fed me, but through her example, taught me of life's unexpected rewards through kindness and hard work.

The catalog for S&H Green Stamps reinforced that idea, too. After sitting for hours, licking stamps and filling up booklets, all I needed for inspiration was to look at the alluring descriptions of those prizes, despite the fact that by the time I finished filling up a booklet, the taste of glue on my tongue completely obliterated any vestige of Ma's supper that night.

There were home economics and business management lessons here, too. This was no accident. Instituting a practice that was very unusual in the foster care system, Agatha insisted that each of us have our own saving accounts. I was six when I proudly walked into the Rochester Trust Company in New Hampshire. Also known as the Lilac City, Rochester was the gateway to the world for me, a point of departure.

On occasion, after Agatha deducted from her social services and social security checks, with documented scrutiny, she presented each of us with a small allowance for completed chores. Ma accompanied me up to the teller, my heart beating a mile a minute with anticipation, as I rose to demi-pointe and relinquished my saved change. Even though the bouffant-coiffed teller mistook me for a little boy, my braids hidden under my hood, this did not dull my enthusiasm in the least. Each time I went back to the bank with my red plaid savings book, I saw proof that if you saved, you gained interest. I thought this was a great deal!

Just as Ma wanted us to learn to save, she must have been the unofficial president of the "waste not, want not" school of thinking. Richard, Agatha's fourth-born child, could remember the Depression years when, as he said, "We were so hungry we used to scrape the burned rice off the bottom of the pot," and he very much believed that my sisters and I were spoiled because we would never have to do so. Richie would always say, "You kids are lucky; you have no idea." In a way I felt guilty, because I knew I was getting the best parts of his mother, no longer struggling between ten children, trying to make ends meet, and that's what her son saw. We probably were spoiled in many ways, compared to how Agatha had brought up her own children in another era, but Ma did her best for all of us and made sure none of us ever took material things for granted.

There were three things Ma hated wasting: electricity, time, and water. I brushed my teeth and washed my face once a day, in the morning, and shared bathwater on Saturday nights. Our hair was washed and pressed once a month. Agatha also had three fears: God, fire, and ever losing Forest Edge. "You must think I have money to burn" was an oft-used quip, as was her admonition to "stop wasting electricity," together with her matter-of-fact observation "Every time you turn the lights off and on, that's five cents."

In this regard, the Green Stamps were instructive, too, since a trip to the Globe, our closest grocery store, provided an opportunity to estimate exactly how many stamps our purchases might yield, which

Ma calculated with her red plastic gizmo, pressing three white buttons like keys on a trumpet, to keep track of her running tab. Grocery shopping, therefore, was never just about food. It was a first stop on the road to attaining modern technology. But Forest Edge was not entirely stuck in the Dark Ages. Agatha had her cherished electric blanket, the RCA television set, and the ungainly green rotisserie that was wheeled out of the woodshed amid much fanfare, to be admired and revered, like a Roman gladiator, strategically placed in front of one of her burgeoning flower beds. It was the centerpiece of the annual cookout.

Without question, Agatha Armstead was the eighth wonder of the world, the original multitasker, with a method to her genius. Take the epic process of canning and processing goods; the rest of us were mere mortals, there to pick, dice, wash, chop, and cheer Agatha on to the ultimate outcome: vegetables, jarred pickles, jams, cranberry and apple sauces, homemade cider, various wines, and of course, her famous beer. By age six I was a canning veteran; I was taught that canning was both art and science and about the perils of botulism and the importance of french cutting and labeling. Aesthetics counted obviously in the peeling, paring, dicing, and slicing of foods to be preserved in Mason jars. After all, items like her coveted dill pickles were given as gifts throughout the year accented by sprigs of homegrown dill and cloves of garlic. It all had to look appealing on the shelf—besides having the right crunch and tang.

Depending on what was being canned, this process could go on for weeks, from the act of gathering supplies to the melting of wax to be used for sealing containers, to the food preparation in the kitchen with bubbling, percolating vats and pots and pans, as Ma hovered over it all like Madame Curie in her laboratory. We were dispatched to collect Grandpa's old beer jugs, and to set them up as a barricade to the kitchen entrance, in the unlikely case of an explosion. Then, when the coast was clear, we were invited back in a steamy kitchen to admire the beauty and the settling aroma of the cooling concoctions. When steam from the boiling pots transformed Ma's synthetic wig into something that looked more like a Berber rug, she would say, "I know I look like *zip in distress*," and quickly remedied the situation by grabbing the bangs of her wig and rotating the front to the back. Everyone fell out with laughter each time she did this. Agatha not only had a brilliant sense of humor but also didn't have time for vanity when there was serious work to be done. Finally, in a sort of ad hoc assembly line, the canning jars were checked for cracks and lids with metal clamps were secured before they were labeled with Agatha's exquisite penmanship. My sisters and I took turns carefully placing the glass jars in the pantry, a built-in icebox in the kitchen, the cellar, our linen closet (where Agatha kept all of her beautiful linen and lace tablecloths), and other spaces in between. She even stored a few jars in her bedroom. When we were done, we were cooked. Not one square inch of our home seemed to be spared from Mason, Ball, and Kerr canning jars.

⟡

I was taught that there were no shortcuts in life to completing a full cycle. It was how nature worked. Moreover, I learned that follow-through and completion were the only means to earning a desired result. And none of this could have been brought forth if not for the power of Agatha's exhaustless ability to envision completion, starting with the inspiration she gleaned from magazines, her primary source for planning her garden before planting. Next, mail-order Burpee seeds were cultivated in little peat pots on windowsills, barely past winter. She taught me to attend to each seedling and sprout with the most attentive care: how to avoid overwatering or being tempted to tear away a husk; but rather allowing nature to release its natural wonder in its own time. To see the first glimpse of green growth poking through was an absolute miracle to me, an experience that I could share with Ma, year after year.

In my six-year-old arms I carefully transported fragile tiny plants to the freshly tilled garden, delighting in watching Agatha's excitement as she was outfitted in overalls and kneepads to buffer her brittle bones. Momentarily, not feeling any pain, she was in her element as she pierced the soil with her trowel, providing just enough dimension for me to follow behind and place the peat pot into the earth, old hands over young hands securing it. We did this over and over until we finished. As I helped Ma to her feet, she always said "Whew, it's getting hot out here." With her hands on her hips and my arm threaded through one of hers, I leaned on my pillar of strength as we admired our work together. The hint of a kitchen towel she used to pad her bra where the hollow had been peeked out just under her neck, as we made our way to get a cold glass of well water. The sight was so familiar to me that it became endearing, and a reminder that she had refused the expense of breast reconstruction.

With *Star Trek* over and the picture tube now reduced to a white dot, Ma reminded us that it was time to return to Earth: "Let's say prayers." On our rusty knees, heads bowed, fingers interlocked, lips moving, quietly reciting words I didn't understand, giving them my own pronunciation, I continued praying the way Agatha taught me to pray, even for those who mean you harm.

On those Sundays when weather prevented us from getting to church we participated at home from our living room, watching mass on our RCA. I did my best to reenact receiving Communion, even if we didn't have the actual Eucharist. And though Agatha was not exactly crazy about my theatrical display, she didn't find it to be blasphemous, so didn't say anything as I took reverent steps up to the television screen, knelt before it, stuck out my tongue to receive the imaginary wafer, and blessed myself before moving back to my chair. Before we went to bed that night, Ma would have the last word, completing the service with a glass of Manischewitz wine, her favorite.

Ma's room was always a haven, where all things fearful or confusing were banished. During a time when I slept with Ma, I jumped into bed first. Here there were cures and potions, clarity and history. There were trinkets, beads, pill bottles, her jars of Pond's cold cream, skin lotions, face powder, fabulous and expensive wigs on stands and forms, clocks, candles, fabric, yarn, rugs, color, and texture for days—all in that compact New England sleeping space. On the rare occasion where I wasn't feeling well, there was always a jar of Vicks VapoRub at the ready, the cure-all that Agatha would rub on my chest, then give me a teaspoon of to ingest, saying, "This'll kill that cold." *And me, too,* I thought, but I never asked why and just swallowed. I could feel the blob of heat making its way down like a slow ball of fire.

One night, I had questions and not enough answers. As I lay there in Ma's bed, I still wondered who those black people were I had seen in my town the week before. How did they find our little enclave? Weren't we the only black people in Maine? I stared at them the way locals stared at me all the time. I guess I was just shocked to see other people who looked like me who weren't Agatha's relatives.

Then there was some other confusion. Where did the Rowell name come from? What did "foster" mean? Many times Ma was asked if we were related; she always noted, "Yes, Vicki is my foster daughter," and I cringed each time, feeling exposed. The church lady asking on that day said, "Well, she looks just like you, anyway," and awkwardly walked off. I didn't believe the lady who had just come out of Sunday service anymore than she believed herself. Couldn't I just be Agatha's daughter?

All such thoughts dimmed when Ma entered the room on the night in question, lighting it with her presence, as she looked down to see that I had laid out her rosary beads and her orange polyester pajamas.

"Thank you, Vicki," she said, beaming, pleased at this small courtesy, just as she was every night.

Sometimes by the time Agatha had begun to prepare for bed, I had fallen asleep, or at least closed my eyes to give her privacy. But this night I wasn't tired and found myself mesmerized by the blue ruffle that ran in a rectangle and hung above the bed in a dreamy canopy, which Agatha had attached to the ceiling with evenly spaced red thumbtacks. It wasn't hard to visualize the four mahogany bed posters holding up the ruffle, or so I imagined that was Ma's vision all along. Illusion. Magic.

"Time to turn over, sugar, and go to sleep," she said, interrupting my blue reverie, making sure my eyes were closed.

I promptly turned over, face to the wall, my nose against the moist air held within the two-hundred-year-old plaster. Ma was not only fiercely modest, but in preparing for her disrobing ceremony, she was protecting my young eyes from seeing her disfigurement. That had been explained without words many times, just as we knew that there was an imaginary line down the middle of the bed, leaving an empty space that protected privacy for the both of us.

This night, however, I needed at last to see for myself how deep her wounds were, how heavy her burden. Still facing the wall, I watched Agatha's shadow in silhouette fighting against itself on the patterned wallpaper. I had to see more; ever so slightly I peered over my shoulder and witnessed the agonizing struggle she undertook to unfasten hooks with her phlebitic fingers bent behind her crooked spine.

I held my breath until her effort and gravity could tear the medieval corset away from her ravaged torso and allow it to fall with a thud to the floor. We both exhaled.

Curious to see what else was to be peeled away, I continued to spy as she removed her wig and pinned it onto a Styrofoam form, moving next to lovingly apply cold cream to her face and throat. "Vicki," she whispered as she plucked up a tissue, not turning around to check whether I was awake or asleep, "always remember, the neck and chest are all part of the face."

Agatha knew all, and sensed, of course, that I had been watching her. She knew that I had seen her breastless body. Curved, bent, wounded. But beautiful. She knew I had seen her without her wig, two thin braids pinned neatly beneath the artificial hair. I lay frozen.

How did she channel away the pain, past and present every day? What was her secret? Later, I would find out.

After winding her West clock and popping a Rolaid, Agatha pinched out the last bits of light and instantaneously left us in complete blackness. In the time that the cricket sang his first notes, crucifixes, statuettes, rosary beads, and clocks were illuminated in a chartreuse glow. The creation of this light, I believed, had to be Agatha's private miracle.

I joined her in reciting the rosary, not understanding why she prayed for redemption. Or maybe I knew that she was as close to God as any human could be, and that through her, I was with God, too. I was still trying to figure out who God was or what God meant. Agatha seemed to sum it all up for me just lying there breathing with her plastic beads between her fingers. This was my fortress. She was my belonging.

Through Agatha, I had been given a foundation that provided guidelines for what mattered: Merit. Study. Hard, hard work. Investment in property and people. Humility, silent meditation, laughter, and music.

This moment in the sixth year of my life, August 1965, ended my carefree youth and was followed soon thereafter by a life-altering experience. I was getting ready to start the first grade at West Lebanon Elementary School and Agatha asked me a simple question.

Double-checking our annual purchase orders from the state for shopping for school clothes, she noticed that I was going through sneakers twice as fast as my sisters. She had only recently replaced my red Keds and already the toes were worn through. Turning the Keds over a few times in her hands, Ma lifted her head and set her chin like a detective out to uncover the truth and asked, "Vicki, why do you keep getting these holes in your sneakers?"

What I next explained to her by way of an answer would radically affect everything, not merely my whole future, but would reshape my past, condensing it all into an impressionistic collage of experiences that had transpired before Ma's discovery of those holes in my shoes.

"From the barn," I ventured. Her skeptical face made me explain a bit more. "I got them trying to standing on my toes."

"Standing on your toes?" asked Ma, curiously. "Show me."

She handed the Keds to me and off to the barn we went.

Leaning on the frame of the organ, I lifted myself onto my toes just like the little girl I saw who toe-tapped on a local TV show called the *Ted Mack Family Hour.* I suspended my weight between the tops of my sneakers and rough-hewn splintered floor.

An expression of wonder came into Agatha's eyes. How could holes in my sneakers make her this happy? I wondered. "Come with me, sugar," she said, as she took me by the hand, humming a tune all the way back into the house and into the front room toward the Steinway. She pulled a piece of Melrose Brothers Publishing sheet music out of her overstuffed piano bench, which held her dreams of yesteryear, and told me to stand in the middle of the room. She gracefully sat down as if to give a recital, then got up again and did something she only did for special occasions. She lifted the cumbersome ebony lid I'd polished so many times, sustaining it with its stand, revealing the wondrous secret workings of her instrument, a golden jewel box with red felt accents, which always dazzled me. Agatha sat back down, placed her foot on the brass damper pedal, spread her arthritic fingers across her ivory universe, and began to *swing.* "Let's have fun, Vicki!" With such an effort, I wanted to do something to please her but wasn't sure what.

Agatha disregarded my hesitation, gently commanding, "Move around the room, honey; do anything, just dance!"

I let the vibrations of Ma's voice and the cords emanating from her Steinway & Sons piano, inspired by a German cabinetmaker in his kitchen, move me, lift me, twirl me, creating shapes like the ones I saw the June Taylor Dancers do on *The Ed Sullivan Show*. Ma, not really needing the sheet music at all, closed her eyes behind her jeweled cat-eye bifocals, recalling perhaps her own inspiration from James P. Johnson and Willie "the Lion" Smith, and one of her favorite singers, Pearl Bailey, her feet rapidly moving across the damper, *sostenuto,* and soft pedals below. We improvised and collaborated, laughing and singing, both of us doing our dance. Then Ma stopped playing, abruptly. I stopped, too, out of breath and perspiring. Nodding her head as if to respond to a question she had silently asked herself, she said it out loud, "Yes, Sugar, there's no doubt about it, we've got to get you some dance lessons."

None of the Wootens, Kings, or Armsteads had ever trained in ballet. Whether Agatha had ever seen a professional ballet or had even a passing familiarity with the art form was doubtful. But not for a millisecond did she consider that she might not be qualified to teach me ballet, or at least to expose me to enough fundamentals to take advantage of the natural talent she believed I had shown her.

Just as Ma began so many of her undertakings, she went in search of magazines and books that might allow her not only to study up on the history and practice of ballet, but also provide her with visuals. Somewhere, possibly in a back issue of a magazine, Agatha located an article that showed the six rudimentary positions of the feet and arms, first documented by the court of Louis XIV and inspired by the courtier dances of Spain. In stark diagrams, stick figures illustrated the positions.

That was how we began together to have ballet class in the living room. Holding on to a heavy enameled doorknob substituting for a ballet barre, I attempted to mimic and re-create the positions. Agatha, with her knowledge of Latin, was able to decipher the pronunciation of the French words. After trying to contort my body back to the natural turnout every baby is born with, unsuccessfully holding the stick figures' positions, I came to the conclusion that though Ma said I had natural talent, ballet was completely unnatural.

Then again, the moment that Ma began to play, giving me an encouraging nudge and the basics plucked from the article she found, I began creating movement that belonged to no school but Agatha Armstead's School of Dance, and all that was soulful, elegant, beautiful, and had style.

The dream that had been Agatha's dream for a performing career began to become my dream. When the Wooten aunts and other relatives visited from Boston, Ma herded everyone into the small living room and insisted that they all be my audience while she played something from "Jack The Bear" by Duke Ellington or a composition by Count Basie. Tentative at first, I came to love every moment, encouraged by that blur of faces as I twirled around the braided rug.

I began to understand, even at the age of eight, that physical struggle was a part of learning how to dance. I also realized something else that became much clearer later on—that my love affair with ballet was a double-edged sword, a dance/fight to channel pain, to stave off exhaustion, to defy gravity, and to make something extraordinarily difficult appear effortless.

To keep the necessary balance, my touchstone turned out to be a story that contained Ma's secret method for channeling pain that she finally confided in me, after nearly two years of exploring ballet together.

Agatha's annual mitten knitting enterprise was under way, another shared activity that made it possible for us to talk for hours about everything under the sun. That is, everything but anything remotely related to sex, gossip, or repetitions of anything said that had cussing in it or taking the Lord's name in vain. Other than that, the sky was the limit. Ma rarely veered from plan or schedule to make the same three dozen or more pairs of mittens; our routine by now was well rehearsed. Using my forearms as spindles, I anchored a single strand of navy blue wool between my thumb and fist—the same grip for holding pencils that parochial school nuns could never get me to change; Ma wound the skein around and around and every so often I would get a whiff of the Chantilly fragrance she religiously applied to her wrists and neck every morning.

When I saw the small-gauge needles moving at lightning speed, *clickety-click, click, clickety-click,* in their own rhythm—knit two, purl one, knit two, purl one—I wondered how such thick fingers could manipulate such tiny stitches so expertly. The answer was Ma's theme—that pure intention could make impossible things happen.

On that note, she began her story. It had happened in the early 1900s, in Alston, Massachusetts, where her family first owned property after migrating north from the Carolinas. As an adolescent, Agatha had already endured the agony of being in a body cast for a full year following surgery to correct scoliosis. Resilient though she was, fearless in many ways, she had a paralyzing terror of the horse-drawn fire engines that came speeding so recklessly around the corners by the Wootens' house. She was sure that one day they would veer off course and careen into her and anyone who happened to be in their path. In a self-fulfilling prophecy, when the tower bells began to toll one afternoon that a fire was burning in the town square, she was on her porch as six white horses pulling the fire truck came fiercely galloping around the corner directly toward her. In blinding fear, Agatha ran into the house and flew up several steps, but just before the top landing, she lost her balance and fell backward, head over heels all the way down to the vestibule landing.

It was a miracle that she lived. Every physician who examined her was shocked that she walked again. Again, for months, she remained in a body cast. In miserable confinement, Agatha taught herself that through silent meditation, not wallowing in her own suffering, she could master the ability to self-modulate pain by offering it to the most deserving and vulnerable—children. Still in a body cast, she returned to school.

One morning in the classroom, upon realizing that she could no longer expand her rib cage, Agatha drew from her most vital resources and managed to run home. Her father, John Wooten, was working on a piece of furniture, and when he saw his daughter's distresss, he grabbed a hammer and cracked open the plaster cast himself.

This was the secret she taught me, an effective technique, as well as a talisman to ward off physical pain or adversity. That story by itself revealed everything about Agatha Armstead that I ever needed to know—comforting and inspiring me beyond measure during rough rides ahead.

Another keepsake would travel with me, long after Agatha was gone—the enamel doorknob that was my first ballet barre from the farmhouse at Forest Edge, which I proudly display in my home today as a reminder that love is eternal.

THREE

THE WOOTEN SISTERS &
THE ARMSTEAD DAUGHTERS

The excitement that filled the air all along Barley Road in the days and weeks leading up to August 14, when the annual cookout commemorating Robert Armstead's birthday was held, seemed to grow exponentially with every passing year; 1967 was no different.

Eight years old, still a ways off from adolescence, I depended dearly on extended family gatherings for a glimpse into the world beyond the sheltered sphere of the farm. Somewhat cut off from the outside world, Ma faithfully stayed current with Walter Cronkite on the nightly news. She followed the work of the Reverend Dr. Martin Luther King Jr., the Vietnam War, the Beatles, hippies, the Black Panthers, and the cultural revolution that was taking hold in most major urban areas. Watching the news was a tradition. A few years earlier, when the Boston Strangler was in the headlines and on the loose, I can remember staying up on Sunday nights with my sisters, watching the nightly news, brandishing Ma's cast iron frying pans, Ma with Grandpa's rifle at the ready, just in case the Boston Strangler came to Forest Edge.

With the exception of variety shows like *Ed Sullivan*, *A Star for a Day*, and *Jackie Gleason*, most of what we watched on television was white. With the exception of the character Rochester, played by actor

Eddie Anderson, who starred on *The Jack Benny Show*, it wasn't until 1966 that I witnessed black characters in a regular series, such as the breathtakingly beautiful Nichelle Nichols as Lieutenant Uhura on *Star Trek*. Nichols sent shock waves around the nation as she was further catapulted into fame and history along with William Shatner, boldly going where no two people had gone before; they kissed! Right there on national television, right there in our living room, right there in front of Ma as I sat between her knees, playing with the donuts she made out of her stockings just above her shin! Oh, my goodness, none of us could believe it and I tried to pretend I hadn't seen it. And instead of Ma saying, "I think you kids should go to bed," she let me watch. She let me watch something she couldn't talk about—kissing, sexual attraction, and, beyond that, interracial love. I can remember exactly how natural that moment felt. At last, I had witnessed a black person and a white person romantically embracing. And prior to that in the ballet world were New York City Ballet dancers Arthur Mitchell, who was black, and Allegra Kent, who was white, intertwined in a passionate pas de deux. Sponsors were outraged, but the nation survived it and grew.

Next, in 1968, was Diahann Carroll, starring in *Julia*. Carroll was incandescent, and I wondered why she wasn't Miss America.

For all that TV lacked by way of diversity, Agatha's annual cookout, a show unto itself, gave me everything television was lacking and then some. I marveled at the various big-city hairdos and fashions, listening to the accents and the tonations of the Wootens and the Armsteads telling their stories. In the swirl of conversation once the cookout was in full swing, many more chapters of history, scandal, and success would unfold.

In addition to being part of the action, I also loved hanging back, just listening to the elders. Storytelling time. The Wooten sisters, sitting in green-and-white plastic woven chairs under the shade, talking about the world and history, their history. They talked about everything; how, *in their day*, a bottle of Pemberton's Coca-Cola, for 5 cents, bought you more than syrup, the NAACP and Paul Robeson, music and education, heroic black leaders past and present, and how sweet Agatha's corn was that year. They shared how proud they were of the successes of their immediate and extended families. They laughed like they were singing and cried like they were laughing.

Moving on from the elders and farther down the field were the younger aunts, sitting on the stone wall, smoking and spilling rich, juicy gossip and, yes, they were talking about sex. I was all ears. There was only so much about the birds and the bees that I could figure out on my own being raised on the farm or from playing kissin' cousins in the barn, which would have made Ma apoplectic if she had figured it out. Her idea of sex education did not extend past the science of botany. But once the cookout got going, many more chapters of fooling around, shenanigans, and seductions were to be had.

There was trouble and tragedy. There were those who fell and those who got up again. As in most extended families, there were branches that thought they were superior to others. According to the cookout gossip, there were wives who didn't deserve their men, and wives who wouldn't leave their men no matter what. One wife took another wife's husband while another woman didn't need a husband at all. While some husbands were adored, others were henpecked. Some were princes, some cads, and some were low-down and just plain wrong.

I vividly experienced the stories told by my extended family. Part soap opera, part sitcom, both fiction and nonfiction, they were more than merely tantalizing. Somehow, paying attention to the oral history of this family, the process, of listening and allowing the stories to become mine, seemed to legitimize my place as a familial member. The cookout also gave me the luxury of bonding with the Wooten/Armstead inner circle of women—the fabulous, sensational, brilliant, powerful, inimitable aunts.

Agatha's three sisters were not kin to me; however, out of respect and affection, I referred to them as aunts: Aunt Marion, Aunt T, and Aunt Ruthie. Agatha's four daughters and five daughters-in-law were more accurately my foster sisters, although I referred to them as aunts as well. Marion, Theodora, and Ruthie shared certain traits and values with their sister Agatha, but each was gifted and distinct, each representing to me different facets of womanhood, so much so that they collectively helped to supplement my education in womanly ways in girlhood and later on.

During the days of preparation before everyone arrived, I found myself scouring our Spiegel catalog to see what new fashions the aunts would be wearing and what I could do to manipulate my country wardrobe in an attempt to emulate them. I couldn't wait to see the face of pride on whichever woman made the dish or dessert that the men would fight over to get the last serving of. Of course, Agatha was the real star of the day, seconded only by the now slightly dinged-up green rotisserie that this particular year she decided to preset in a prominent place so that everyone could admire it anew.

Out-of-towners would stay at motels or in guest quarters in the attic. Little did our guests know that behind an attic wall, inadvertently sealed off by contractors years earlier, was a treasure trove of one-of-a-kind, antique, carefully packed and wrapped Christmas decorations: bulbs of all shapes, strings of bubble lights, old-fashioned red and silver tin garlands—holiday collectibles that Agatha had lovingly gathered for decades. I begged Ma to break open the wall the way her father broke off her plaster cast, but she refused me, saying, "It would cost too much." Every time I passed that wall I would pause and remember all of that beauty, buried just beneath the surface.

Ma took the lovely presentation of our home very seriously. Before the cookout, her homemade curtains were starched and pressed, as were the good bedroom and bathroom linens. Forest Edge was a picture postcard everywhere you looked. The fields had been cut. Hay was baled. My sisters and I had helped with the extra chores, setting up the badminton net, bringing out the softball gear, and making sure the screened-in porch had new playing cards for tournament-style bid whist games.

Agatha began food preparations weeks in advance. With her masterful timing, as the big day approached, everything was ready—abundant, irresistible, perfect. Beers, wines, canned and jarred goods were carried up in numerous trips from the cellar and were ready to be savored. Breads, cakes, cookies, pies, and other desserts competed for room on tables and countertops.

The dreaded ancient hot comb made its appearance the day before the cookout. An event. The two-hour ordeal typically required Ma to wash a month's worth of farm dirt out of my long fuzzy locks. I would emerge from our 1960s Sears Roebuck electric hair dryer with a colossal 1900s James VanDerZee–esque doo. Ma would rub a dab of Vaseline between her hands before applying it to my hair. As the comb rested against the red-hot coil, the scent of residual hair from a previous straightening session reminded me that I'd better not move. Ma would say, "You better sit still; I don't want to burn you." I held my breath as she pressed at the nape of my neck. *Sizzle, sizzle* I would hear as the hot comb skillfully glided through my tresses. Ma pressed hair as expertly as she pressed clothes. Agatha would let me run across the kitchen to feel the breeze, the freedom, before weaving my hair into two clean neat braids once again.

That next day, shortly after sunup, the first car would signal its arrival, beeping its horn at the start of Ma's property. The excitement was palpable. Chevrolets, Impalas, Wagoneers, Cadillacs, and motorcycles all came sputtering, vrooming, chugging, bumping, kicking up dust as they barreled down the dirt stretch of Barley Road and pulled into our makeshift parking lot—the field.

My sisters and I were showered with compliments and comments. "What's mother feeding y'all—you're growin' like weeds."

Against the stone wall, old used doors sat on top of sawhorses and served as an epic long buffet table covered in pressed tablecloths. Quickly, the table became obscured as family and friends arrived and added their own mouthwatering recipes. Some of the perennial favorites were applesauce cake, corn on the cob, and, as much as I hate to say it, our homegrown fried chicken.

Agatha, the belle of the ball, red lipstick and eyebrows applied, always managed to somehow greet each and every guest upon arrival, with her gift of making everyone feel welcomed, special, and included. Vibrant, poised, loving and loved, she stood, this one-of-a-kind force of nature, receiving compliments about her beautiful farm, the incredible buffet, and, without fail, the intoxicating aroma of her flower bed.

Ma gave all of her guests the option of joining her for a special mass with her priest. Most of us kids stayed clear while a smattering of adults joined her underneath the sober overhang of a lone apple tree in the middle of the field. Jokes and stories were already revving up. We would talk about the time Ma told us a lightning bolt came clear through a window and out another, UFO sightings, found dinosaur fossils set in big rocks, but no one believed us kids. It was customary for Agatha's children to spontaneously break into the song, a melody that their father, Grandpa, used to sing to her, "If I could be with you one hour tonight. . . ." I never heard the end of the song because of the contagious laughter that would erupt every time the song was sung.

Agatha and her sisters took their rightful place at the center stage of this gathering. They were stellar, the epitome of class, each in her own orbit, yet interconnected in a solar system that we were all so lucky to travel in. The Wooten sisters were, as anyone could tell you, something else.

In 1907, the Wooten family that migrated north from New Bern, North Carolina, consisted of four-year-old Agatha and five-year-old Marion. While John Wooten left behind numerous members of his family—with relatives whose lineages dated back to the 1700s when the King of England vacationed in coastal New Bern, the second town to be established in what became North Carolina—most of Mary Jane King

Wooten's family had by this time put down roots in the greater Boston area.

Of the twenty freeborn children of a slave owner's son, Samuel King, and his wife, a former slave in Charleston, South Carolina, more than half of them elected to pass for white when they moved northward. Boston was their preferred destination, because they considered it the hub of the civilized world.

Many of the Kings—Mary Jane's siblings—rose to high stations, living on Beacon Hill and the like. Miles across town was Roxbury, where their black mother and white father lived in a comfortable though not so prominent address. To visit their mother, they did so by prearrangement, so to keep their secret. But Mr. and Mrs. King could never visit them at their homes. The agreement was strictly abided by and never challenged.

The constraints were onerous but everyone knew their lot would be much worse in the South, so Mrs. and Mr. King remained in the North. Agatha's grandmother, Mrs. King, had only one request, which her devoted husband granted—that she be returned to Charleston, South Carolina, when she died. Agatha's grandfather Samuel King kept his promise and accompanied his wife's body home on the train, their family in attendance. He had such disdain for slavery in the South that he refused to be buried there, in spite of his beloved wife's last decision. Instead, when he died in 1908, he was buried in Mount Hope Cemetery of Massachusetts.

When the Wootens arrived in the Northeast, there was clearly a large and well-established family network. Some, like Grandpa King, who lived long enough to spend time with his granddaughters, gladly welcomed the North Carolinians into the fold, but others were more standoffish. In the former category was the dazzling Aunt Cash, one of Mary Jane's sisters. Without exception, she swept her Wooten nieces under her wing—not only Marion and Agatha but also the much younger Theodora and Ruth, who came along almost a dozen years later—and gave each of them a taste of glamour and style that their own parents could not have provided.

Aunt Cash was probably the original woman of independent means in their lineage, going on to invest heavily in property with savings she inherited from her late husband's tailoring business. At a time when most states wouldn't give property deeds to people of color, the only way around that was to work through a white attorney. Aunt Cash paid whatever extra money she earned to her lawyer and he would, on faith, make the payments. Many African Americans lost their homes either due to bad business deals or the inability to pay taxes. But for those who could make the payments, during the '20s and '30s, opportunities arose for Negroes to acquire property in fancy areas around the Cape where foreclosures cropped up daily—like the magical gingerbread house that Aunt Cash bought on Martha's Vineyard in Oak Bluffs, an area that became the black bourgeois section. By the early 1960s, though, the laws had changed. Aunt Cash had never gotten the deed switched to her name, something she had never told family members about and something that was not uppermost in her concerns at the nursing home where she was living out her last days. Her original lawyer had already passed away and so, too, would have the ownership of her jewel of a house on the Vineyard, if not for another lawyer who had followed the property's history and went the extra distance by making repeated visits to the nursing home in the hopes of finding Aunt Cash lucid enough to sign papers to prove she was the rightful owner—and to stipulate an heir.

During a time when the civil rights movement of the 1960s was just gearing up, when the favorite son of Massachusetts, John F. Kennedy, reached out to a nation to broaden its vision and to think beyond differences, this never-named lawyer—who stood to gain nothing other than the knowledge that he had done the right thing—was at last able to obtain her signature and her decision to deed her house to the third-born of her Wooten nieces, Theodora.

In later years, I would have occasion to visit Aunt T, as we all called her, and her grandchildren there, crossing over on the Woods Hole Ferry, mingling with the high society side of the family.

Aunt Cash was also famous in family lore for her magnificent head of lustrous black hair that cascaded down to the tops of her thighs, which she typically wore in a long braid that she could sit on. In their upper-crust Boston accents, the four Wooten sisters all said the same thing: "Aunt Cash's hair was so thick, she would get migraines from it." Finally, she subjected herself to scissors and transformed her black mane into soft curls. That was how I last saw her, when I was five years old and went with Agatha to her funeral.

I later figured out that one of the reasons Agatha encouraged me to become close to her sisters was because of the extremely positive influence their aunt Cash had had on them. Following in their aunt's footsteps, each of the Wooten sisters was ultimately self-made, and all four were also property owners. Very early on, that stirred something profound in me. Proprietorship was power. The more uprooted I became in years to come, the more I yearned never to move or be moved.

The influence of their mother, Mary Jane, was clearly strong, too, yet she remained more of an enigma to me. From most perspectives she was tough, probably because of the kind of life she had lived by remaining in the South as a woman of color when most of her siblings and her parents went north. Most of her grandchildren would say that they remembered being scared of her. But in spite of her terse demeanor, Mary Jane was revered for her character and abilities. Her employment was initially what was then called "out in service"— which meant that she cooked and cleaned as a domestic in the homes of the well-to-do. Soon enough, because she was so in demand, she earned a level of independence by taking in laundry and hiring her daughters to help in their heralded pressing work. Mary Jane Wooten's real claim to fame, however, was her cooking. In the late 1940s, her culinary talents and recipes were featured in *Ebony* magazine's monthly column by Freda DeKnight. No wonder Agatha and her sisters were such outstanding cooks.

While the Wooten sisters took after their mother in their homes and gardens, their temperament was more warm and affable, like their father's. By trade, John Wooten was a furniture maker with a top reputation in woodwork, caning, and upholstery, which explains why Ma became an expert in caning and furniture repair. Even though their father had never finished grammar school down South, he was apparently such a brilliant self-taught mathematician that he went on to tutor youngsters who found out what a wiz he was at numbers. The Wooten girls inherited his intellectual prowess, not only in academics and in their capacity to learn, diving into complex subject matter and professional interests outside of their background, but also in having such passion about everything they undertook. Above all, it was probably his talent at the violin that most influenced his daughters, each of whom was unquestionably musically gifted.

Or such is the opinion I developed in connection to Auntie Marion after going to hear her rehearse for an organ recital at St. Joseph's Catholic Church in downtown Boston. At this juncture, in early 1967, some months before the annual cookout, Agatha had started to ask my social workers to request a subsidy from the State of Maine for me to take bonafide ballet lessons. Until they approved the cost and a local teacher could be found, she was intent on exposing me to more arts and music. To that end, we made the trip into Boston, during which Ma filled me in on the unpredictable turns that her sister Marion's life had taken.

Born in 1902, just a year before Agatha, Marion had also been beset by many of the same health crises that Ma had been through. As a young girl, Marion also had surgery for scoliosis. Later, she, too, was diagnosed with breast cancer and underwent a radical mastectomy, causing her arm and hand to become swollen. Remarkably, this did not affect her playing the organ.

Their likenesses didn't stop there. The two petite beauties resembled each other very closely and had the same pure, authentic essence. Both five foot even, arms always wide, single breasted, both with love. Marion had a gentleness and an ever so slight reserve that contrasted with Agatha's more outgoing personality.

With Marion's musical gifts evident early on, her parents managed to send her to study piano at the prestigious New England Conservatory of Music. She was flooded with offers but chose to recommend that her sister Agatha take advantage of the opportunities, at a time when she believed that it wasn't practical to be a wife and mother and have a career at the same time. Putting the creation of a family first, Marion married Arthur Leroy Collins and they were soon blessed with a son—Arthur Leroy Collins Jr., or Sonny as we all called him— as well as a daughter, Margaret.

Then, quite suddenly, three years into her marriage, Marion was widowed. Arthur was stricken with tuberculosis. Marion resorted to moving back with her children, into her parents' home in Alston, but she was determined never to be a burden on them and their household.

As it happened, a number of years earlier, after years of miscarriages, Marion's mother, Mary Jane Wooten, had miraculously given birth to not one but two more daughters. Theodora and Ruth were still very young in that time. Marion vowed to support herself and her children, and to add to the welfare of her parents and younger sisters. To that end, she went to work out in service, as a live-in housekeeper and cook, in swanky Roslindale, Massachusetts. For the next eleven years, she was able to see her children only twice a week.

Never would I forget hearing this part of her story, or the image it gave me of Aunt Marion, an accomplished pianist who might have gone on to play on the world's most illustrious stages, having to swallow her pride and her dream, having to put on an apron and work as a maid. I imagined moments when she would slip off her apron and sit upon the piano bench, unable to resist her truest self.

Moments like that must have sustained her until, thankfully, there came a time in the 1940s when she was able to return to the career that had been put on hold, and she was able to pick up, more or less, where she left off—as an accompanist for the popular black songstress Dorothy Richardson. In other words, like they say, it ain't over 'til it's over. By now she had met and married Alfonzo Williams, and the two were eventually graced with a daughter, Mary Jane Williams.

The importance of sacrifice was a value that Marion embodied in many ways, a value that she obviously passed on to her kids. Her first-born, Sonny, joined the navy and fought in World War II, as did her daughter, Margaret, who served as a captain in the Nurse Corps of the army. Mary Jane became a champion of early education and went on to be the executive director of Head Start in New York, a program in which I had been lucky enough to participate before I went off to school, thanks to Agatha's insistence and persistence.

In the meantime, Marion found a way to combine a musical career and her life of religious devotion when she became the lead organist for St. Richard's Catholic Church.

It was a real honor that Ma chose to take me to hear Marion's rehearsal. But when we arrived at the cavernous, empty church and took our places in a lonely pew, I privately wondered what the fuss had been about. There was Auntie Marion, looking smaller than ever as she sat down in front of the massive organ. But all at once, at the striking of the first note, I felt my body begin to shake. The reverberation of the sound emanating from the brass pipes pulsated through me, leaving me motionless, speechless, and dazzled. Aunt Marion's command of melody and phrasing made an unforgettable impression on me, as did the sight of her—unhindered by scoliosis or any other previous infirmities, or by her diminutive, crooked form—in her grand dominion of music. It was as if I could hear the story of her life told in the emotion that she poured into her playing, freeing herself from her earthbound state, overcoming limitation, flying and connecting to infinity: another personal eyewitness account of the transformational power of art.

During a visit to Aunt Marion and Uncle Al's home on Montrose Street in Roxbury, I wove my way through stacks of Uncle Al's newspapers that he refused to throw away, making my way to the scent of a freshly baked lemon meringue pie.

During my adolescence in Boston, when long separations from Agatha found me missing her desperately, I would make my way to Aunt Marion's house. On one occasion she wasn't there and all I could do was sit on her front porch and cry for the whole neighborhood to see. Otherwise I was content with the briefest of visits—even if just for a hug, to nestle into that familiar contour, and to see that kindest, gentlest of all creatures, a woman who understood pain, loss, towing the line, never giving up, sacrifice, and never losing her dream or her passion.

Theodora Wooten Roberts, built like Eleanor Roosevelt, with conservative pressed gray hair, had an intelligent composure that was her special brand of beauty. Aunt T was private, and proper. Though Aunt T enjoyed playing the piano like her sisters, she did not pursue a creative career. Not at all a rabble-rouser or a trendsetter, in her own determined manner she had blazed a trail in the Wooten family by graduating from Boston Teachers College—working summers as a waitress on Nantucket—and then going on to work as a teacher at the Thomas Gardner School among others in Boston for forty years. Her husband, John Roberts, worked forever for Payne Furniture, a prestigious Boston store, the kind in which you barely stole your own reflection in the store window.

Between her beautiful Boston brick house and the home on Martha's Vineyard that she inherited from Aunt Cash, Aunt T had every reason to be proud of the level of success and stature she had attained. I believed the secret was a combination of things Aunt Theodora epitomized—the power of education, consistency in pursuit of higher goals, and acute organizational skills.

It was by no accident that John and Theodora's only child, Maryanne, was the family's golden girl, the debutante and shining star whose future was unlimited. Untouchable in beauty, poise, and social standing, Maryanne was in the top of her class in nursing school, engaged to one of the most eligible, debonair African American bachelors in her circle, when the unthinkable happened and she was struck with polio on her twentieth birthday.

At a time in the mid-1950s when Dr. Jonas Salk's vaccine was still new and many people were skeptical about the side effects, Maryanne was tragically not vaccinated—even when cases among her age group were rising. Maryanne, drawing from a well of willpower and faith, refused to go down for the count, telling her parents and everyone who asked that she was going ahead with all her plans. "I'll walk down that wedding aisle on my own," she promised, and, of course, with crutches, she did exactly that.

Maryanne Roberts Bradley then proceeded to become a nurse at St. Elizabath's in Boston, where, without much of a disability from her wheelchair, she practiced for thirty-five years. During the days when she had been in training to become a nurse at what was Peter Bent Brigham Hospital, later known as Brigham and Women's Hospital, Maryanne learned that her grandmother Mary Jane Wooten had been admitted for blocked arteries and acute heart disease. For all those years that many members of the family had feared their matriarch, Maryanne was one of the few not at all intimidated—something her grandmother loved about her. Now, at the end of Mary Jane's many days, how comforting it must have been to have her granddaughter with her, gently and lovingly attending to her, holding her hand and telling her not to be afraid. Several years passed before I understood what a blessing it must have been for both of them. Little did I expect that decades later history would repeat itself with Agatha and me, in the same hospital.

⌒⌒⌒

Born a year after Theodora, in 1919, Ruth seemed to mix together all of her sisters' exemplary traits with her own savoir faire. Her arrival at the annual cookout instantly raised the bar for style and elegance. Aunt Ruthie was pure glamour, beauty, brains, and ambition. She played the piano, as was the Wooten daughter tradition, but her professional path was as an executive secretary, the pursuit of which led her meteorically to the pinnacle of the political world in Massachusetts and around the world. As the secretary to Governor Paul A. Dever at the State House in Boston, Ruth Wooten Williams made U.S. history by becoming the first African American woman appointed as executive secretary to a U.S. governor.

In my childhood, Ma explained how her sister Ruthie received a Western Union telegram of congratulations from the legendary Josephine Baker.

MRS. RUTH WILLIAMS—1951 JUN 12 PM 12:04
SECRETARY OF GOVERNOR PAUL DEVER
GOD WORKS SLOWLY BUT SURELY I AM SO HAPPY AND
PROUD OF YOU AND OUR RACE
BLESS YOU—
JOSEPHINE BAKER

Aunt Ruthie was in newspaper(s) across the country. This was not only important for black history, but also important for women. One Boston paper wrote,

> Mrs. Ruth Williams . . . the first Negro to be appointed private secretary to a governor of Massachusetts. Prior to her appointment as secretary to Gov. Paul A. Dever, Mrs. Williams worked as a civil employee at the State House here since 1941 . . .

Aunt Ruthie's legacy gave me hope while Agatha continued to send appeals, on my behalf, to the State of Maine to underwrite the expense of pointe shoes. The birth of great expectations had taken place in my psyche.

Given the society circles in which Ruth Wooten was ensconced, nobody could believe that the man who turned her head, fine-looking though Harold Williams was, could barely read or write. Aunt Ruthie's attitude was that his shortcomings weren't anything that couldn't be addressed with adult education. After she began teaching him to read, he attended night school and earned his GED in record time. The next thing the family knew, Harold Williams had become one of the premiere real estate brokers on Cape Cod and would remain so for nearly fifty years.

Meanwhile, Aunt Ruthie owned homes in Hyannis and Falmouth, and a vacation home in Jamaica. She and Harold traveled the globe and supported the arts and celebrated six decades of marriage.

After Ruth left the Boston State House, she went into business for herself and invested in a popular hair salon for ladies of color. She showered Ma with gifts of expensive wigs. Short, long, straight, curly bobs, flips, and teased updos. Gray, black, auburn, you name it. I loved to try on every single wig, making faces and creating characters, causing Agatha and me to roar with laughter.

Later, after persistent urging from all her sisters, Ma took time off to travel, returning to places she had once been—St. Kitts, Antigua, Jamaica, and to her favorite destination in the world, Montserrat. California was out of the question. "They say it's gonna' fall off into the ocean" was her pat reason. But those former French colonies in the Caribbean beckoned her. For one special vacation, she sent her most fashionable wig, which she had named Suzie, to Aunt Ruthie to have the salon wash and style it. It left Forest Edge a small mashed-up heap of hair and came back in a gilded hatbox, styled to glorious perfection and pinned to a wig stand inside the box. How could anyone not adore Ruth Wooten Williams?

Well, everyone did adore her but she ruffled feathers a time or two. Aunt Ruthie had a tough business sense that was unrelenting. She wanted to win and she had to win, but sometimes she stepped hard on toes, if they got in her way. The part of Ruth's story that resonated the most with me was the fact that she and Harold had adopted a beautiful girl named Barbara. All I knew was that Barbara was raised as if she was their own, which was the attitude that I felt from nearly everyone in the extended family.

When the 1967 cookout kicked up into high gear, Aunt Ruthie and Uncle Harold glided down Barley Road like movie stars. Aunt Ruthie was the first to ask how my ballet lessons with Agatha were going, and the one who seemed to take the most delight when Agatha and I offered a few moments of entertainment.

Practical journeywomen, the Wooten matriarchs were cut from the same cloth. Their approval and encouragement was imprinted in my spirit and bones forever.

The 1967 cookout was significant to me because it would be my last year living full-time at Forest Edge. I did not know this yet, as I hurried off to the softball field where the teams were being chosen.

This softball game was a serious matter. Everyone under the age of retirement played, everyone except Aunt Velma, and ex-wives who were no longer invited. Aunts like Adrena and Ruby, all wonderful, all missed. Aunts I loved but could no longer see; here one cookout, gone the next. I tried to understand and accept the complex curveball of divorce. Anyway, Aunt Velma, Uncle Ronnie's second wife, who had not been blessed with children, did not budge from the spot she first claimed upon arrival—where sunblock and a bit of shade from the oak tree foliage protected her fair skin from the summer rays. She did not sit; she lounged in the most languorous, long-legged pose, reclining back on her self-supplied chaise. Her two pampered giant poodles sat on either side of her with fancy hair ornaments I wished I had in my own freshly washed hair. The three of them turned their heads in unison at the most meager of angles to ogle us country bumpkins. Velma was one of the untouchables.

⌒

When I was between the ages of eight and twelve, three of the Armstead children followed their mother's example and opened their homes to me as I followed my ballet scholarship. They became backup foster parents for durations of anywhere from a weekend to several months.

Included on that list was Auntie Kay, Agatha's firstborn, who was the only one of the Armstead offspring to live at Forest Edge year-round on her own two-acre parcel. When Agatha went to the hospital for the radical mastectomy, it was Kay who watched over my sisters and me. Aunt Kay lived in a maroon-painted trailer, outfitted with old car seats for living room furniture, creating a whimsical, inviting atmosphere. The trailer had been cut open like a tuna can more than once to create additional space for her growing family. I figured Aunt Kay must have inherited her steely toughness from her maternal grandmother. Her complete no-nonsense cool served her well. Aunt Kay and I clicked, hatchet or no hatchet. Without apology, a cigarette hanging from her mouth, worn pink sponge curlers in her hair, she exchanged few words with me. There was a sadness behind her eyes, and I felt it; we felt each other. She was the oldest of Agatha's daughters and I was the youngest. I understood that the foster sister I referred to as Auntie Kay lived a life much different from mine. I loved being in her uncomplicated presence. There was intense peacefulness about it. My theory was that maybe she channeled pain, too, in her own way.

On Saturday, after a full week working at the factory, the slightest smile formed on Aunt Kay's face as she watched *The Newlyweds*. Kay had once been a newlywed, a young beauty, working as a hostess on passenger trains, from South Station to New York City. Kay introduced me to survival skills many women never learn—living without any extras, no frills, no fat, only necessity, a poker face, another plane of consistency.

Her unwavering stoicism was remarkable. When her husband left her, with five children to raise by herself, she went on, without histrionics, living her life and never looking back. Maybe she learned her cool demeanor in her childhood, and had figured out how to take crisis on the chin and keep it movin'.

Auntie Barbara—who lived upstairs in an early 1900s brick town house Agatha owned in Roxbury—was the polar opposite of her sister Kay. Barbara had a fabulous disposition, and anyone who met her noticed her hourglass figure. Mother of three, and a longtime factory employee of Raytheon, she was married to Uncle Norman for more than forty years. Norman had been stricken by polio in his young life but went to work every day as an elevator operator.

Playing in the softball games at the cookout, Uncle Norman was a standout athlete. Aunt Barbara cheered him on as he swung the bat and sent the ball over the ridge of tall pines and into the woods. It was impressive. Barbara epitomized wifely and womanly pride in her man. To see Uncle Norman make it to first base in a series of choreographed skips, hops, and limps, then fall down, wrestle himself up again, then fall down a second time, laughing and continuing to run in spite of his polio, made him a champion in my eyes.

Barbara gladly took the two acres that her mother offered her and kept a pink trailer on it. I was fortunate to have a close enough relationship with her that she could be honest with me about the difference between hygiene in the wilderness and hygiene in the city.

"When you come to Boston, Vicki, you have to change your clothes more than once a week," Barbara said. I was embarrassed, but I took the information in stride, not realizing it would come in handy later.

Aunt Joan was another straight shooter. She was tougher than Kay—gangsta' tough, hard as nails when she had to be—mixed with the same warmth, humor, and affection that I got from Barbara. One summer when Agatha jetted off to her cherished Montserrat, I went to stay in the projects of Lynn, Massachusetts, where Aunt Joan lived with her husband and their seven children.

As my foster sister, aunt, and now respite mother, Joan laid it all on the line: "You'll eat what's on the table or not at all." She warned me to forget about my finicky eating habits, my culinary likes and dislikes; there would be none of that in her house. I would have to eat the liver and rice just like everyone else and I did.

I remember all the commotion when I overhead that Aunt Joan's husband, a security guard at the time, had committed suicide. Aunt Joan, like her sister Kay, was left with seven children to raise by herself, which she did successfully; she would later say to me, "Vicki, the best medicine is learning how to laugh." This was Joan's way of dealing with her pain, of which she had plenty.

Sylvia confirmed for me that a person could be born into a family and be completely different from all those in it. Agatha's fourth daughter, Sylvia was named after her paternal grandmother and was soft-spoken and fragile, a flower. She was graceful and gentle, undoubtedly a Wooten woman. I watched her, the mother of three who adopted two more, unload her station wagon, finally arriving after a long drive from Long Island, New York, with her husband, Bill, who was afraid of cats. Later Sylvia would have to endure the tragic loss of one of her beloved sons, Barry, a painter and artist, whom I kept in touch with, further aggravating her delicate constitution.

As the cookout began to wind down, more out-of-towners started to leave. Among them were the Philadelphia Armsteads—Uncle Roger, who worked as a postal worker, his then wife Marilyn, and their four sons. Aunt Marilyn, a statuesque redhead, was Marilyn Monroe sexy and she knew it, flaunted it, and made no apology for being the modern-day Venus of the family.

Who could have predicted that Roger and Marilyn's son, Roger Armstead Jr., would one day be party to an arranged marriage? Who would be his bride? My sister, Sheree. Agatha carefully cultivated a courtship between her grandson and her foster daughter. Prior to the marriage, Sheree had become pregnant when she was seventeen by her first love. To see Sheree, a young mother, find family stability after such a tumultuous youth made me think I might do the same for myself one day.

The unpredictability of life, love, marriage, and children was a running theme at the cookout, that year and every year. As the Robert

Armstead Jr. crew began to pack the car to head back to Dorchester, they represented to me the bedrock of marital and family stability. Aunt Joanne, mother to four children, had a gracious, calm spirit. Sometimes there was a hint of an outsider in her, as though she didn't completely belong to the club, something with which I couldn't help but identify. Or maybe I had gravitated toward her because of her kindness.

Over the next several years, she and Uncle "Junie," as we called him, were happy and compatible, from all appearances. Junie was a Boston cop, part of the elite K-9 force, with his much-loved police dog Geta as his German shepherd sidekick—and later a half wolf/half German shepherd he insisted on training in his backyard, causing a bit of a ruckus in the neighborhood. Out on duty one day, Uncle Junie heard a woman screaming, went to investigate, and found her being accosted. An officer of the law and a compassionate citizen, Junie rescued her. The woman happened to be white and was an ex-exotic dancer. Junie, feeling no compulsion to justify his actions, moved the woman and her daughter in with his wife and children, and then fell in love with her. Not in any particular order. Not long after, Joanne retreated quietly to build a life for herself, and Junie brought the woman and her daughter to Maine to meet Ma. The little girl and I played together as Ma pulled from her reserves and all of her best Emily Post etiquette in an attempt to make this son's guest feel welcome. I couldn't help but look at Uncle Junie and this wounded woman and think back to when Dorothy visited Forest Edge with a black soldier. There was something incredibly bare about both women, something heartbreaking.

When Uncle Ronnie and Velma signaled that it was time for their departure from the cookout, I lingered close by, holding my breath, knowing that Uncle Richie planed to make a special request of his brother Ronald. Before final good-byes were said, Uncle Richie told his brother that their mother was trying to locate a ballet school for me. He asked Ronnie, "What would you and Velma say to sponsoring Vicki with her ballet classes?"

Ronnie didn't say no, and he didn't say yes. He laughed, and laughed some more. He couldn't seem to catch his breath. He all but said, "Are you crazy?"

I stood there frozen, composing myself because I owed that effort out of gratitude to Uncle Richie, and deference to Ma, who did not deserve to have my hurt show at the end of her special day. Within minutes, I brought myself to join her in waving good-bye as the Connecticut Armsteads and the two tired poodles drove off in their Cadillac into the dusk.

Staying at Forest Edge in the attic guest quarters were Raymond and his new wife, Francine. The first time Raymond brought her to meet Agatha, the sun was setting and she appeared out in the front garden as though backlit, like a goddess. There I was in my usual dusty braids, slack-jawed at how effortlessly her long, flowing hair framed her face and her almost adolescent body. In her sassy ruffled midriff shirt, she was right out of the centerfold of *Jet* magazine— Beauty of the Week.

Francine pulled off a look like it was magic. To achieve that glorious head of hair, every night she rolled it on humongous curlers, the kind you saw in Spanish Harlem. She traveled with her own egg-shaped beauty-salon-type hair dryer, hood and all. There was a lot she could teach me. But it was more than the look. Francine, only about nineteen years old when Raymond married her, taught me about Attitude. She was a guide to flirting, social dancing, betting at cards and at the racetrack, and being sexy at all those things. Being fabulous, standing there, flaunting her fineness.

Nobody else had ever shown me that kind of vanity. She had collections of earrings, shoes, perfumes, cosmetics. White frosted lipstick with white frosted eyeshadow to match. It was theater, baby, and I wanted a little of what Francine had. She started me off when she told me to put my earlobes between two ice cubes. Shortly after piercing my ears with a needle and thread as she tied a knot at the end, she said, "Sometimes beauty hurts." I was on my way.

Later, Francine caught me off guard when she said it was amusing that I was planning a career in ballet. If she didn't take my ambition seriously, however, someone who did early on was my Aunt Laura Armstead, Uncle Richie's wife. An attractive, extremely fastidious, highly motivated mother of two, Laura had married Richard Armstead, a police officer, to escape an oppressive environment where she was growing up with a divorced father and a stepmother. Tall, with a reserved poise and a clear intelligence, Laura received her teaching degree from Boston State College and taught in the city's public school system for forty years. When I later lived in her household, I would have a very difficult time adjusting to her cool demeanor, as Agatha's maternal warmth had been such a staple. At the same time, I admired the devotion she showed to her two daughters, the extra hours she contributed to making sure they had access to everything she didn't— private schools, speech therapy, ice skating, and, yes, ballet.

That's why, when Agatha reminded Laura, "And don't forget to check on some names of ballet schools for Vicki for next summer," Laura nodded her head and promised to do just that.

What is most prominent as the curtain fell on that particular cookout, as with every yearly celebration, with the happy hordes leaving, some to stay over, some to wander down to their trailers, others driving back to the big cities, is the sight of a petite sixty-five-year-old woman—who year-round collected seeds and romanced the idea of greatness from a garden not only for herself but for all who wanted to sit at her banquet table—giving each and every one a part of Forest Edge as they departed.

That is collectively what I learned most from the Wooten and Armstead women: the joy of giving. For Agatha, it was her moment of greatest pleasure as she cut her best blooms from her garden, wrapped them in newspaper, and lovingly gave them away.

Over the years, I collected treasures that aunts, sisters, mentors, friends, and mothers had given me in every form imaginable. I saved every letter, note, and postcard—all holding remarkable energy.

All of my aunts were extensions of Agatha. She is best remembered standing in the middle of the dirt stretch of Barley Road, with night approaching, gazing with satisfaction at the little faces pressed up against the glass in the backseats of cars, arms reaching out windows to wave good-bye, her waving back, long after the cars have driven out of sight.

PART TWO

MENTORS, FOSTERERS, GRANDE DAMES

(1968–1983)

*For those filled with the spirit of the true dance, it is a lifetime of giving.
Art conceals art to reveal on stage the appearance of effortless expression.
The desire consumes. There is no satisfactory substitute. Once felt, the
only release is to perform. Inspired by the legend of Karsavina or Nijinsky,
Fonteyn or Nureyev, the child must dance. And school's rigorous discipline
is happily endured to that great end—the first performance.*

CHARLES MURLAND,
"CHILDREN TO THE DANCE"

FOUR

ESTHER BROOKS

Agatha firmly believed that when a child turned ten years old it was reason enough to celebrate. She did not think that turning sweet sixteen was as important a milestone in a child's life as living an entire decade, 3,650 days, on Earth. That really impressed her. She had already faced the fragility of a child's life when her baby Ralphie, one of the twins, died at five months old. Agatha knew that childhood could be cruel as well as short. After all, she was the one who had to extract me from a heartbroken Bertha Taylor when I was two years old.

As my ninth birthday approached, Agatha began planning a tenth birthday party for me. She knew with certainty that I was on my way to somewhere, so she decided to take the liberty of celebrating my ninth birthday late and my tenth birthday very early, combining that purpose with a going-away bash. All of the children on Barley Road were invited to the Saturday afternoon party. The highlights were Ma's homemade cake and a game of Pin the Tail on the Donkey. With tape attached to a paper tail we delightfully played the game with a neighbor's actual burro. For this party, Agatha gave me my first introduction to party planning. Every detail was addressed and carried out to the fullest extent. She passed me her Brownie camera, instructed me to look down into the small square magnifying lens, frame the party guests, and press the button.

Agatha wanted this day to be momentous and memorable. We both knew I was a year shy of turning ten, yet the gravity of what was before us dictated that perhaps we would not be together for my tenth birthday, and she wanted me to have the same experience she had given my two older sisters.

For nearly a year, Agatha had conducted a full-court press to locate an accredited, accessible, and affordable ballet school for me. Her effort was fueled not only by a belief that ballet was going to be important in my future, but also by my passion to dance and by my desire to study. By the spring of 1968, however, her search looked to be a losing proposition.

That was until the phone rang on the evening of my last day of third grade. We shared a party line with a number of neighboring farms, but each house had a coded ring. For instance, the Amadons had three consecutive rings, the Gothwhites had one ring, and Forest Edge had two. We all shared a common trust that we wouldn't listen in on each other's conversations. Such we assumed to be the case when Agatha listened intently to the caller. Saying very little, she nodded her head, as if confirming information she already knew. Before hanging up, she did say, "That's the ticket, Laura; we're cookin' with gas now! I'll make arrangements with Vicki's social worker and be in touch."

In her earnest effort to find a ballet studio for me, Aunt Laura almost came up empty-handed until one day at Joseph P. Hurley School, where she taught, there was an announcement about a public ballet performance offered to students and their families. The Cambridge School of Ballet was issuing the invitation in order to promote their summer scholarship program and to announce that auditions were being held one week later. Not only was the Cambridge School of Ballet one of the most prestigious training and performing schools in the Northeast, situated at one of the most illustrious addresses on Massachusetts

Avenue, in the Odd Fellow Building just off Harvard Square, but there was something even more relevant: the scholarship program was specifically for students who couldn't otherwise afford tuition.

A flurry of preparations began at once. Not knowing of any particular ballet protocol, Agatha took remnants out of her sewing supplies and, by hand, carefully sewed sherbet-colored interfacing strips—in lieu of ribbons—onto my black, mail-order pointe shoes; not the traditional color or fabric.

The plan, strategically conceived, was for me to take the bus to the downtown Boston Trailways station where Uncle Richie would be waiting as I stepped off. He would then drive me at once over to Cambridge for the audition, all timed for me to be at least an hour early in order to roll up my pants and put on my toe shoes.

As we discussed the big day ahead, Agatha made sure I understood the level of competition I would encounter. We both knew that my interpretive dances at Forest Edge were coming to a close. I also understood the value that came from the introduction to ballet, along with the gift of discipline produced from my diligent practice of relevés with the support of a doorknob. For one hour, daily, with the musical accompaniment of our sunburst clock, *tick-tocking*, I faced the living room door and dreamed, humming and talking myself into believing that there was a stage and a theater past the door, through the wood slats and plaster and into infinitum.

In nearby cultural centers, especially Boston, it was certainly another world—full of aspiring dancers who had already been exposed to classical music and training, not to mention the advantage of resources unavailable to me. But I had three clear advantages: natural talent, a desire to succeed, and a willingness to work hard for what I wanted.

Not yet so evident was something else that would serve me in the long haul: a competitive streak. I had no choice but to excel, whether it was winning the fifty-yard dash in the second grade or competing in a sled competition down Barley Road. I had to win. This was a double-edged sword, as I would discover, but for the good part of it, I credit my sister Lori for sharpening this edge in me. A social worker who used to visit us described Lori as being quite competitive with me. Looking back, I find this to be odd, because we were so different: Lori was always quiet, delicate, unemotional; I was outgoing, talkative, and full of feeling. When I was literally chasing after butterflies and catching frogs and grasshoppers, Lori stood stoic, somehow already knowing life was not a fairy tale.

I loved my sister and assumed in her own way that she loved me, too. But her coping skills were such that she couldn't allow herself to be embraced—as much as I tried. For her, armor was synonymous with survival. In that regard, Lori was more strategic than I was. In terms of emotional survival, I learned the hard way later. On the other hand, I knew from the age of six what I wanted to do in my life, and that was a lot to ask others of my own age to embrace, let alone my slightly older sister. It was only natural for her to resent me at times for what became known as my "special interests."

Lori's eventual path into law enforcement and forensics couldn't have been predicted. Nonetheless, she would excel in that field, which benefited from her kind of cool temperament and the discerning strengths that she had developed since childhood. Although we were destined not to be close in the way that sisters can be in adulthood, she forewarned me early on not to be in a rush to get out of foster care and helped me welcome competition, rather than fear it.

As prepared as I could have possibly been under the unprecedented circumstances, on the Monday morning that followed my specially timed birthday party of June 1968, I breathlessly watched the taxi round the bend on Barley Road to pick us up. The moment for departure had arrived and I couldn't wait to leave.

"Slow down," Ma cautioned as I ran down to the dirt road in half as many steps as usual.

Before I knew it, the last vestiges of Forest Edge receded behind us, as we bumped along passing the familiar sights of West Lebanon,

Maine. Past Ole Bull, a hollowed-out cave where Indians once lived and where a Norwegian violinist in 1871 gave concerts because he believed it had perfect acoustics. We passed the Congregational church built in 1835 where Agatha sent me for Bible studies one summer, past the post office that was actually a part of our neighbors' house, past the Lebanon town hall built in 1833, before we eventually cruised across the state line into New Hampshire.

Once we got to the Trailways stop, I faced one problem: having to say good-bye to Ma. I blinked back tears forcefully, denying them to fall, swallowing every urge to cry. I detested "so long," "see you later," and especially "good-bye"—there was nothing "good" about it.

Agatha did all she could to reassure me, wrapping me into her sideways concave hug, and then stood back to gaze at me with loving approval. She began, "Mother is very proud of you." I nodded, taking in every ounce of her encouragement. Repeating what we had already been over, she went on, "You've practiced hard; be yourself and you'll be just fine! And remember, don't talk to strangers." Agatha reminded me that the minute I got off the bus, Richie would be there to pick me up. With that, she sent me on my way.

After I boarded, I knelt up on my seat to peer out the far side window for one last look at Ma—standing by herself under the gold lettering of Woolworth's five and dime, exuberantly waving good-bye with a brave smile. In an instant I understood the impact of Agatha's birthday gift to me. I was alone in body but not in spirit. Therefore, I was not afraid. In effect, she sent me off into the world with the support of my country village on Barley Road. Ma took hold of her brown wool scapular draped around her neck, and in response, I pulled out the Saint Christopher medal she had given to me for my journey. Without words, we said everything that needed to be said. She had taught me everything I needed to know to navigate circuitous roads ahead.

Excitement was now replaced with intensified sadness with each revolution of the Trailways wheels. I felt myself inexplicably detaching from Agatha as more and more distance came between us. I measured her shrinking frame between my thumb and index finger and in the smallest of spaces I held the greatest unconditional love I possibly could for a human being. We trusted what we had between us. I was nine years old and on a bus pulling me away from the "Lilac City" and toward a gateway to the world.

Both the driver and the beverage hostess—the Trailways version of an airline attendant—had been enlisted to look after me. The hostess said, "Vicki, if there's anything you need, you just ask, all right?" She paused, then added, "You're very grown-up to be riding the bus to Boston by yourself. How old are you?"

"Nine; I just turned nine."

The bus driver chimed in with his heavy Boston-Irish accent and said, "Don't you worry about a thing. I'll get you to Boston safe and sound in a jiffy." His booming voice was reassuring. I sat back in my reclining burgundy chair thinking about all I had seen and all that had been done to get me on that luxurious bus.

Just as I was convincing myself to view the day as a grand adventure, no matter the outcome, the bus did something I had never felt before. It hopped with a down-up motion, lurched, swerved, and finally screeched to an earsplitting halt.

Our formerly jocular bus driver was now very serious. I had no idea what had happened and did not want to ask a soul as I had sworn not to talk to strangers. Instead, I knelt up on my seat and looked out the window and saw something unbelievable: an older black man laying on the ground, completely immobile, the lower half of his body pinned under the bus. His eyes, bulging with terror, looking straight up into mine. My first thought was, because it was what I sometimes pondered whenever I saw an unfamiliar black man, *Is that my Daddy?*

As all the passengers filed out of the bus, including me, I spied the

suffering man's wooden cane on the wet asphalt and wanted to give it
to him but I wasn't permitted near him.

It seemed as though hours passed before emergency crews were
dispatched, tow trucks arrived, and the transference of luggage onto
another bus was completed. Numb by now, I knew that I would never
forget the mercilessness of random tragedy and the despair in the old
man's face. For the remainder of the trip, I wondered if the nameless
man had lived or died. At last, the bus pulled into the Trailways station. Waiting there as I descended the steps was a stalwart Uncle
Richie, proudly wearing his policeman's uniform, framed by the backdrop of tall Maine elms in the Boston Commons, gifted by Judge
Humphrey Chadbourne to John Hancock after the Revolutionary
War. His expression told me that he was fully informed about the accident. It was late and there was only a slim chance that the auditions
were still under way. The day was getting bleaker.

Uncle Richie, a seasoned Boston cop with a determined attitude,
knew every backstreet there was and could speedily navigate us across
town, and into the other world of Cambridge.

In record time, we parked in front of the Odd Fellow Building, I
leapt out, raced inside and up the grand staircase, taking the steps
twos and threes, and dashed down the hall and into the almost empty
massive ballet studio.

At the far end was a stunningly elegant woman with a cigarette
clasped between two fingers, jangling the assortment of bangles she
wore on both forearms as she lifted it to her mouth and then exhaled,
staring off in deep thought. She turned to see Richie and me standing
apologetically just inside the studio. She pivoted and glided in my direction, in such a manner that she seemed not to walk like other human
beings but rather to float. "I'm sorry," she said, "the auditions are over.
We finished nearly an hour ago."

Her voice and accent were rich, exotic—the embodiment of the
knowledge I yearned to have. I could not help but stare in admiration

not only at her arctic blue eyes and the wisp of smoke swirling up from her like a genie escaping from a lamp, but also at the backdrop of the ballet studio behind her. This was my first view ever of a real studio—with massive mirrors lining the walls, a ballet barre running down the length and width of the studio, gilded royal flags with fleur-de-lis and eagle emblems giving it a grandeur I could not have dreamt in my most expansive visions.

I was about to accept my unhappy fate when Uncle Richie took a stab at explaining why I was late. The woman listened with no reaction. I did not dare look at either one of them; instead, I fixed my attention on another little girl scurrying around with great ease and familiarity. She smiled at me, which encouraged me to think that everything would be all right. The next thing I heard was that unmistakable, elegant voice, "Well, dear, you're here now, let's dance, shall we?"

This was my first encounter with the extraordinary Esther Brooks. We soon learned that she was the founder and artistic director of the Cambridge School of Ballet, and that though the summer program had been filled and exceeded capacity, she would not turn me away without the chance of auditioning first. Esther summoned Christine Murad, the little girl who had smiled at me, a student no more than nine years old herself, and asked her to show me to the dressing room so I could change into my leotard and tights. What? Nothing in the article Agatha had found remotely mentioned anything about a leotard and tights. What was Esther talking about? I told her that I had pointe shoes and that was all. Esther showed no judgment or surprise as she asked Christine to help me find something in the lost and found steamer trunk. So, off we went.

I had never met a little girl with such maturity and confidence before. She led me down an L-shaped hallway into a dimly lit dressing room to an enormous old steamer trunk with brass latchings. Christine's strength reminded me of my own as she single-handedly hoisted open the lid of the trunk. We both giggled as we buried ourselves from

the waist up in the antique trunk, furiously searching for a leotard and a pair of tights that would fit me. Within minutes I was changed, back in the studio in a pair of pilled red tights, a black leotard, and my black pointe shoes with striped interfacing for ribbons, looking more like a confection than a ballet dancer.

Esther smiled in approval, masking any amusement she may have had over my apparel. All that mattered now was what came next, as she began by asking me to show her the different rudimentary positions of the arms and feet. I sailed through this part of the audition, earning approval from her. The second part of the audition, however, moved us to the corner for tour chaînés déboulés, a rapid series of turns across the floor on a diagonal, all with French terms that had not been in the Forest Edge curriculum. Unfazed, Esther, in the most perfect French, her first language, demonstrated the movements, and I then followed along.

"Good," she said. With a quizzical expression that seemed to have her quite perplexed, she asked, "Vicki, where did you study ballet?"

"I learned from a book."

"From a book?" Though Esther's English was impeccable, when she asked this, I could hear hints of an eclectic accent shaped, I would soon learn, from a childhood spent in France, China, and points in between. She was astounded. "Did you say a book?"

"Yes, Ma . . . I mean my f-f-foster mother, Mrs. Armstead, Uncle Richie's mother, Agatha, I mean my mother; she taught me."

I got through that horribly complicated explanation. I took a deep breath to control my stuttering and inner trembling. I seemed to have confounded her even more. To a woman whose raison d'être was her devotion to the transformational power of the arts, it was almost as if I have been sent to her as validation of her beliefs and ideals. For me, she had been sent as the mentor of a lifetime.

The result of the audition proved to me that the luckiest place in line can sometimes be the last. Ma, now acting as my publicist, may well have written the articles published five days later in the two Maine newspapers that served West Lebanon, both with the headline "Vicki Rowell Will Attend Ballet School":

> Congratulations to Vicki Rowell, nine-year-old foster daughter of Mrs. Agatha Armstead of the Barley Road, West Lebanon, on winning a $700 scholarship to the Cambridge School of Ballet in Cambridge. She auditioned in Boston, Monday, and passed with flying colors. The award was made at the school. Vicki has never had any previous lessons.
>
> Her classes begin June 24 and finish just before Labor Day. There will be dancing lessons, trips, and other activities from 10 a.m. until 5 p.m. each day. She will stay with Mr. and Mrs. Richard Armstead in Dorchester.

On the Tuesday morning after the audition, after spending the previous night in Dorchester, we planned to spend the afternoon with Ma, pack everything that I needed for the summer, and return that same night so that I could settle into my new routine.

Even though I was going away only for two months, an undeniable sense of finality hovered around us, as if we all knew that the time away might just be longer than that. We all recognized that inevitably I would be changing while Barley Road would stay much the same.

Uncle Richie loaned me a large blue-and-cream-trimmed suitcase for me to pack my things in—a piece of luggage that would become synonymous with my nomadic life for the remaining nine years of my term as a ward of the state. Solemnly, Ma and I placed the suitcase atop the dining room table and opened it. She proceeded to fold in love with every article of clothing she packed. Barely looking at each other, we knew that by nightfall I would drive away without her.

That moment came much too soon, even though I was late leaving and Uncle Richie was waiting for me down the road at his trailer. Ma accompanied me from the kitchen to the back porch. Hugs and good-byes were exchanged. I started off into the cool summer night air and

Not long after I was born I went to live with Bertha Taylor and her husband in Gray, Maine (*top*). In raising me (*bottom*) as an infant, she was supported by her good friends and neighbors Laura Sawyer (*bottom left*) and Retha Dunn (*bottom right*).

When I left the Taylors at two-and-a-half years old, I went to live with Robert and Agatha Armstead in West Lebanon, Maine. Here, Agatha and Robert are surrounded by their bridal party at their 1920s wedding in Boston.

Here is Agatha as a young mother in the 1930s when she worked at Hoveys department store in Boston. She was always a stylish woman —never caught without red lipstick, arched eyebrows, and a hat.

Agatha and Robert on their bucolic sixty-acre farm in Maine before their daughter Barbara's wedding. She is wearing an Agatha C. original— sewing was a passion of hers, and she not only made clothes for herself but for all her children. She also insisted on baking the cake for the wedding, including making all the decorative icing. She stored the three-tiered cake in the cellar to keep it cool until after the ceremony.

Agatha purchased Forest Edge and this 200-year-old farm house with the two thousand dollars she earned by welding during World War II. In the dining room, she is lovingly surrounded by my sisters, Sheree, Lori, and me. Sundays were a time for family togetherness and, of course, Agatha's sumptuous meals.

Agatha loved celebrating the seasons. Here I am with a pumpkin as big as me from our garden (*top*). My sisters and I, in the usual bangs and braids, are showing off our new, used clothes from the Vashon family, good friends of Agatha.

Agatha in Maine shortly after her radical mastectomy. In the early 1960s options for reconstructive surgery, if any, were limited and expensive. Agatha was a very practical woman.

Aunt Ruthie, Agatha's sister, with Governor Paul A. Dever at the Boston State House. She was the first African American to serve as an executive secretary to an American governor, which was noted in papers across the country.

Agatha, now in her sixties, is with her trusty Brownie camera ready to snap off a shot. In the background is her bed with its famous homemade canopy and matching dust ruffle.

Here are three of the Wooten sisters at Aunt Ruthie's home in Jamaica: Ruth, Agatha, and Theodora.

Esther Brooks teaching me and other students at the Cambridge School of Ballet. Even though many of us were quite young, Esther took a very serious approach to teaching us classical ballet and its history. Her ethics quickly rubbed off on me—I spent long hours in search of perfection.

Here I am with some of my foster mothers—me with Sylvia Pasik Silverman and her daughter, Robyn, at my home in California (*top*); Rosa Turner (*center*); Barbara Sterling and me having a great time (*bottom*). *Photographs courtesy of Robert Hale*

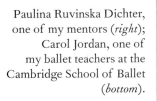

Linda Webb, my social worker. *Photograph courtesy of Robert Hale*

Paulina Ruvinska Dichter, one of my mentors (*right*); Carol Jordan, one of my ballet teachers at the Cambridge School of Ballet (*bottom*).

My mother, Dorothy, came from an old Maine family. Here are two of her relatives, Sarah Pressey Collins and her daughter, Zillah Collins, in Castine, Maine.

Dorothy with two of her sisters when they were young. Their father was a fisherman in Castine and decided against becoming a doctor like others in his family.

Dorothy and her three sisters—(*left to right*) Lillian, Elizabeth, Dorothy, and Edith. I have always been struck by the haunting image of the dead tree in the background.

My mother in 1980 in Bath, Maine, three years before she died.

This odd photograph was taken by Dorothy's family. I brought the single rose placed in her casket.

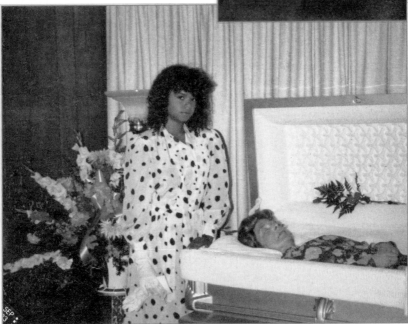

A NUMBER OF REMARKABLE WOMEN HAVE BECOME MY "SISTERS" OVER THE YEARS AND HAVE HELPED ME CONTINUE TO RAISE MYSELF.

Patricia Knight (*left*)

Susan Jaffe (*right*)

Nancy Morrison (*below*)

Margie Cortez (*left*)

Sarah Neece (*below*)

Dolores Marsalis and Jasper Armstrong Marsalis (*below*)

LaTanya Richardson Jackson, me, Samuel L. Jackson, Nancy Wilson, Kasi Lemmons

In my daytime and primetime television experiences, I had the honor of working with two men of the highest integrity: Dick Van Dyke on *Diagnosis Murder* (*top left*) and William J. Bell on *The Young and the Restless* (*right*).

I am very fortunate to have Esther Brooks, my first ballet teacher, in my life. Here I am introducing her to Wynton at the opening of Jazz at Lincoln Center, a very special evening.

As the mistress of ceremonies for Americans for the Arts, I am standing with the CEO of Casey Family Programs, William Bell, David Rockefeller, Veronica Hearst, and Americans for the Arts President, David Lynch.

Wynton and I celebrated our son Jasper's baptism with a wonderful reception. Here we are joined by Jasper's godfather, George Wein, and the former New York City Mayor David Dinkins.

Spending time with my children, Maya and Jasper, is my greatest joy.

In 1994, I arranged the first gathering of Dorothy's children. It took tremendous courage for my brothers, sisters, and I to come together with our families. We shared a lot of laughs, and even shed some tears. We all came away from that weekend feeling more connected and have stayed in touch since then.

walked into the field of high grass, scattering fireflies as I glanced up at the sky that seemed almost excessively studded with stars, and then back at Ma standing there under the glow of a naked porch light, beaming the brightest of any light source.

I walked forward, all the while looking back over my shoulder, not wanting to take my eyes off that misshapen silhouette that I loved— Agatha Armstead. She had foreseen this moment of my departure many moons ago, maybe from the instant she first sat down at her Steinway and gently commanded me to dance.

Esther Brooks was born with arresting beauty, destined to grace the world's most illustrious stages and concert halls, as both an actress and a ballerina. She had an unsurpassed intellectual brilliance that put her in the most esteemed cultural circles abroad and in the United States, but her true calling was empowering others, especially children, through teaching classical ballet and providing opportunities in the arts. She felt that if she introduced them to a discipline, they could eventually free themselves from the chaos that poverty so often inflicts on the very young. She hoped that this discipline, if learned, would give them some of the tools needed to embrace whatever careers they might choose for themselves as adults.

Esther was not afraid of her own power, nor did she apologize for it, something that made her disarmingly successful at what she did—with an innate business prowess she could have run major corporations—and that also made her sometimes controversial. A powerhouse in and out of the studio, without question, she made things happen. People shook in her presence.

With her bangles chiming to the count as the accompanist played in the background, Esther invariably began class with a simple plié. It never failed to amaze me that the mastery of the most basic ballet movement could be as important as one day nailing the perfect double pirouette onstage. Esther held the keys to opening those doors—secrets handed down from legendary dancers, choreographers, and teachers who had mentored and taught her.

Over the next thirty years I would weave together the strands of Esther's remarkable biography. Her astonishing curriculum vitae was known by everyone who was anyone in the dance world, including none other than George Balanchine, one of Esther's more famous admirers and mentors, Muriel Stuart, Pierre Vladimiroff, and Alexandra Danilova.

Before I knew much of anything about her private story, I sensed that Esther's childhood had been clouded by a solitude that was similar to mine, but was different from the disenfranchisement of a foster child. And we both learned to anchor ourselves through the power of classical ballet. From a prominent well-to-do family, she was born in Paris, France, and at the age of twelve, in the late 1930s, went to China with her parents. Esther dearly loved them—her father, a navy officer, was American, as was her mother, who was considered to be one of Europe's leading beauties.

Esther's social conscience developed early in response to the grinding poverty of the Chinese masses as well as the thousands of destitute refugees. Perhaps something in Esther rose up, even at fourteen, wanting to right injustice. And perhaps it was these encounters that became my good fortune and the good fortune of hundreds of other "poor" inner-city children.

Her other anchor, of course, was ballet. In Paris, Esther had begun training at the age of eight with Olga Preobrajenska, one of the most renowned teachers in the early 1930s. When Esther went to China, she studied with Audrey King, whose influences as a teacher, choreographer, innovator, and social activist all shaped her protégée. That first year while training under King, Esther made her stage debut with the Shanghai Russian Ballet and performed in *The Tarantella* and in *Swan Lake*. Her mentor could have been partly responsible for Esther's independence and her insistence on confronting injustice and intolerance, even at her own expense. Audrey King, in fact, later battled apartheid in South Africa by founding the Johannesburg Youth Ballet. (In 1976, the Johannesburg Youth Ballet performed for the first time with black and white dancers together onstage, in a "nonracial" corps of young dancers who turned the evil institution on its head, all of which coincided with the Soweto student uprising. After founding the company, Audrey King created a ballet entitled *Waratah*, a staging of the mythical story of an actual shipwreck off the coast of Africa, in which a white baby is rescued and raised to adulthood by a black community.)

When Esther left China and said good-bye to her great teacher, she was sent by her parents to live in a convent in Hollywood, California. Why a convent? Maybe all her grand ideas of saving the world were unnerving, especially with the ravages of World War II spreading across the continents. Maybe it was on account of her increasingly perilous good looks. In any case, her parents felt in a convent she would be protected from the evils and enchantments of Hollywood.

Esther stayed at the Convent of the Immaculate Heart for two months until she was asked to leave. One evening a nun caught her reading a book called *Out of the Night,* which is now considered a socialist classic. The book was immediately taken away from her, but a week or so later, she was in the nun's room, sewing, and her spool of thread rolled under the bed. When she went to retrieve it, she found her copy of *Out of the Night* with a bookmark strategically placed where the nun had left off in her reading. Esther became irate at this hypocrisy and was described as "insolent." That was the end of her days at the convent.

This circumstance propelled her into the foster care of Adolph Bolm, the legendary Danish dancer, who was friends with Igor Stravinsky and Cecil B. DeMille. Bolm was one of the core architects at the nascence of American ballet. The former stage partner and promoter of Anna Pavlova, among countless other ballet luminaries, Bolm and his company gave Esther the opportunity to make her American debut at the Hollywood Bowl in California. In her late teens, she moved to New York City to study with George Balanchine's Ballet Society at its inception. Mr. B's dictatorial direction even extended to telling her, over dinner one night, how precisely she must eat a plate of escargots—in a clockwise direction.

Fending off the most eligible of suitors, Esther succumbed to the virtuosic musical charms of the Russian violinist Paul Makovsky, whom she married in 1944, and with whom she had a daughter, Alexsandra. By 1948, the Makovskys had divorced, and Esther returned to France to dance with the Ballet des Champs Élysées and then with Ballet Russe de Monte Carlo. Two years later, amid travels throughout Europe, she met Peter Chardon Brooks. His gift for whistling classical music, journalism, and very dry wit not only captivated but complemented her as well. She had met her match, later marrying the award-winning journalist and having three more children.

Settling down in Cambridge, Massachusetts, the mother of four next gave birth to a dream that swiftly transformed into reality: the founding of the Cambridge School of Ballet in 1953, and soon thereafter the Cambridge Ballet Theater. The school and company were supported by foundation grants and championed by state and national leaders, namely Senator Edward M. Kennedy, Thomas "Tip" O'Neill Jr., Elliot Richardson, Thaddeus Beal, and Dr. Freddy Homburger, consul of Switzerland.

At a time when the public interest in ballet was at a low ebb, Esther further conceived the innovative idea of having Cambridge Ballet Theater perform in area public schools, thus making classical dance and music accessible and affordable to audiences of all ages and all walks of life.

By 1966, Esther—already a pivotal force in a dance renaissance taking place across the country, with American classical ballet coming fully into its own—had a brainstorm that would become her most enduring contribution. It came from a memory that stayed with her for many years of a boy who ran through a palazzo in Rome and nimbly boosted her wallet from her pocketbook, without disturbing her hand-kerchief or her gloves. The typical reaction by most would have been to bemoan the loss and report the crime to the policia. But Esther's first reaction was to admire the child's artful dexterity, imagining what a superb violinist he might have become, if given the opportunity. She fervently believed that if she could have found that pickpocket, "He could have been the next Paganini!"

Esther's implementation of that memory, a scholarship program for children without means, was in its first year when I auditioned for the Cambridge School of Ballet. I not only studied classical ballet but was given lessons in music, art, and modern dance and was taken on excursions in and around Cambridge to widen my scope beyond the inner city.

Despite the support she received, Esther did have detractors in differ-ent camps. In the more working-class neighborhoods that bordered the liberal haven of Harvard, residents were aghast that black children were being imported over to their side of the river, a rancor that increased with the racial tension spreading across the nation and that would later erupt across Boston with one of the worst busing crises in the country. Meanwhile, some of the black radical leaders were critical that we were being brought over to Cambridge, rather than having resources go to-ward establishing schools in black neighborhoods around Boston—even though highly supported cultural and arts schools did exist, such as the Elma Lewis School of Fine Arts in Roxbury.

Everyone gave Esther grief over the terminology she used. Her original idea was to help children living in poverty experience the power of discipline through the arts. Esther was told, however, by a Boston social worker who paid her an hourlong visit in her office, that using the word *poor* to describe children was unacceptable. The social worker stated, ". . . we have moved on from that. We now use the terms disadvantaged and underprivileged." Also in the meeting was the ac-claimed African American choreographer Billy Wilson, then one of my dance instructors at the Cambridge School of Ballet, who had this to say, "Honey, I was poor but I wasn't a bit disadvantaged." Esther continued using the word *poor*.

I had faced some of my own difficulties in navigating the terms to use to define myself and my social status.

Esther well understood the limitations of labels and refused to allow words alone to *describe* my status, or anyone else's. Nothing kept her from helping to *elevate* our status.

Her deepest conviction was that if she could save children from poverty through education in the arts, she could also save them from the downward spiral of hopelessness, homelessness, and crime. She was adamant when she told the *Boston Herald* in one of many interviews, "Incredible talent can be found among deprived ghetto children who really work hard when given an opportunity," and she went on to note that at the end of any given day she often had children who didn't want to go home because they felt safe and happy at school. Not only that, she pointed out, "The children are single-minded in the work, some coming to classes four to six times a week."

Esther did indeed save hundreds if not thousands of lives, both directly and through the example she set as a mentor and a teacher on a national and international level.

Starting on that very first class, June 24, 1968, upstairs in the ballet studio at the Odd Fellow Building, I saw emphatically that Esther literally never missed a beat as she kept an eye on every single one of her two hundred and ten students who attended that summer. I would catch Esther watching me and one other student closely, singling me out from time to time with her focus and her heart, attentive to my absolute desire to learn everything.

She gave me frequent muscle adjustments, placing one hand on my rib cage and the other on my shoulder to encourage me to relax, to breathe. Most serious ballet students knew that this was a sign of interest by the teacher, not being critical but recognizing promise. I favored the left side of everything, from pirouettes to jumps, and naturally loved romantic music scores.

Everything about the Cambridge School of Ballet those first months was like cotton candy. All of the summer program kids, like me, all caught up in the magic, grew together, many of us spotting each other at the train or bus station, riding out of poverty and the projects and into the other world of lofty Harvard Square. We were so eager to get to class that T-shirts could be seen peeking out from under leotards with no tights, just bare legs and shorts, most of us holding our slippers in our hands with brown bagged lunches while others arrived empty-handed, hungry but full of hope.

We were introduced to French, opera, how to score and read music, how to paint and sculpt. We created scenery and stage props for an end-of-the-summer performance, our own Versailles. We were all entrenched with the idea, teachers and students alike, that this artistic haven had unified us. Each adventure unfolded into the next.

Because I showed promise, as the program was drawing to a close, Esther and the Cambridge School of Ballet extended a full scholarship to me, and to several others, for the entire school year.

Agatha cleared the way for me to continue to stay with Uncle Richie and Aunt Laura in Dorchester, promising that she would check in on me as often as possible. Since she still owned a brownstone in Roxbury, that meant I could stay with her whenever she visited the Boston area. Even so, the separation from each other was increasingly painful.

Solace was found by holding firm to that ballet barre in Cambridge. Knowing of the sacrifices made on my behalf, I was an especially serious student. Esther and the rest of the teaching staff encouraged me in every respect. Early on, I was touted as being a natural lyrical dancer. Adagios required a delicate somberness, a gentle quality, and a lot of control. Not only was I learning my strengths, but also how to be part of the great ensemble. The throngs of children in my classes—some like me and others who weren't—all became my friends, part of my new family. We were connected in the kinetic energy of one common goal: to learn, to respect, and to depend on one another, with rewards based on merit. There were *no* shortcuts.

The exposure to classical music was often as exciting to me as the steps themselves. I soon understood that everything began with a message from the music. The composers who first caught my ear were Chopin, Debussy, Schumann, Shubert, Mendelssohn, Mozart—all played by our accompanists in class, gifted pianists who were accomplished in their fields, often modifying complex scores to fit the exercises or combinations at hand.

I was a sponge, soaking up every drop of history, reading books, going with my classmates to art films like *Stars of the Russian Ballet*. I read articles, listened to the odysseys of our teachers who described their faraway lands of origin, memorizing the fantastic-sounding names of who taught them and how they were taught.

Esther believed that it was important for her students, even those of us who were only nine and ten years old, to be introduced to the history of ballet. We were taught how the feasts and celebrations of the Italian aristocracy in the 1400s involved elaborate balletic presentations. Then there was Louis XIV, who commissioned magnificent productions at Versailles and even danced in them. We learned about the Russian choreographers, about the evolution of the Vaganova syllabus, in which we were taught in part with its codified, demanding approach that sought to utilize the whole body in an integrated, optimum way. We also trained with teachers whose dominant influence came from the Royal Academy of Dance School, which had brought together the leading choreographers from many nationalities and backgrounds.

Esther helped cultivate the love for history that was already in me. Just as family histories were always fascinating, it was important to know where my forebears of ballet came from, which gave me standing. Through that history, I now belonged to the family of others who were connected to the ballet world, with royal ancestors I could call my own and know that in their company, I was never a guest.

Esther encouraged curiosity about all forms of art and culture, a passion for me that would continue to grow over the years. Looking at photographs of paintings by Degas, Toulouse-Lautrec, and John Singer Sargent, I swore that I had lived in those scenarios of dancers that they painted. My favorite Sargent was his *El Jaleo*, a large canvas that I discovered during a visit to the Isabella Stewart Gardner Museum in Boston. One of his more famous works, it is of a flamenco dancer performing in low light, one hand grasping her skirts and the other arm outstretched, playing the castanets. As an adult I would discover other connections that went beyond the strong emotional reactions I had to John Singer Sargent's paintings. It turned out that he had been commissioned to paint portraits of individuals directly connected to the Cambridge School of Ballet—Mr. and Mrs. Peter Chardon Brooks, Esther's in-laws, as well as a family member of the school's treasurer, Reverend Augustus Hemenway. Both families had significant histories of overcoming difficult circumstances to attain levels of wealth with which they became major philanthropists on behalf of children and foster youth like me. It would seem like a series of divine connections that made Sargent's work all the more glorious to me.

Esther also lit a passion in me to travel. At night asleep I sometimes danced in my dreams in foreign, exotic settings; by day I imagined myself in Russia dancing with the Bolshoi for the most critical audiences in the world—performing thirty-two perfect fouettés, that single-legged high-velocity multiple turn performed by the lead ballerina in *Swan Lake*. It would be the Bolshoi, in fact, that I would later witness when I attended my first full-fledged ballet performance in Boston, with Maya Plisetskaya performing *Spring Waters*. I may have gasped out loud when she threw herself halfway across the stage into her partner's arms. That absolute and unconditional trust in someone else was unbelievable. Could I ever feel that certainty that someone else would never fail to catch me? It seemed impossible. But what I did think possible was that one day if I had a daughter, I would name her Maya. And indeed I would.

Esther taught me lasting life lessons that went beyond the ballet studio. I learned that I was loved and welcomed, as were we all. I learned the simplest, most universal truth: that one person could make a world of difference in someone else's life, even if only by caring enough to make sure carfare was available for getting to ballet class.

Esther compelled me to embrace my surroundings just as Agatha had done so at Forest Edge. I learned that the Charles River ran through the city but didn't have to divide it, and that I could attend the Harvard sailing and rowing practices while I lunched with fellow dance students, free for the watching. In the fall, I discovered the magnificent chestnut trees. On one occasion, I found myself standing on the narrow steps above the elegant Radcliffe campus. Before me was a kingdom of chestnut trees flush with fruit—my very own Maine. I ran freely across the campus, scooping up as many as my plastic Capezio bag would hold, nearly snapping the string over my shoulder. There was beauty and history everywhere I wandered: along Brattle Street, into the lively circus of Harvard Square, and through the Harvard Commons. I didn't need an excuse or justification for being there. Even at nine years old.

In only a handful of months I had developed levels of independence and seriousness that were important for me to succeed in the long haul. In this context, foster care had given me an advantage. I knew what pressure felt like. It had been the blueprint of my life: I knew what black or white meant in more ways than one; all or nothing, no middle ground, no excuses and no tears. As time went on, I would learn more and more that one missed step could mean the end of career in the classroom, and one misstep in my personal life could mean the end of a living arrangement. I would know how to shrink to the point of nonexistence when necessary or transcend into a queen during rehearsals for a *variation*. I know how to suspend hope; I had done it at every planting in Maine. I trained, mentally and physically, night and day in prayerful anticipation of being awarded support from the National Endowment for the Arts or possibly a Ford Foundation scholarship the following year. So much was riding on a plié.

As I headed into my fourth grade of elementary school, Esther and her fellow teachers were robust in their praise of my development thus far, pointing out how supple my feet were, how natural my arch and turnout were, and they were effusive over my flexibility, which allowed me to do a ninety-degree arabesque. As the result of what would total less than a year during which I was graced with a mentor named Esther Brooks, I would be given the means to attend the Cambridge School of Ballet on full scholarship for most of the next eight years, leaving me with the undisputable belief that, as Henry Adams wrote, "A teacher affects eternity."

My memories of staying with Uncle Richie and Aunt Laura in their home in Dorchester span different periods that began that first summer, along with a later stay during most of a school year. Adjustment to an atmosphere that was so different from Forest Edge wasn't easy, although I tried not to forget the generosity the family of four—including their two younger daughters, Brenda and Sheila—extended to me.

The Richard Armstead home at 23 Page Street, built in the 1940s, was a clapboard painted a shiny brown with yellow trim. The downstairs level of the house was a rental, while the upstairs was where we lived. Its most prominent feature was a balcony, which I thought was very rich at the time. I slept on the pullout couch in the living room during that summer and then later when I stayed for a school year.

While Uncle Richie kept busy with his work on the police force, Aunt Laura meticulously managed to balance her full-time work as a public school teacher with being a mother of two and maintaining a most orderly home, in addition to the attention she gave to her perfect appearance and bearing. Though I didn't always like this kind of regimentation, I didn't dare challenge the order of things. If Aunt Laura insisted that I clean the kitchen chairs with a toothbrush to get all the crumbs out of the seams, I did it. Everything she did had a purpose.

That drive had been bequeathed to Laura by a long line of women, most directly by her mother, Charlotte Louise Moore Cook Haywood, who was born in 1915 in Newton, Massachusetts. An avid reader, Charlotte bought loads of used books and encouraged Laura to read as well. Reading enabled Laura, an only child, to escape and to connect with the characters she read about, and through them, she too took a serious interest in many pursuits: skating, tennis, swimming, dance, and piano, studying at the New England Conservatory of Music. Laura was further buoyed by her mother's constant praise of her success as a student, and then reminded her of what she could accomplish if she continued to gain knowledge. One of Laura's fondest memories that she shared with me was of the time her mother took her to a concert performance of the great contralto Marian Anderson. Afterward, her mother took her backstage to meet the legendary artist—a life-changing event.

Above all, Charlotte believed that hard work was for the greater good of the family's future, and she passed that philosophy on to her daughter, Laura, who, by her example, reinforced that belief in me. Charlotte's numerous jobs included cleaning houses, working as an elevator operator and at the BF Goodrich rubber factory for more than twenty-five years, operating an army forklift, and sorting mail for the United States Post Office for twenty-two years. Moreover, she was one of West Newton's first black female entrepreneurs, having owned and managed a small variety store in the 1950s. She retired at the age of seventy-five, a pillar of strength and determination. Laura credited her mother as her first and best teacher in preparing her for her role as an educator. With a bachelor's degree in education, Laura accepted her first teaching position in 1958. She went on to teach and influence her own children and hundreds more during the forty-three-year teaching career that followed.

Aunt Laura believed strongly in setting, accomplishing, and

maintaining goals not only for herself, but for any child who came into her life. She also believed that when there was an opportunity to cultivate a child's interests and ambition, such as mine in classical ballet, that opportunity must be acted upon at once. As a child I felt that Aunt Laura was unemotional and no-nonsense, but I later understood the gift that she passed on to me from her own lineage was how to be an independent, hardworking career woman.

Sometimes the lesson is held in a toothbrush: to be thorough, to turn over every stone, to persevere until the last crumb has been wiped away. Aunt Laura likewise taught me the power of paying attention to detail. She unapologetically demonstrated that a person's loving care doesn't always show itself in an embrace.

Looking back, I have come to appreciate the honesty of that kind of love and those invaluable lessons that Aunt Laura passed on to me. As a nine-year-old, however, I had to work very hard to keep a stiff upper lip whenever I was hurting. Unfortunately, this set up a pattern of holding in and hiding feelings. Instead of voicing fears and legitimate concerns, I learned to keep them secret.

Not long into my stay in Dorchester, I first experienced a physical symptom that had no earthly explanation, something I felt that I could tell no one about. No one. Not Uncle Richie, not Aunt Laura, not Esther Brooks or any of the teaching staff, not even Agatha. It seemed like a fluke the first time it happened, without warning or cause, when I noticed that my hands suddenly became excessively moist with perspiration. I tried wiping them on my clothes, but that only exasperated my circumstance. When it happened a few weeks later, and then a week or so after that, I knew this wasn't random. Why was it happening? Was I being punished for having a bad thought? Was it a form of stigmata? Was it connected to being born out of wedlock?

If only I had confided in someone who might have helped me search for an explanation, I might have warded off the undercurrent of thinking there was something wrong with me being a foster child.

Instead, I carried this heavy burden of a secret and soldiered on, only seeking refuge in prayer in the confessional, where I sought out forgiveness through contrition.

In the fall, to my immense relief, Agatha decided to move to Roxbury with my sisters for the school year. She was now in her late sixties and the Maine winters were becoming much too harsh for her. In planning for her later years, she had held on to the brownstone in Roxbury—where she had lived before moving to Forest Edge full-time—so this was more of a return to a previous home that it was a move to some-place new.

Agatha's Roxbury brownstone at 48 Burrell Street was adjacent to a burnt-out brownstone full of dumped trash and oversized mice. Ma tried to rid us of the threat of vermin by catching them and drowning them in Mason jars filled with scalding water—a sight that horrified me. Other than the unfortunate decline of what had once been an up-and-coming neighborhood, being reunited with Agatha was all that I really cared about.

This move to Roxbury, in fact, was also a way of continuing to honor the wishes of our mother, Dorothy, who never stopped in her valiant campaign for her daughters to be together. Combined with the challenges of snow and freezing temperatures at Forest Edge, this was Agatha's public reason for coming to Roxbury, but I suspected the main factor in her decision was that she missed me as much as I missed her.

Roxbury was formerly known as "Rocksbury" for its plentiful supply of puddingstone, a combination of glacial debris and volcanic lava. English colonists established "Rocksbury" in 1630 as one of seven villages in the Massachusetts Bay Colony. In the 1940s and 1950s, Roxbury became home to thousands of African Americans who migrated from the South to escape Jim Crow. They were now included in the melting pot that already consisted of Irish, Italian, and Jewish immigrants. Once home to Fredrick Douglass, Malcolm X, and Simon

Willard, and just three miles south of Boston, the "Bury" offered three centuries of impressive historical buildings and landmarks.

Sadly, the same Roxbury that had been the center of important industrial trade and farming, a place that had boasted baroque and Renaissance revival architecture and that had once claimed Franklin Park, designed by landscape architect Frederick Law Olmsted, had met with a downturn in the 1960s with increasing poverty and social unrest.

On the streets in the fall of 1968, it was evident that the assassinations of Dr. Martin Luther King and Robert Kennedy had left everyone shell-shocked, with race riots taking their toll on the poorest neighborhoods, and anger over Vietnam, drugs, crime, and violence spreading.

In this atmosphere, Agatha was pleased to find the haven of St. Patrick's Grammar School, which was within walking distance from her brownstone on a well-kept block. She felt it was important that Sheree, Lori, and I receive the benefits of a private school education, and she made sure that we followed the safest route to school and back. In my case, Agatha was careful to plan the most secure commute for me from St. Patrick's to Cambridge by bus, and two trains and then home again after classes.

I regularly turned down rides from parents of ballet classmates who lived in better parts of Boston, although in the winter I sometimes couldn't resist.

"Thank you," I would gratefully say as we approached an attractive burgundy three-story home on my street, "you can drop me off here," claiming it as my own home. Quickly stepping out onto the dimly lit sidewalk, waving until the car was out of sight, I ran for my life down the middle of the street until I was safe inside our apartment at 48 Burrell Street.

Besides being reunited with Agatha and studying three afternoons a week at the Cambridge School of Ballet, I had a growing social life and a promising academic fourth-grade year at St. Patrick's. Even though the nuns tended to be stricter than my teachers at West Lebanon

Elementary School, they were generally kind and they were also interesting personalities.

Early in the school year, Sister Catherine Williams corrected me about an assignment while poking me in the chest as her beady eyes peered into mine, which I'm sure were wide with terror. The habit she wore exaggerated the humiliation of being singled out, in front of the whole class, for doing something differently. Was this how school was going to be in the big city? It took great effort to keep the lump in my throat from rising above the bow tie that was attached to my Peter Pan collar.

There was another nun with untreated psoriasis that she constantly itched and scratched to the point of bleeding. One day when my new friend Lauren Turner and I were whispering in English class, I was reprimanded and given detention. After the final bell rang, I made my way to the detention room and was met by Sister Psoriasis. It was just the two of us that day.

Glumly, I sat there in silence, still unsure of how to tell time; I watched the light begin to fade, knowing that there was just one last bus that I could catch to get over to Cambridge to ballet class in time. Finally, before I had been dismissed, I stood up and began to collect my books and my plastic Capezio bag with my ballet clothes in it.

SISTER *(scratching menacingly)*: And where do you think you're
    going? Detention isn't over.
ME: I have to get to ballet class.
SISTER: Oh, no. You're not going anywhere. Sit down!

"I can't be late or I'll have to sit out the whole class," I said defiantly and stepped toward the door.

Suddenly she ran toward me and I picked up my pace, racing down the hall. Terrified, I outpaced her, running down the stairs, taking two steps at a time. Becoming winded, the red-faced nun stopped and leaned over the banister, screaming at me as I dashed toward the exit.

SISTER: Why can't you be like all the other girls?
ME: Because I'm not!

Other than that encounter, the teachers at St. Patrick's were very supportive of my interest in dance. They encouraged me to perform in the spring recitals—in such standard fare as a baton twirler in *Yankee Doodle Dandy,* dancing to "When Johnny Comes Marching Home" for the Veterans Day program, or as one of the daughters in *Fiddler on the Roof.*

All of my teachers were proud of an article about me and my participation in the Cambridge School of Ballet that appeared in the *Christian Science Monitor*—another Agatha Armstead coup that was as pragmatic as it was promotional. Rules were being bent to allow me to maintain my status as a ward of the State of Maine, even though I was living in Massachusetts part of the year; the feature story made everyone involved feel that the extra effort undertaken on my behalf was worth it.

To be featured in the *Christian Science Monitor,* an international newspaper, was incredible. But when Esther Brooks selected me to appear on television to demonstrate ballet fundamentals, I couldn't believe something so impossible was happening to me. It was *The CBS Newcomers* show, starring Dave Garroway, a pioneer broadcaster of morning and late-night television shows. After starting on the NBC network in 1949 with *Garroway at Large,* three years later, on January 14, 1952, he was the founding host of the *Today Show,* one of the longest-airing morning news shows that is now celebrating more than fifty years on the air!

My first television appearance was a storybook experience. The lights, the camera, and, yes, the action left me spellbound. When the segment ended, Mr. Garroway applauded from his desk, ready to turn to the next guest, who was poised and sitting beside him. Still standing at the barre on the set, I stared at the exotically radiant woman. I had seen her before; she was pure Hollywood. She was Eartha Kitt! Later, backstage, she was with her daughter, a beautiful, blond-haired little girl. I thought how lucky they were to have each other.

Many of the nuns commended me for my appearance on the show, also noting that they were pleased by what dance had given me. Sister Francis Lillian, always kind and thoughtful, reminded me that no matter how hard I was working to also take time not to work so hard. "Enjoy life," she recommended. "It passes by so quickly."

After seeing the Garroway program, an elderly sister decided that she and a few fellow nuns would teach me the steps of Irish dancing, more specifically the Irish jig. Along with the rest of my class, I was delighted to watch these stoic nuns metamorphose into free, unrestricted beings. Slightly lifting their skirts to demonstrate, they jumped, laughed, snapped, clapped, scuffed, and stomped themselves into near hysteria. They were liberated and happy. Their energy was infectious, making me want to join right in; that is, until I heard the elderly nun say, "Please line up in girl boy order. We'll rehearse the steps first, then I would like you all to link pinky fingers with your partner."

My heart sank as I felt a tingling of wetness in the tips of my fingers. My dance partner was the "it" bad boy, Baron "Pudgy" Lewis, who wasn't pudgy at all but skinny, and not the most forgiving kid on the block. I desperately wiped my hands against my navy uniform jumper, only increasing the involuntary sweating.

The elderly, bespectacled sister sat down at a tired upright piano as Pudgy reached his pinkie out to mine and we tentatively linked. Horrified, I could see the minute beads of sweat as they began to appear. I prayed that my partner would be distracted by the steps as the sister began to count with a spirited clap: "And a one, and a two, and a three . . . let's go . . . Scrape-hop, scrape-hop, a one, two, three."

Fully formed drops of sweat glistened on the tips of my fingers. Now I prayed the music would stop. The nun was in a personal frenzy, striking the keys, eyes closed, transported back to Ireland, oblivious to little brown children kicking up rosin with their worn shoes.

I could feel Pudgy's cold stare. Collected perspiration created a tiny streamlet between our upright forearms. A drop hung at the tip of my elbow before falling onto the wooden floor, mixing with the rosin. All in slow motion. Splash. I looked straight ahead. The music stopped. Small fingers unlinked. I stole a glance.

It was a moment out of Charles Dickens's *David Copperfield,* which I later read, copying down this quote:

> . . . and at parting, gave him my hand. But oh, what a clammy hand his was! . . . As ghostly to the touch as to the sight! . . . It was such an uncomfortable hand, that, when I went to my room, it was still cold and wet upon my memory.

Smarting from embarrassment, I promised myself that I would never allow this to happen again. I decided to avoid close physical contact that might set off or expose my symptoms. Without being conscious of it, I somehow turned the idea of my affliction into a form of self-protection. But at an awful cost.

Whenever Agatha wintered in Roxbury, for periods that might only be a few months or extend into a year or longer, she didn't think for a minute that because she was approaching seventy years old she shouldn't be employed. To the contrary, she felt that the high urban cost of living for herself and her foster daughters warranted her return to the workforce. When she applied for a position with the Social Security office in Dudley Station, a notoriously rough neighborhood where all the commuting lines convened, they were honored to have her, especially as a senior citizen, as she brought much experience from an earlier position working for the State House in Boston.

Agatha walked in a cloak of white light, but traveling at night could be treacherous, and I worried about her coming home from work in the evening. Ma maintained that there were angels watching over us, even at Dudley Station.

That's what she assured me whenever I had to go see the dentist there. Besides the neighborhood, I found the Warren Dental next door to the Dudley Station to be suspect anyway. Ma insisted we go there instead of Grover Dental at Northampton Street when the office announced they weren't taking Medicaid anymore. Either way, no one wanted to deal with the insurance requirements provided by the various state agencies that had to be billed for my visit. They would tell me, a nine-year-old, "We sent your original to Augusta to be paid, but it was sent back 'not approved.'" The standard response also included a note that informed the dental office, "Please find a copy of our dental fee schedule for the State of Maine children." All of this transpired as the secretary inevitably became exasperated, along with the other patients waiting to be seen. Everyone knew my business, everyone knew I was a foster child, and everyone knew I was on some sort of welfare. I just wanted to go home.

Not far from the dentist's office was where one of Ma's mystical encounters had taken place, at the John Eliot Burying Ground—a cemetery that dated back to 1630—when a woman approached her to ask for money. Ma gave her a quarter. Something substantial. The woman thanked her, then proceeded to bury the coin in the above-ground cemetery. Ma tried not to stare, so then looked away and within two blinks of an eye the woman vanished into thin air. This wasn't strange in Agatha Armstead's cosmology. Ma explained to me, "Obviously the woman was an angel just testing me."

That story made sense to me as someone who would always believe in the mystery of circumstances and that not everything that happened had an obvious explanation. I would come into contact with that woman in various guises on many occasions in my life.

The first time was in connection to an incident that had taken place early that fall of 1968 when I was returning from ballet class on a new route that Agatha had just mapped out for me. We had only recently moved to Roxbury and our telephone hadn't been connected yet.

In case of an emergency, I carried an extra dime and a piece of paper with the number of Agatha's daughter Barbara, who lived in the up-stairs apartment at the brownstone. After I dutifully repeated to Agatha exactly what the route was, she was satisfied that all would go well.

And it did, until I arrived at a major underground artery, Washing-ton Street Station. This was where I was supposed to change trains but the lack of familiarity confused me as to how to proceed next.

A young black man in a green leather blazer saw my confusion and offered his assistance. I declined, shaking my head no, knowing it was wrong to talk to strangers. Still lost a half hour later, I looked down from a platform and saw him at the bottom of a flight of stairs. This time I accepted his help.

Speaking softly, he suggested that I call home and let everyone know I was going to be fine, and then directed me to a pay phone in the sub-way. I took out the dime and Barbara's phone number just as the man slithered into the telephone booth with me, closing the door behind him. My hand shook as I dropped the dime and dialed.

With relief, I heard Barbara's cheerful, "Hello," and I began to ex-plain that a nice man was helping me find my way back home. But be-fore she could respond or I could continue, he grabbed the receiver from my hand and hung it up.

In the blur that followed, I saw a swirl of many people passing by the phone booth, rushing to get to the same place I was desperate to get back to: home. My natural survival instincts now alerted me, indicating that I was in great danger as he took me by the shoulder, pushing me out of the subway, toward the construction site for a new Jordan Marsh department store, and then down a dirt path in back of it.

Walking with serious trepidation, I asked, "Are you sure this is the right way?"

The man replied, "Yes, it's a shortcut." Now completely obscured by walls, he slammed me against a brick building and warned me, at knifepoint, "If you run, I'll have to cut you."

Fright and flight battled for supremacy as I felt the heat of my own urine pour down my legs, wetting my leotard and tights. But in the split second he paused to raise his hand, I ran for my life. Those moments between moments when time can't be measured, I flew. Racing furiously down a dirt path, gasping for air, I went past the construction, all in more of a blur.

With his angry panting behind me, I pushed faster, soon stumbling frantically back down the subway stairs. Unable to breathe, I began to convulse, when I turned around to find him on my heels. Inexplicably, out of nowhere came an elderly woman, who raised her cane in his face, warning him, "You leave her alone!"

I begged her *not* to leave me alone, and she didn't. The old lady limped with me to the train connection that I needed to make, appealing to another perfect stranger who delivered me all the way home. She was most definitely one of the angels Ma had long tried to teach me about.

To my further relief, I managed to avoid questions from Agatha that night, as I stood with my back to her, washing out my leotard and tights, crying into the sink.

For the rest of the year, I rode the train in complete terror, knowing that he was looking for me as much as I was looking for him—a necessary process for sharpening my survival skills.

By late fall 1968, even though life in Roxbury—the "Bury" to us locals—had begun to toughen me up somewhat, I was still very much a fish out of water, especially in contrast to the girls in my fourth-grade class at St. Patrick's. Lauren Turner was a true case in point. As pretty as she could be and the most popular girl in our class, Lauren was a real toughie, and even led a clique, a kind of black Catholic schoolgirl gang.

Imagine my surprise one day at school, when I happened to show up wearing the same green cardigan she had in her own wardrobe and she sent one of her sidekicks to tell me, "Lauren Turner's gonna beat you up if you wear her sweater again."

Not saying anything, I gave her a blank stare. I was proud of my green pilled cardigan; it was the only one I had, and I fearlessly wore it the next day.

Not only did Lauren Turner not beat me up, but when she discovered that my Zodiac sign was Taurus, like hers, we became best friends. From early on and into adolescence, Lauren amazed me by how comfortable she was with using her sensual good looks to taunt and tantalize the boys. Her striking almond-shaped eyes and their exotic tilt were made even more pronounced by how tightly her various Afrocentric dos were pulled back. She had a high forehead, glisteningly perfect skin, and all she had to do was cast a look in the direction of some boy and she would have him coming and going, like a bull with a ring through his nose that she could pull at will. Lauren had mastered *attitude,* that feminine stance, which in the 'hood is a very different thing from the ballet pose of attitude that I knew.

"Vicki, put your feet together," she said one day early in our friendship, rolling her eyes at my constant "corny" turnout. I tried putting my feet together in parallel but then it became apparent that while my ballet training had me tucking my tailbone under, girls in the Bury were flipping theirs out. I just had to learn how to stand two different ways. Lauren demonstrated a slightly separated fourth position as I followed along. "Good, now, put your hand on your hip, and rock back." She was the prima ballerina of our neighborhood.

I still needed practice in my stances, the various attitudes, the sucking of teeth and gum-chewing techniques. I still had to learn that hair wasn't just hair in the 'hood; it was a lifestyle and could define who you were. Everyone wore different versions of Afro puff hairdos except for me and one other girl, Clarissa Townes, who had green eyes, light skin, and long, long brown braids. Eventually, I was given enough grief that when someone told me if I washed my hair in vinegar it could create an Afro, I gave it a try. Not only didn't it work, but my hair smelled like vinegar for at least a week.

Then again, as a serious student of ballet, I had to learn another set of hairstyling rules. Traveling between different worlds as I did on a daily basis, I became very skilled at adapting. This is an essential tool for any foster child, not merely to fit in, but to do so with frequency, sometimes at a moment's notice. Yet it was also important to have my own ground to stand on, my own sense of self, a sense of where my home really existed. Dancing gave that to me. It was freedom and safety. My church. My sanctuary.

Dance class was where I was headed, in fact, for another shot of inspiration, on what was a memorably crisp midafternoon of that first Monday of December back at St. Patrick's after the Thanksgiving holiday. With nothing else out of the ordinary, I went through my usual odyssey of transportation, taking a bus, two trains, and a trolley from Roxbury to Cambridge.

As I walked down Massachusetts Avenue, the smell of smoke was distinct and I could see the commotion ahead. A crowd of familiar and unfamiliar faces, spectators, police officers directing traffic, and photographers, along with firefighters gripping hoses, crisscrossed the avenue from all directions, still extinguishing the last stubborn vestiges of what had been a ferocious blaze. In total shock, I saw the remains of the Cambridge School of Ballet. It had been burned to the ground, only the brick shell remained. On all four corners, people gathered, aghast at the sight. I stood there with them, looking up at "my world" in smoke and flames. The smattering of students, mostly from the Bury, were commanded to return to our respective homes immediately. But I *was home* and could not be moved. I could not leave my dream. Instead, I stepped into the cut of a factory doorway across the street and watched the spectacle in horror. In shock, I had no recollection of how I got back to 48 Burrell Street that fateful afternoon.

It was later confirmed that the fire was set by locals—two white teenage boys, one of whom was allegedly the son of a high-ranking police officer—because of anger over the influx of black students. My fear was soon realized—that everything had been burned in the fire: irreplaceable, one of a kind, Russian tutus that had been given as gifts to Esther, which she had carefully preserved as patterns for new ones, as well as costumes, sheet music, pianos, school and office records, ballet films, photography and books, furniture, *my trunk*. Memorabilia. A lifetime of work. In a way this was the closest I would ever come to witnessing a public lynching. It was also the first time I learned that Esther had lived for many years with police security because of the death threats she received. This taught me the sacrifice required of leadership.

When the last embers were out and the smoke had cleared, Esther insisted on returning to the wreckage to salvage anything that was left. On a hunch, she decided to search for the school's safe, and her husband, Peter, climbed down into the pit of ashes, managing to both locate and open it. Inside, where they had been originally left to stay dry, were several pairs of perfectly intact, new pink satin pointe shoes. A tiny miracle, but one that would sustain Esther during the regrouping process.

Within two weeks we were up and running again in our new home in the basement of the First Church in Cambridge Congregational, built in 1633. Located across from Radcliffe campus, it told me that I was still in the Ivy League. Esther took out ads in local newspapers, alerting her students and their families to return to class at once.

Esther stayed long enough to pass the torch to her successor, Carol Jordan, but when I learned in the spring of 1969 that the Brooks family was moving to Florence, Italy, I was inconsolable. In the same time frame, Agatha moved back to Forest Edge. The escalation of violence and crime in Roxbury were taking too much of a toll on her weakening body. We decided together that I should stay in Boston and continue my studies with the Cambridge School of Ballet and not return with her to the farm. There were a series of back and forths, however, that would at least reunite us for short periods, both in Roxbury and at Forest Edge. While Sheree and Lori would continue at St. Patrick's at

certain points, staying with different Armstead family members, the
three of us were rarely under one roof from then on. For the time being, I returned to Dorchester to live with Aunt Laura, Uncle Richie,
and their daughters.

My tenth birthday, which we had celebrated almost a year earlier,
had finally arrived. It coincided with the start of my slow extrication
from Agatha, marking the beginning of my adulthood.

Esther's departure from my immediate sphere left a permanent
ache. At the same time, the teaching she had instilled in me was also
permanent. In so many respects she would remain peerless. In the
power of her wisdom, the power of her power, the graceful lilt of an
arm; her voice.

Starting from that first year that Esther went away we began ex-
changing correspondence. One of my favorite letters from her came
that following Christmas from Florence, addressed to me at Forest
Edge, where I was visiting for ten days:

Dearest Vicki,

*Your letter was mailed so long ago that I am truly ashamed not to
have written you long before this. Will you forgive me? You can't
imagine how much I think of you, and miss seeing you. It made me so
happy to hear that you were on toe, also to hear that you are working
hard. Mrs. de Mille wrote me that you had improved a great deal. If
you keep working like that, some day you will surely be a beautiful
dancer, and I will be proud that I had some small part in your dancing
life. . . .*

*We will all go down after Christmas to the south of Italy to stay for
two weeks in a little village called Positano. It is on the Mediterranean
sea and built all up and down the side of a mountain. No cars are allowed there because the streets are much too narrow and steep, so if you
want to go somewhere and it is too far to walk, you go on a donkey.
Now you can think of us all riding around on donkeys and laugh.*

Dearest little Vicki, have a lovely Christmas. I shall think of you on Christmas day and will wish you then as I do now, all the happiness in the world, both in the present and in your future. . . .

Mountains of love, and a sugar plum tree full of kisses,
Esther Brooks

FIVE

Rosa Turner & Barbara Sterling ... & Linda Webb & Carol Jordan

Between the ages of ten and fifteen, I benefited extraordinarily from the influence of several teachers, advocates, and surrogate fosterers who generously contributed to my growth, helping me make the difficult leap into my teen years. In particular, four women stand out as representing distinct roles in raising me.

There was the steady force of Carol Jordan, Esther's successor as director of the Cambridge School of Ballet, who was to prepare me, like no else could have, to compete at the highest levels of my discipline. Adding to the array of social workers who pulled strings on my behalf was Linda Webb, assigned to me when I was twelve years old because of my status as a "special case"—on account of my living out of state, studying classical ballet on a full scholarship, and not always living with Agatha, still my official primary foster mother. Barbara Sterling was a respite caregiver, representing the many willing part-time fosterers who couldn't commit for an entire year but could foster me in my early teens for a weekend at a time. Rosa Turner became an official temporary foster mother during a good portion of a school year.

Each of the women who raised me in these years left me with lasting lessons that came from their unique talents, while Rosa Turner, as though clairvoyant, most showed me the road into the future, letting me see there were treacherous roads ahead on my way to adulthood and providing me with the sustenance for my survival.

All of these individuals, together with the agencies and institutions that were supporting me, collectively sent me the empowering message that they sincerely believed in me and wanted me to win. That sparked my desire not just to be *good* at ballet, but to be *great*. To be great, however, meant being fearless—to reach high, risk failure, falling, getting up and starting over. Lessons to be learned.

No doubt Carol Jordan recognized that drive in me and cultivated it, taking over where Esther had left off, bringing her own brand of foundation building to the school and to me.

Ms. Jordan, as all the students referred to her, was English, born in the working-class city of Birmingham. She not only left behind the poverty of her youth but, through unflinching determination and strong, classical athleticism, had overcome what was not the optimum physique for ballet. Ms. Jordan had nonetheless worked tirelessly to develop every muscle in her body, even her instep, eventually ascending the ranks as a teacher in the Royal Academy of Dance syllabus.

In 1920, when RAD was conceived in England, the founders brought together the most esteemed names in the ballet world from different nationalities—including British, French, Russian, and Danish. Carol's influence came from that versatile background and she also taught in the Vaganova system.

In Russia in the late 1800s, Agrippa Vaganova had faced her own challenges as a dancer, because, it was whispered, "Vaganova doesn't have the beauty to be a prima ballerina." During the last year of her performing career she did indeed master the role of prima ballerina, and upon her retirement as a dancer, she taught some of the most legendary dancers, including none other than prima ballerina assoluta Maya Plisetskaya.

Those were the rigors from which Carol Jordan drew to become the stalwart of balletic discipline that she was. She exemplified the necessity of relentless training and performing experiences, never underestimating the lesson, no matter how small the venue. I was honored, at age twelve, when she chose me for a liturgical dance that I performed to Erik Satie's *Morceaux en forme de Poire,* as part of a program presented at the First Church in Cambridge Congregational where we studied. For added inspiration, I loved the program notes that were handed out to the fairly sizable audience in which it was affirmed that the ancient tradition of dancing was to show delight in a relationship with God, an "inevitable and normal part of worship."

This was why, after all, the church had been providing a home for the Cambridge School of Ballet to hold classes in its basement, in support of the mission to provide artistic education and scholarship to so many children throughout the greater Boston area. The connection was not lost on me between what was happening in my corner of existence and what the worldwide mission was—to raise children up out of poverty everywhere. These were some of the seeds planted in me, allowing me to feel part of something integrally important, beyond myself. It mattered that somehow my performing that Sunday morning helped raise money to feed children thousands of miles away. This was an introduction to acting with purpose and the power of reciprocity, made possible wherever you stood or danced, and by Carol Jordan's efforts—who sent me the loveliest notes, writing, "Thank you darling for the hard work & the joy you put into the ballet."

With incredible energy and conviction, Ms. Jordan led by example and lecture. There never was a class or rehearsal that she was late for. She demanded the same from her students. No nor'easter could keep her from teaching and neither could her two pregnancies. She demonstrated grands battements, pirouettes, tour jetés with ease and grace at every stage of her developing motherhood. This was proof to me that a woman could always excel by doing what she loved, and it was evidence that motherhood was filled with an energy that did not impede a woman's passion; in fact, it seemed to increase it.

Ms. Jordan was known as a taskmaster. She occasionally dictated choreography with her hands, expecting me to calculate, translate, and then execute the combination. I learned that the brain was another muscle and could be developed and trained just like any other. The developed skill to decipher hand movements, emulating choreography, would prove invaluable later in New York during my professional career and in other professions that required memorization.

It may have been apparent to Ms. Jordan already as to how many of us only in our preteens would continue with ballet once we had completed high school. Perhaps as few as ten dancers would pursue a career out of hundreds of students. Even so, she expected the best from each of us. Latecomers had to sit out the entire class. Not one hair should attempt to be out of place. She did not permit excessive jewelry and despised leg warmers or any article of clothing that hid the body from her critical gaze. She knew each and every one of our bodies as if they were her own.

Carol Jordan would say, "Muscle tone is the ability to move out of the way of a speeding car." It was Carol's insistence on this that played a key role in saving my friend Patricia Knight's life in years to come.

Ms. Jordan's special message for me came during the very first class I took with her and made its way into every utterance she made in front of me. In contrast to the limitations of her body, she emphatically wanted me to remember, "Never take natural talent for granted," reminding me what Maxim Gorky believed, "Talent is work."

With that, she had license to push me to go past what came easily and naturally. On one unforgettable day, Carol Jordan tapped into my focused space as I held the barre with my right hand, my left leg in à la seconde, and transferred her energy to me, as if by osmosis. I could feel a kind of opening, a freedom, a release in the ball and socket of my hip. The discovery that I could sustain this difficult position by understanding the architecture of my muscles was exhilarating.

We looked directly at each other without words, a moment made more meaningful by Carol Jordan's knowing nod. We both knew that I had found that invisible connection, placement, also known as the center. I gained confidence in my craft knowing that Ms. Jordan had the expectation that I could. As early as the sixth grade when I was twelve years old, she had instilled in me the sense that I was to be one of a handful of pupils exiting the Cambridge School of Ballet: to put all of my training to the test, to embark on a professional career, and ultimately to make my mark.

This confidence was further fueled by the rest of our ballet instructors. Rosalind DeMille, the daughter-in-law of Cecil B. DeMille, had been the first to announce that at ten years old I was strong enough to go en pointe, a rite of passage for every ballet student.

The naturally gifted Marie Paquet inspired all of us. A former ballerina with Gerald Arpino's Joffrey Ballet, Marie did everything with ease, even the way she walked and talked. She floated as she whispered instructions—"Pas de bourreé en tournant"—making each movement seem as though it ought to be effortless, even in combination: "Chassé, pas de bourreé, glissade, grand jeté." To watch her was to watch a fairy. In class I sometimes wondered if I reached out to touch her whether my hand would pass through her. There was absolutely no evidence of effort when she danced.

Tatiana Babushkina was my true inspiration. The Ukraine-born, heralded prima ballerina who had danced with the Ballets Russes was a marvel of consistency, a common thread among so many of the women I most admired. As a metaphor for perfection, Tatiana—with her ballet skirt tucked just under the bottom of her leotard to reveal that much more of her perfectly shaped legs—frequently carried a yardstick in order to measure the height of our extensions. Her technique was unflappable. I was mesmerized by the strength and crisp speed of her feet. Like diamonds they pierced the air, stirring up rosin as she executed intricate combinations. My impulse was to applaud not only at the end of class in a *reverence*—a show of respect to the teacher and the accompanist—but during class. I knew that I was in the presence of greatness—a bona fide prima ballerina. Tatiana epitomized what Martha Graham believed, that "where a dancer stands is holy ground."

She was further validation that my serious studies mattered, that I mattered, and that I indeed was related to ballet royalty that she embodied: the high instep, her perfectly proportioned body, her thick Eastern European accent never lost to my ear, carrying her history and her privileged ballet knowledge. It never failed to amaze me how far she had traveled in her life to teach me in the basement of a church.

In the years leading up to my twelfth birthday, I was what social workers described as *well adjusted*. If there was any doubt as to the fullness of my young life, I had only to flip through the pages of my expanding brown scrapbook, which I enhanced by painting flourishes on the front in gold glitter nail polish. Here was yet another device for keeping track of experiences and relationships, which Agatha had encouraged me to institute. The collection of newspaper clippings, dance programs, notes from teachers, dried flowers, ticket stubs, photographs, napkins, and any scrap that held a memory were all captioned by me in my sprightly cursive handwriting—almost as though I was writing to a future version of myself—with references of shared events with my diverse assortment of new friends.

The gift of friendship, sisterhood, was something I didn't take lightly. Not surprisingly, most of the friendships that were made in these years became lasting ones.

Patricia Knight and I knew each other from ballet, starting from that very first summer scholarship session. Patti danced on an unshakable plane, refusing to be bullied or made to adhere to any demands— even those of ballet—unless they made sense. It wasn't that she didn't want to muss her press and curl with unnecessary perspiration; it was that she had other priorities, including an eye on education that eventually led her to conquering the corporate world. All it took was her staid, "I have an exam tomorrow and need to get home to study." I knew that if I wanted a ride home from Cambridge that night, I'd better throw my street clothes over my leotard and tights in a hurry. Patti was no joke, serious in every way. Mature beyond her years.

In a small-world scenario, Patti's parents, hard, hard working Jamaican immigrants, lived in Dorchester and knew Uncle Richard and Aunt Laura, which meant that whenever I was staying with them we could commute together. Patti's no-nonsense mother, Mary "Pearl" Knight, understood the importance of the arts in life and as they applied to high education. Pearl passed on to her daughter her own practical thinking, and, moreover, strove to give her child the best—from private schooling to extracurricular enrichment—in order to ensure success in whatever she pursued. In addition to this vital support from her parents, Patti was strongly influenced by Carol Jordan's determination and commitment.

Tall for her age, with a quiet, poised demeanor, Patti was invariably able to listen the way most everyone else preferred to talk. Indeed, the fact that no one knew what she was thinking could be intimidating, something she would employ to strong advantage in the corporate arena.

Remarkably, I never saw Patti cry. Not ever. If she was annoyed or upset, her face would remain implacable—except for the tiniest arch of her eyebrow. How to find that state of Zen mystified me for years, though it didn't surprise me when I heard in adulthood that it had helped her overcome a near fatal accident and its aftermath.

We had by then established a pick-up-the-phone-never-miss-a-beat friendship, and late one night I received a call from Patti to tell me about an incident that had happened while she was on assignment in London as global director for the Gillette Corporation.

Unbelievably, Patti had found herself in exactly the crisis that Carol Jordan had used as an example so many years earlier—she was crossing the street and saw a car coming straight toward her. Ms. Jordan's voice reverberated in the memory of her muscles, brain, and cells. Had she not been able to jump and roll over its hood, falling to the pavement, one can only speculate about the dire consequences. She immediately rose to her feet, declining emergency medical treatment, and walked away.

Years later, I had to ask, "Did you cry?" Patricia answered, "No." She attributed her spared life to Carol Jordan. Throughout her corporate career Patti continued to take ballet classes, which returned her to a time and a discipline that were familiar and enjoyed. "Dancing makes me feel good" was how she described it; that feeling good and being good do not require perfection—something Patricia Knight exemplified even in our early days.

Another lifelong friendship made early on was with my ballet buddy Robyn Silverman, destined to be a sister to me in more ways than one. Robyn was like an Olympic gymnast in her unbridled approach to dancing. In continual amazement of how she had no fear of falling, I watched her throw her body full bore into whatever was asked of it. In contrast, I detested striking anything hard or anything hard striking me. Being her friend emboldened me somehow when it came to the passion for ballet we both were pursuing. By the same token, Robyn made me feel that she admired me for my independence, which challenged her. On those and other respects we built a lasting friendship, despite our different backgrounds, as we were destined to become even closer in our high school and adult years.

I also came to know Jackie Legister from ballet class. A Jamaican beauty, who loved every inch of her voluptuous self—not at all the conventional physique of a ballet dancer but more of a burlesque dancer for the Moulin Rouge—Jackie had a lackadaisical manner of moving and getting through class that drove Carol Jordan to distraction. Of course, I took ballet much more seriously, but Jackie's "evry' ting gonna be all right" spirit helped me consider that life might not be as serious as I thought.

At school, Lauren Turner and I were still the greatest of friends. I continued to work on my hip stances and tried to learn the latest urban dances, in addition to the cool lingo that went along them, not to mention the lyrics to the never-ending list of R&B songs.

Everyone in the Bury could sing. There seemed to be talent showcases and scout searches every other weekend. But as soon as I opened my mouth to join in, Lauren invariably gave me a look that said *Don't do it!* Everyone knew I made up my own lyrics and sang a little off-key. But I was making up for lost time. At Forest Edge, Ma only had old 78s in the attic, so I still had a lot of catching up to do.

To be really hip, I had to learn how to jump rope. No, you don't understand. *Jump rope*. It was mandatory. Incredible skill was required. It was a language: double Dutch, Chinese jump rope, onesies, twosies, checkers, hand clapping games. It was scenic: Black, Puerto Rican, and Irish girls in uniforms, some with greased-down sideburns and big gold earrings, everyone swinging rope and swinging to the rhythm of made-up lyrics in a school yard. If you couldn't jump, you'd better know how to swing—no, *swang*—how to slack the rope and gauge the distance between it slapping the asphalt and the top of the most elaborate hairdo. It was status, respect, identity. I loved the sound as I stomped the schoolyard asphalt hard and breathed in the crisp New England morning air.

Still, I never thought that I could really be hip enough, until an event that happened in the spring of 1970 taught me that I could, simply by paying attention. Everyone was talking about a hockey player named Bobby Orr. I had never been to a professional hockey game, but by living in Beantown and opening up my ears I got an immediate education about the importance of the Boston Bruins.

The entire city was electrified by Orr's redefining the role of defenseman in the National Hockey League. Orr and Phil Esposito galvanized every man, woman, and child from Roxbury to Marblehead with a sense of hope. It didn't matter if you were Irish or Italian, Dominican or Puerto Rican, African or Chinese—it just mattered. Countless people came together for one common goal: rooting the underdog to victory. Even I, not knowing a lick about hockey, knew the odds were stacked up against the Bruins who had not won a Stanley Cup Championship in twenty-nine years.

But I received the most incredible birthday gift on May 10, 1970, when Bobby Orr, just twenty-two years old, scored the winning goal of the Stanley Cup Championship. He defied gravity, arms and legs outstretched, frozen in time forever, scoring against the St. Louis Blues. I was equally impressed with Derek Sanderson, the Bruin who made that quintessential assist, passing Orr the puck. It further solidi-fied my belief that nothing is done alone, that even great men need support. It proved to me that impressive triumphs always had assists; that mentoring happens everywhere and in everything, inspired through genuine action. The importance of that heralded victory reso-nated with me for years to come.

Two years after Agatha decided to return to Forest Edge, I went through a period of wondering whether ballet was worth it. It seemed possible that the lack of a secure home base increased the frequency of the episodes of sudden, excessive sweating of my hands and feet. This was a clue that there might be a stress connection, even though I couldn't put the pieces together as such.

I went from receiving an Honorable Mention in the spring of 1970 to a D the following school year, reflecting my growing distress at being separated from Ma.

Everything came to a head during a visit to Maine before the start of seventh grade. When it was time to say good-bye I just could not tumble into that abyss one more time. It had occurred to me that I was now coming home for every possible holiday, even Valentine's Day. On those interminable, claustrophobic bus rides from Boston to Roch-ester, New Hampshire—with sealed windows and a thick fog of smoke that caused me to consciously learn to breathe in as shallow a way as possible—I had plenty of time to think about my decision.

If I had to choose between ballet and Ma's love, the latter was what mattered most. True, I had found a sense of confidence and belonging with my ballet family in Cambridge, and although I might be the odd man out back on the farm, so be it; home was where Agatha Armstead was. Ma was alarmed by the suggestion that I take a break from ballet, knowing that technique would be lost. Our compromise was, "Well, sugar, we'll just have to find you a school right here." As impossible as that had been four years earlier, Agatha not only located a ballet school in Rochester, New Hampshire, but also found a teacher by the name of Mrs. Brooks. She arranged weekly transportation there and back. On top of all that, she cleared the expenses with the State of Maine, making sure that the costs were approved in advance.

With that, a reverse in course was made. I became a farmer once again, attended Berwick Newichawannock ("river of many falls") Junior High School, and enrolled in the Lindy Brooks School of Dance, situated in Mrs. Brooks's garage, to be precise. European, with an air of show biz about her, my new teacher entered her top students into area and regional dance competitions. This was a complete 360-degree turn from the rigorous Royal Academy of Dance and Vagonova rudiments that had been ingrained in me for the last four years.

Agatha hired a local farmer, a young man who was a member of the Heath family, to drive me to and from class once a week. It was a sobering change after the hustle of the big city to ride home in the rusty pickup, occasionally startling a deer darting across the road, as I gazed out at moonlit fields.

As the truck wound its way through the narrow dark roads of West Lebanon, only the red embers at the end of the driver's cigarette reminded me that he was still there. At moments I worried that he might turn down an unfamiliar pathway but he always delivered me safely to Barley Road. He was completely trustworthy, never arriving late, always respectful.

His circumstances were modest. He lived in what was basically an underground cinder-block bunker, with one floor aboveground, together with his children and wife. This was to conserve on heat during the winter months.

Agatha told me about the farmer's wife, recalling that she had been quite a beauty and was famous for her wild bareback riding. One day her horse became startled, reared up, and threw her backward. She tried to hold on to its mane, but lost her grip and slid backward, violently hitting her head—an image I could never shake. Ma believed that the impact from the shattering blow brought on the multiple sclerosis from which she now suffered.

The first time I witnessed one of the rare visits made by the couple, upon Agatha's invitation, was shocking. I had never seen a man so attentive to his wife, nor seen such a young woman so feeble and distorted. Moreover, the sight of Agatha leading them over to our best antique living room chairs was unprecedented. The satin upholstered chairs with carved wood lions' heads on the arms were strictly offlimits to kids or most houseguests. Under other circumstances, whenever uninitiated company had the nerve to sit in that chair, I usually held my breath, knowing that they'd be advised to move. Not so these two, whom Agatha treated like visiting royalty, and who were visibly improved, when they left, by her kindness.

The reality was that I, too, was visibly improved being back with my Agatha. But the school year was not over before it was soon realized that I was losing my technique. I had to make my way back to Cambridge and get back to a real studio—with a real pianist, not a record player that skipped. I needed to be where I belonged. Ma and I were temporarily stumped as to what to do, so I returned to the doorknob for my barre and Agatha playing a jazz standard for accompaniment. Not a minute too soon, Carol Jordan called.

After receiving the latest photograph of me at a recital in Spaulding High School in New Hampshire, attired in an abominable sequined canary yellow tutu and yellow tights, sent to her by Agatha, Ms. Jordan was aghast that my hard-earned years of technique were in jeopardy. She put it as diplomatically as she could, saying, "Mrs. Armstead, I will do whatever it takes to ensure that Vicki returns immediately to Cambridge."

Agatha was most appreciative but explained that with her age and her health, she would be unable to house me in Roxbury and that besides my not having a place to stay, funds from the Ford Foundation for ballet school had been forgone and that it would take time to requisition the State of Maine about paying for tuition at St. Patrick's. Under the womanly banner of "where there's a will there's a way," the two agreed to put their heads together. Agatha got on the phone and relaunched her ever-successful campaign for temporary places for me to stay while Carol Jordan secured immediate lodging for me with a fellow ballet student, Sharon, who lived in the suburbs.

Thus ended my sojourn in the old Yankee country of my youth, where Mark Twain and President Franklin Pierce sought strength and inspiration. I knew that this was the end of maple sugar falls and mackerel summer skies, January thaws, and all the back and forth.

My return to Mother Maine had been a refresher course, important to reinforce the values not only of enduring physical strength, but durability in mind and spirit as well. She reminded me that if I didn't shovel my way out, I would remain snowbound; if I didn't pull water out of my well, I wouldn't drink; if I didn't lift grain bags, my animals would die and if I didn't spread manure and pitch hay, I couldn't pick the fruits of my labor. Once again, I witnessed the truth that abundance was predicated on what you poured into the soil—*your* soil. The lesson was simple and never easy.

I returned to Boston reenergized—the center of my entire cultural universe as far as I could imagine at thirteen years old. Whatever the specific magic that Agatha worked during that stay, I never knew. But something about me had changed. If I fell while trying my wings, I had to take a leap of faith in believing that someone would be there to catch me.

None of the logistical arrangements and changes could have been possible without the intercession of my social worker, Linda Webb, a quiet reed of a woman, who tirelessly pushed the impassive bureaucrats in Augusta for more purchase orders for ballet slippers, pointe shoes, leotards, and tights, and who seriously bent rules to get me across state lines. And that was for starters. Who was this intrepid thinker who risked her job on my behalf? How did I pull the lucky number and have her assigned to my case?

The answer to both questions is one and the same. As a graduate of the School of Social Work at the University of Southern Maine and an employee of the Department of Human Services of the state of Maine, Linda had been identified as having a gift with "special" cases. Before being assigned to follow my foster status and my unique set of circumstances, her narrow specialty had been working with children in adoptive and foster homes who had learning disabilities, and she opened doors for them from preschool to college. Linda genuinely enjoyed her work, not so common among many social workers bogged down with insurmountable caseloads, especially because of the opportunity to assist those few who had a desire to go on to college, and to help their foster and adoptive parents with the complicated application process.

Linda was indeed special. That's how my "special" file landed on her desk. She embraced challenges as well as successes, bringing to her path as a social worker a Mainer's practicality and a belief in good works instilled in her from her upbringing in the church. When I later sought her out in my adulthood, she confided in me that part of her motivation to pursue social work was from having grown up in an unstable home. Though she described her family as loving and supportive, the household was also plagued with alcoholism. In her teens, her parents divorced, leading to a traumatic period.

"I would have designed it differently, if I could have," Linda remarked with a philosophical laugh, as if to acknowledge what another world it would be if we could all redesign our family lives retroactively. And yet, she also believed that adversarial circumstances make people stronger, that difficulty in a child's life often leads him or her a heightened sensitivity and compassion toward others. That certainly had been true in her life. Social work was clearly her calling.

During visits or phone calls to alert me as to why the purchase orders for my ballet slippers were taking so long, she patiently explained, "Yes, Vicki, we do have discretionary funds at DHS for *special* interests for some of the children, but a *special*"—there was that word again—"purchase order has to be facilitated for ballet slippers."

Discretionary, facilitate, purchase order, Department of Human Services, special interests, guardianship—all these big words. Before long, I got into the habit of carrying a little dictionary with me to decipher what everybody was talking about in my little bureaucratic life; as an adult it became routine for my bigger one. However, I didn't need a dictionary or a thesaurus to understand what my social worker meant by discretionary purchases.

The tug-of-war over purchase orders for ballet slippers had been ongoing even back when Agatha was still in Roxbury. One of the hitches was that it was twice as hard to get reimbursed for special discretionary purchases; Ma usually waited for the cash proxy in the form of a slip of paper with the State of Maine's official seal on it. Even when we knew Linda Webb was eventually going to come through, the waiting was so epic that my feet might have grown another half size in the interim. "Any day now" was Linda's familiar refrain. With the exception of one big toe, my feet were crammed into slippers two sizes too small, restricting me from fully executing the steps. I would resign myself to dance as if I had the support of an entire ballet slipper around my foot, attempting to execute a double pirouette while feeling the cool Marley floor beneath me. Besides being a lesson in patience, the power of those purchase orders taught me the true weight that a piece of paper can hold. A future.

In contrast to her quiet manner, Linda Webb's written requests to the State of Maine on my behalf were pieces of fiery persuasion, culminating often along these lines:

> Since Vicki is so serious about studying ballet, has demonstrated a significant amount of talent, and does wish to make a career of this, it seems we have an obligation to assist her in attaining this goal as we do with other foster children.

Throughout the years, the arrival of the purchase order was followed as soon as humanly possible with a trip to the heart of downtown Boston to buy pink tights at Albert's Hosiery and then to Capezio's for ballet slippers. It was practically a holiday. Everything about the purchases made me proud, including my black-and-white-printed plastic Capezio bag that I swung like a badge of honor until the lettering faded and the string broke or until the next purchase order came. High on a shelf, beyond my reach—and that of the purchase orders—were glossy patent leather ballet boxes that all the rich girls had; in pink or blue, the boxes had a ballerina in a tutu and tiara on the front. There was a compartment that snapped shut for slippers and one for fresh ballet clothes. The boxes were the equivalent of passing by the Ritz-Carlton. Look but don't touch. But I could look and dream.

Linda Webb represented the humanizing of the system to me, additionally personalizing her role through frequent contact almost exclusively through correspondence and phone calls, working for a social cause, children—me.

To the credit of the State of Maine, Health and Human Services, I clearly understood that there were those, though typically faceless, who cared in Augusta and Portland. Though I was living under HHS-regimented constraints and guidelines of colossal size, time and time again Linda Webb emerged from a crushing mound of paperwork to make it manageable, proving that I was more than a case number, that

I was a person—a necessary understanding for every foster child. Every child, period.

Twenty-five years later, I explained to Linda that I had to find her because I always wondered about the lady who cared so much, who went beyond the call of duty. She took chances and made what other people deemed impossible, possible. She never took shortcuts or settled because it was too, too, too much work.

Had she ever wondered about me?

Linda smiled sweetly. "I wonder about *all* of the children I worked with." She then added, "But it hadn't occurred to me that it was even a possibility that I would hear from any of you."

By the time I tracked Linda Webb down, she and her husband were already the parents of two grown sons they had adopted at infancy. Modest about her many accomplishments, Linda felt most proud of how her sons had grown up to become independent, good young men. As their mother, her priority was to trust them and trust herself, to encourage her sons to embrace exploration of their own origin, talents, strengths, and weaknesses, to acknowledge that they had birth parents. I admired her courage and honesty.

Equally important was for Linda's children to understand how rooted they were in her being. I already knew how fortunate those two young men were to have Linda as their parent and mentor. No one needed to tell me that a woman didn't have to give birth to mother a child.

Slender and unassuming, her hair always in a simple bob, Linda employed an economy of language as she asked me questions. In one conversation, she spoke with rare candor about herself by sharing her dream of a world at peace. That dream was at the center of her calling to social work. Linda suggested that if people made an effort to respect and appreciate each other's differences and not just tolerate them it would lay a foundation for peace.

Linda Webb *was* peace. I loved the oasis of calm she created for me, how she sensed that though I was a strong child, I was also vulnerable.

Our talks and my ability to tell her what was happening in my day-to-day experiences was the closest I came to having therapy in my youth, something I later would emphatically advocate for all foster children. I trusted her implicitly and named her in my nightly prayers, in which I listed alphabetically all those individuals in my extended families whom I loved for loving me.

Eventually, of course, my case would be reassigned, but until that time, I absorbed all that she gave me, especially one piece of advice I never forgot.

"Vicki," Linda began, then she paused as though searching for the right words and went on, "it's important to take time, to step back. We all tend to want to do for others, and most of us get pleasure out of it. But don't forget to think about who *you* are and what nourishes *your* soul." That right there was the powerful wisdom that I carefully folded up and tucked into my back pocket, remembering every now and then to apply it. Linda Webb was the social worker who never let me down but only pushed me forward.

I had to navigate the road of ultimate acceptance. Of no one's making, I was never meant to be raised by one mother, but by many. It was during these years of my early teens when I saw Dorothy for the last time, during that meeting in a Howard Johnson's. I was powerless when Agatha, riddled with illness but determined to carry out this visit between Dorothy and me, insisted on traveling from Maine to downtown Boston.

I didn't know if I should embrace Dorothy in front of Agatha. Would I be betraying the mother/daughter loyalty between Agatha and me? I desperately wanted to hug them both but couldn't. Dorothy was an inconvenient intruder. I felt fraudulent in her presence. How could I be the *me* I had become when Dorothy's painful truth stood there, quivering, mumbling at me? Without intent, she exposed everything I was ashamed of, everything I wanted to forget or deny, threatening my secret identity. What if someone saw us together—how would I explain? I could no more ignore Dorothy's illness than I could reciprocate her odd affection. My dispassion concerned me as much as my helpless wish to rescue her from something I had no comprehension of.

Her merciless shaking was something I couldn't begin to fathom. As an adult I would learn from a renowned Harvard professor and psychologist, Alan Hobson, that Dorothy's tremors were due to years of antihallucinogens, serving as a sort of chemical lobotomy.

My mother's suffering and anguish haunted me and maybe that was the part of her that kept us connected. What I am sure of is that Dorothy never surrendered. Upon multiple releases from the Augusta State Mental Hospital and other facilities, each time she would immediately board a bus and show up unannounced to see her children. She never yielded in her fight that I be placed in the most loving hands possible. In her way, Dorothy taught me to never give up if you truly believed in what you were fighting for.

Sewing and knitting together all the pieces of fabric that the women raising me had provided so far, I began to see the makings of a dress. I was experiencing what goes on for so many foster and adopted children, particularly as we enter our teen years and young adulthood. With emancipation looming it the distance, it was a time of reflection and uncertainty, searching and scrambling for any shred of affiliation.

That may explain how I bonded so strongly with Barbara Sterling, the Jamaican-born mother of my friend Jackie Legister, who had many Agatha-like qualities. Her home became an unofficial weekend respite dwelling for me. My first glimpse of Barbara had come at a lecture demonstration at Harvard's Sanders Theatre, which was offered to the public by the Cambridge School of Ballet staff and students. While Jackie was statuesque and exotic, her mother was short and plain. Then, the moment her daughter pointed her toe and lifted her arm, Barbara Sterling's face lit up the room, which it continued to do whenever Jackie made the smallest of ballet gestures—even the slightest épaulement, or movement of the head and arms.

This was gorgeous maternal pride, enhanced by metal teeth. Jewelry in her mouth? This was fantastic. I had never seen such a thing in my life. Theater, baby! Her already megawatt smile became magnified by the gold crowns on several prominent teeth.

When I began spending respite weekends with Barbara and the rest of her family in Bedford, Massachusetts, among many enticements were the talks that I had with my weekend surrogate mother and the stories that unfolded of her life. These were the stories of dreams handed down from mothers to daughters. Barbara's mother in Jamaica had herself dreamt of coming to the United States but had instead sponsored her daughter's journey here. Living up to that investment, Barbara Sterling worked three jobs, owned three homes, and raised three children, and had arrived in America with only three suitcases. Her dream was to be a ballet dancer but knew it was not to be and so passed her dream on to her daughter Jackie—who would eventually take it to New York City to study at the Alvin Ailey School.

Barbara poured a limitless flow of love into all her children and those around her, including me. She was so optimistic for all of us.

My love connection with Barbara Sterling was manna in the desert of my wanderings. Primal and necessary. And there was another aspect to these stays that connected me to what I imagined might have been the island home of my ancestors on my father's side. A passing thought at times, it was later made more plausible when I learned that he might have well been Jamaican.

It could be a subzero temperature outside but it vanished inside Barbara's house, where winter and the outer world were mocked. It was here that I learned about the intoxication of steaming chicken and dumplings, thermostats kept at ninety-five degrees at all times, and that I never felt unwelcome. I loved everything about the heat of the hearth and the heart of that house. Never still, there was a bustle of people coming and going. Women gathered to gossip. Grown men drank Red Stripe and Guinness Stout. Mixed with a raw egg, and down the hatch it went. My ears were seduced by a new language, a patois so rhythmic I swore they were singing their call-and-answers to each other. The music skipped, danced around and through me. Familiar, resonant, making me feel safe. It touched something old inside my being.

Barbara Sterling was an earth mother to me, a root woman. To walk into her home was to walk into a living blanket. She was refurbishment along the relay race of my teens, cheering me on from the sidelines as I danced on, toward my next stop in the home of Rosa Turner—a fosterer, mentor, and a one-of-a-kind grande dame.

In the summer leading into the ninth grade at St. Patrick's, Lauren Turner had come to Maine with me for a visit at Forest Edge that included, of course, Agatha's never-to-be-missed highlight of the year: the annual Robert Armstead memorial birthday cookout.

Our now ancient S&H Green Stamp rotisserie was on its last legs, as were some of the relatives who were getting on in years. I was able to share a foreign yet wonderful way of life with Lauren—farm life and my true home. She and I had come a long way from the fourth grade when she threatened to beat up the girl with pigtails for wearing the same green cardigan that she owned.

Before it was time to go back to Boston, during my usual conversation with Ma about accommodations for me for the next six months or so, Lauren volunteered that it would be perfect if I could stay with her.

"Could I?" I asked Ma, not daring to get my hopes up too much. Lauren was the closest thing to having a sister at that point in time and her suggestion sounded perfect to me, too. At the cookout, to which Lauren's parents had been invited, we ambushed both Agatha and Rosa, excitedly campaigning for something we thought made sense.

Mrs. Turner was apprehensive for good reason, as I would learn later, when the reality of blood being thicker than water would raise its ugly head. But before that happened, as the result of an intensive lobbying effort that Lauren undertook with her mother, Mrs. Turner acquiesced, saying, "Fine, Vicki can stay here as long as her social worker approves."

Welcome to Grant Manor Projects.

The area where Agatha's brownstone stood on Burrell Street was older and more run-down compared to the newer Grant Manor Projects where the Turners lived in Roxbury—but in a neighborhood and households scarred by the ravages of heroin and alcohol addiction, domestic violence, poverty, vets with posttraumatic stress disorder, all ratcheted up by the fury over busing. The court's ruling in Massachusetts to make sure schools were integrated was noble in theory, but everybody was up in arms about who went where and why. The crime rate skyrocketed and, like always, the poorest neighborhoods bore the brunt of it no matter what color they were.

This was the more sophisticated version of the era's notorious Orchard Park Projects, without an apple tree in sight. My new address on Northampton Avenue could be said to have been the Harvard of the 'hood. It was a springboard to my future beyond my term as a ward of the state that would teach me about survival in the real world—and then some.

At first blush, it was easy to observe that Rosa, true to her name as a stunning flower among the thorns, seemed not to belong in such a setting. But on further observation, it was apparent that her radiant presence had been earthbound on purpose—right there in the ghetto, sent from above to impart her womanly secrets of beauty to all. Literally. Rosa Turner was an Avon representative, in the truest sense of that vocation. She was the perfect palette—breathtaking, with smooth cinnamon skin and auburn hair and a dainty spray of freckles on her high cheekbones. Rosa's stark beauty was the kind you see in ghettos all over the world and wish Scavullo or Demarchelier or VanderZee could be there to capture in a photographic essay. That was Rosa Turner.

What was the fragrance that surrounded her at all times? This was a question I pondered that first night as I settled in for the night.

The answer came a few days later. Rosa smelled like fresh air. Pure, wholesome, feminine. Her bedroom was a shrine to womanly beauty products—lotions, creams, balms, scented emollients specially concocted for elbows and feet, hair shampoos, conditioners and treatments, sprays and splashes, colognes, perfumes, soaps, makeup. She wasn't the Avon lady for nothing, and, boy, could she move some Avon.

There wasn't a person in the vicinity of Roxbury, including the patients and staff at Boston City Hospital, who didn't know Rosa Turner. Black, white, Hispanic, struggling, affluent, women, and men. I met individuals in the upper tiers of Boston's elite cultural circles who somehow knew Rosa.

What was she doing in the chaos of the 'hood? Adding more by fostering me?

This wasn't easy to answer initially, because Mrs. Turner hadn't signed on to sit me down and tell me the story of her life. Over time I had a chance to take a peek at some of her secret coping skills, like her passion and talent for bowling. I was invited along with Rosa's family to cheer her on as she made an appearance on a local television show called *Bowling for Dollars,* a program that paid out big prize money if you bowled a strike. Watching Rosa hurl her bowling ball down the center of the lane, I knew it had to be about more than a strike; it was a personal victory.

My job was to learn everything that a fourteen- and fifteen-year-old could about living in the 'hood and being a lady about it, but first, I had to attempt to learn how to fight. In the middle of the busing insanity, I defended my Italian friend, Debbie DePalma, and then, as a result, got jumped by a gang of black girls I knew. This was survival of the fittest, where adapting to unfolding circumstances gave you the keys to the kingdom. It was where my dance training helped in leaping onto roofs of parked cars in order to escape stray Doberman pinschers; where *leathahs* and leathers were two entirely different things. I saw movies that only real life can script: Pimps with processed hair more laid out than their women, in full-length mink coats and wide brim hats cocked perilously to the side. Cadillacs and pinky diamond rings. Where fires were set because people were poor, angry, or just plain cold.

Inside the Turner household, there was another kind of fight to learn. If I wanted something, I had to speak up for myself, and I sure as hell had better put my things back where they belonged. Rosa ran a kind of pawn shop or *pound* operation, charging twenty-five cents to get back personal items from her that we didn't put away. If I couldn't afford to buy them back, she tossed them after a certain amount of time.

This was all I needed to make sure that I wedged part-time jobs in between schoolwork and ballet classes, singing my own fourteen-year-old's version of "She Works Hard for the Money," which that Bostonian Donna Summers would make famous. I waitressed at Howard Johnson's and then took a job scooping ice cream at Brigham's, a popular restaurant chain in and around Boston; my location was in the red-light district.

Did I like walking down sidewalks with the crush of last night's broken beer bottle glass stuck to the soles of my shoes? Hell, no. Not at the time. But it was also the best learning experience I could have been given.

To every lipstick-smeared prostitute who made his or her way past the manager's watchful eye, I gave a little extra ice cream. Agatha had taught me not to judge, only to be of service. *There but for the grace of God.* That was only one lesson.

In a greater sense this period was teaching me independence, letting me know that ultimately I alone needed to be responsible for my things and my welfare. In the meantime, however, I wasn't without the constant concern of Agatha, who never stopped checking up on me, knowing full well that teenagers need pocket change and a feeling of autonomy. She would say lovingly that she sensed I wasn't "flush with money" and would send me a little something. When she couldn't be there to protect me completely, she put me in the hands of God, fully and faithfully, writing to me in this era:

> *I know you're going to call me square but if you find yourself in a precarious position, make an act of perfect contrition. You are sorry for your sins, not because you will be punished for them but because you have offended God. That will get you into Heaven, if you say it meaningfully. Don't forget the Virgin Mary, She's marvelous . . . the souls in Purgatory need your prayers and so do I. I love you very much.*

And so I kept pluggin' away, slipping chocolate-mint ice cream to the disenfranchised, saving my pay and tips in a shoebox full of coins that I spent hours rolling into paper cylinders, while starting a permanent coin collection with the foreign and old coins.

Rosa taught me well. She didn't want me losing my hard-earned savings to my own stupidity. Or as she said, "I don't want your 'dippy' twenty-five cents." It was tough, constructive love; a love that required arm's-length distance, not gushy, lovey-dovey love, but the kind that forced me to take an honest look at my reality.

Rosa was my heroine. Fatherless, she made her own way in spite of the odds stacked against her. She did it her way, too, in the ghetto, as a mother of ten not including me—a provider, fighter, supporter of the arts, bowling ace, foster parent, Avon lady. An entrepreneur and a teacher as well, Rosa encouraged and mentored me to become an independent contractor for Avon, layering what Agatha had already taught me about being a businesswoman.

I decided to sell Christmas candles in the neighborhood, a process that meant riding up and down elevators in the projects, holding my breath so as not to inhale the stale smells of urine and garbage, and praying not to be jumped for my commissions. When I struggled in filling out my first sales spreadsheet, Rosa helped me with her expert math skills. More important, I saw by her example the rewards associated with commerce and the repercussions of being disorganized.

Eighty-six Northampton Street was Roxbury's Grand Central Station. Teeming with family, children and grandchildren, a grandmother we all called Nana, extended family and people who called themselves family, and more men in the household than I'd experienced before, the law of the land was basic: I had to find my place by following directions and not adding to the drama. When testosterone was in overdrive, and when verbal and physical violence flared, I had to learn to keep my mouth shut and get out of the way.

The art of pressing introduced to me by Ma at Forest Edge was taken up several rungs at the Turners', where I proved myself by pressing a crease you could slice bread on in the Turner boys' jeans. Not that they couldn't do it themselves. Most men in the 'hood, I learned, could press clothes like nobody's business. It was part what their mommas taught them and part vanity. Still, I liked to show my stuff, licking my index finger and touching it to the iron, listening for the sound of that sizzle to know that it was red-hot and ready to go.

Lauren, my foster sister and best friend, was my tour guide in the mysterious world of the opposite sex, letting me know how the flirting and dating *thang* was supposed to go down in the big city. I learned about rent parties, an innovation the Brahmins might have referred to as fund-raisers—basically, ingeniously designed open houses to help the hosts make their rent. By paying two dollars at the door, I could find my place in the crowd, any unclaimed floor space where I could move my hips to artists who became part of this era's amazing inheritance: Aretha, Marvin Gaye and Tammy Terrell, James Brown, the Intruders, the O'Jays, the Four Tops, the Floaters, the Chi-Lites, Tavares, LaBelle, Barry White and the Love Unlimited Orchestra, the Whispers, the Escorts, Martha and the Vandellas, New Birth, Nancy Wilson, Billy Paul and Billy Preston, Earth, Wind & Fire, Johnny Mathis, the Temptations, Rufus and Chaka Khan, Smokey Robinson and the Miracles, Stevie, Isaac Hayes, Rose Royce, Gladys Knight and the Pips, the Fifth

Dimension, Al Green, the Commodores, Average White Band, and the Jackson Five. That's what we called havin' a *par-tay*.

A lavender florescent light backlit my supercool partner's blown-out 'fro, in which he had planted his pick—complete with black power fist attached to it. There was nothing like a laid-out brother from the 'hood. He smelled as good as he looked. Cocoa butter mixed with Afro-Sheen was the neighborhood cologne. Nobody went anywhere without the influence of Madam C. J. Walker or John Johnson's hair care products.

My education was vast. In the year or so that I was at the Turners, I learned about getting my period, the medieval belt and straps and what tampons were, about bursting hormones, having a boyfriend and a first kiss. Also: how to slow dance and grind, to feel the male anatomy because I wanted to, not because someone was forcing me to. I learned the definition of a fox. No, a *foxxx*! About what *fine* really meant. About getting in trouble, being tough, and daring to be.

Mrs. Turner was explicit about where to walk and how to carry myself with a don't-mess-with-me attitude, making sure she repeated every time I left the town house, "Walk on the opposite side of the street and don't pay those fools on the corner any mind!"

Sometimes I couldn't resist walking down the more dangerous side of the street, for no other reason than the ability to stand on the same ground as the other inhabitants of these woods. In my periphery, I picked up on the dance that black men dance when walking down the street, owning it with an inimitable beat used only for that purpose. *Aaand-a-one, aaand-a-two, aaand-a-three, aaand-a-four,* the right shoulder tipping ever so forward, an indecipherable skip in his step. I liked that dance these men did. It was called tippin'.

On the corner, my street corner, there was the local bar. Broken green glass and men playing dice. With pints of something, especially on Fridays, they'd lean on the only thing keeping them upright—buildings, lampposts, each other—slurring their much rehearsed: "Hey baby, come mere and give Daddy some of that suga'."

The daddy thing came up in all kinds of ways. If it had dawned on me that my lot in life was to have many mothers, it was probably right about here that I started to think maybe I wasn't ever going to have any male parent, surrogate or otherwise.

The metaphor for the void created by the lack of a father was the handcrafted leather wallet I carried from a very early age, and still do. It had been made for me with only love by Mr. Collins Taylor of Gray, Maine, my first foster father. Inside the wallet were my most important identification materials. There was my prized blue Social Security card, reminding me of my institutional government patriarchs, a library card, and my CIA ID card. Having nothing to do with being an agent in central intelligence, this was a social club from school. The initials stood for Christ In Action. Among my various pieces of identification, carefully concealed in my wallet, everywhere I traveled, was an unsent letter to my phantom father.

The drift to becoming my own daddy continued. After all, the priests had me calling them my Father and the drunks called themselves my Daddy; hell, I might as well fill the slot myself. I'd answer to any name—Pa, Pops, Papa, Dad, Daddy, Dada. Warrior, provider, protector of me.

To formalize my ascension as my own father, I started to collect clothes with which I later cultivated a look and everything: men's suit vests cinched in at the waist with a belt, and a brim to top off the outfit. Whether or not someone else found my apparel odd was beside the point. This was me having a shred of power, a chance to reclaim something—someone—lost to me forever.

Rosa Turner didn't hover, because she didn't have time to. She had her own family, with some of her kids grown and some not. She had to navigate the drama, like the violence that exploded one evening where her defense was a bottle of Tabasco sauce that she broke over her husband's brow. I had no idea if the blood that spilled from Mr. Turner was real or Tabasco sauce.

This was the same man who had complained about the meager

support check they received as foster parents, when he said to Rosa, "She's only bringing in $87.00 a month and drinks too much of our milk." I heard that with my own ears.

Something happens to a child when they hear themselves scornfully valued by a dollar amount. They either let it affect their esteem or they don't. I had to keep telling myself not to own those words, not to be dependent on dollar amounts, which were just paper, remembering that I had emancipation three years around the corner.

But where was I supposed to turn with those feelings? I didn't want to complain. It wasn't my place.

When there were violent episodes, Rosa must have observed that I didn't judge, run away, or tell my social worker or Agatha, and she decided, maybe not even consciously, that she could trust me with her secret—one of the few ways outside of prayer that she allowed herself to channel her pain. It was something called *opera*.

Rosa read that the Metropolitan Opera was coming to Boston to perform *Madama Butterfly* at Hines Auditorium in the Prudential Center and invited me to go with her. *Madama Butterfly?* My classical music knowledge notwithstanding, I had never been to see an opera, and as a recently more toughened up teenager had no idea what to expect. Rosa assured me that the singing and the story would stay with me forever. That was an understatement. Over the space of less than ten miles she delivered me from out of the chaos into the magnificence and splendor of the opera. A miracle.

I was transfixed by the elaborate production set up in a convention center, as well as the metamorphosis of the cavernous space that I had seen once before—with Agatha, when we attended the Boat Show, without the intention of buying our own yacht, but just as an excursion out of Roxbury and to enjoy lofty dreams.

More than what I saw onstage from the upper balcony where we sat, I would never forget the transformation of Rosa and her intense focus on the miniature performers far below. As if on some internal cue, she reached into her purse and retrieved a little case that held what turned out to be opera glasses, which I had never seen before. Rosa, unaware of me watching her, allowed tears to cascade down her perfect profile. Suddenly she returned to the moment, self-conscious, and apologized with a small smile for her indulgence, even though she knew she never needed to apologize to me or anyone for who and what she was.

Here I sensed Rosa's other secret, a form of defiance against any force that would stand in the way of her entitlement. Part escapism; part redemption. Whether it was the Metropolitan Opera, the Bolshoi, or taking me by the hand to see Alvin Ailey at the Orpheum Theater, to experience the brilliance of Judith Jamison or Donna Wood, she was entitled. By taking me, so too was I. It was beyond comprehension to me that these weren't final performances. How could perfection be repeated, night after night?

The crowning glory for each performance was always the curtain call. How did prima ballerina Maya Plisetskaya have any energy after performing the demanding role of Odette-Odile in *Swan Lake* or in *Spring Waters*? As I looked through Rosa Turner's opera glasses, I began to understand the invisible miracle of energy begetting energy. On one knee, with what seemed to be fifty pounds of red roses in one arm, the other outstretched, every lithe muscle extended to the very end of her long fingertips, Maya spoke words without words, expressing her thanks as though she was speaking only to me.

When standing up and applauding wildly wasn't enough, I couldn't help from joining with the rest of audience in verbalizing praise, borrowing Rosa's Italian, which I had first heard her use for *Madama Butterfly*.

"Bravo!" I called quietly in my fourteen-and-a-half-year-old voice. I liked the sound of that. "Bravo!" I called even louder, then shouted, "Bravissimo, Maya!"

How did my foster mother Rosa, living in the projects, know how to speak Italian? How had she so seamlessly taught me, without me even knowing it?

In these surprising ways, Rosa Turner introduced me to theater, on and off the stage. Experiences as dramatic as Greek tragedies and as electrifying as Duke Ellington's *Liberian Suite,* or as conventional as a trip to Disneyworld over spring break, where I joined Lauren, Rosa, and her mother. Seeing the fearlessness of women in pyramid formation on water skis left me speechless and wanting to return to the ballet studio and practice being unafraid. Rosa contributed another meaningful chapter in my education about the need for defiant courage—the insistence to be counted, to show up at the opera, the ballet, or Disneyworld; to show up in life, without apology or justification.

Rosa and I shared a history of illegitimacy, as we were both born to unavailable fathers. Unlike my story of never knowing who my father was, Rosa grew up knowing that she was the daughter of jazz legend, alto sax player Johnny Hodges—but was hardly acknowledged. I remember how somber it was at the Turner household when Mr. Hodges died. Although Rosa was noticeably nervous about going to the funeral, where all the jazz luminaries would be in attendance, she girded herself and traveled to Harlem, anyway.

She defied convention by asking for one of her father's saxophones but was flatly denied it by his widow. Rosa didn't like having to tell that story, partly because it revealed her vulnerability and mainly because the last thing she wanted from anyone was any kind of pity.

That was the most important lesson from her to me, one that could not be soft-pedaled or sweetened: that feeling sorry for myself was not an option. Such was the message I received on an evening in May when I returned from ballet class on a night that happened to be my fifteenth birthday. In the maelstrom of the activity earlier that day I had hoped that some kind of surprise party would be waiting for me. When I came home and saw not a sign of a celebration, there was nothing to feel but bitter disappointment. No one even remembered. I decided, birthdays were overrated, a belief that I reinforced for myself from then on, usually planning for the most minimal of remembrances, more in honor of Dorothy Collins Rowell than myself.

I had crossed an invisible line, expecting my temporary family to remember the day I was born. I had hoped for too much. Time to add more armor.

Over the course of the year, Lauren hadn't appeared to be bothered by the fact that her mother and I had developed a close bond. That seemed to change when I became Rosa Turner's Avon girl, happily shuttling products and collecting money from her clients at Boston City Hospital, where she worked. Not that Lauren wanted the gig; in fact, no one else seemed interested in doing that grunt work except me. The problem had to do with the complexities of relationships. I had encroached on delicate mother/daughter territory without knowing it.

When I returned to Northampton Street from delivering Avon orders to customers, my head full of interesting adult conversation, Rosa sat me down on her plastic-covered furniture, and began explaining things to me. I knew then that our relationship would have to shift, and that these were not her words. She had to choose. I sat there, still. For a while, I thought my chest might break in two. I took several moments to arrest the lump in my throat, to find a way to breathe again.

As the school year came to a close, I had to make a difficult decision for myself. I was standing in Rosa's bedroom, watching her fill Avon orders from her personal apothecary of lotions and potions, when she invited me to stay on for another school year. I was tempted, dreading another separation, another good-bye, but I respectfully declined. I'd lost a closeness that I could never get back, and I had traveled the road long enough at that point in my life to be able to read between the lines.

Many thoughts swirled in my head as I packed up my belongings that June. I would always love Rosa for so many reasons. I left Roxbury armored and ready for whatever the world had in store for me.

Rosa and I remained in touch throughout the years, during which time I had occasion to revisit my most vivid memory of her. Under the stairs was a storage space so small one had to duck to enter. This was where Rosa could escape and feed her other passion, sewing. Illuminated by a small light on an industrial sewing machine, she sat with her broad back to me as I peeked in. The tilt of her head showed a tuft of auburn hair, her glasses low on her distinctive inheritance, which no one could take from her or give her permission to own—her father's nose. I knew that she was somewhere far away in her mind, as she bent over her tiny stitches, surrounded by reams of fabric in her cubbyhole. Alone. At peace.

SIX

SYLVIA PASIK SILVERMAN

After nearly fourteen years of widowhood, Agatha Armstead—believing that enough was enough and too much was foolish—decided that she had mourned Robert Sr. for a sufficient amount of time and that it would not be improper to receive the attentions of a suitor. Peter Cassell was several years older than her, a native of Montserrat whom she had first met fifty years earlier at choir practice. We were all shocked, but not because Ma should choose to have romance in her life, not at all. In her early seventies, she was still full of passion, femininity, and exuberance; of course she should have a loving companion, especially now that her years of raising children, grandchildren, and foster children were coming to an end. What I couldn't understand was how Peter Cassell, an octogenarian at the time of their wedding, had blinded Agatha into not seeing his miserly, controlling side before it was too late. What cost companionship?

When I left the Turners', I moved into Peter's house on Whiting Street. He made no effort to hide his pathological jealousy of my relationship with Ma, which he refused to acknowledge as a relationship at all, because, he said, I was not her daughter by birth or adoption. "How can you love her?" he asked Agatha. She took the path of least resistance, taking into consideration that he had no children of his own, and did her best to try to placate him.

There was a certain element of convenience, if not security, in Ma's relationship with Peter, which did keep her in the Boston area for six months out of the year. We could be together as I closed in on my last years at the Cambridge School of Ballet.

To keep everything on an even keel, Ma encouraged me simply to be patient with Peter, promising that he'd warm up soon enough.

I didn't mind sleeping in the attic; I had done this more than once and it was rather charming. But the situation took a turn for the worse when a pestiferous Peter started rummaging through my things while I was out of the house. Peter rationed and hid food, threatened to cut off the phone, and wouldn't allow me to use his washer or dryer, believing my contemporary fashions would ruin his older machines in the basement. This meant Agatha sent my clothes out to be laundered.

I was treated as a tenant, rather than a family member, and required to say goodnight to Agatha before Peter's bedtime—not one second after; otherwise I found their apartment door locked and lights out. When the holidays approached, Peter—proving to be the quintessential Scrooge—forbade us from having a Christmas tree, no explanation given.

"Where will we put our presents?" I asked, once my bewilderment had a chance to register.

"Under the piano bench," Peter said.

To make the best out of these increasingly uncomfortable dynamics, and money being the issue, I decided to create some holiday cheer for me and for Ma by decorating the banister between our floors with a garland of plastic-wrapped candy canes. What seemed diplomatic by taping them up outside the locked door of their apartment in a neutral zone ended in disaster.

Later that December Sunday, a noisy crackling sound brought me running down the steps from the attic, where I was undone by the sight of a bare banister and a heap of rejected candy canes on the floor that had been ripped off in one felt swoop. That sight and the shock of seeing all of the fifteen hundred pieces of a jigsaw puzzle packed back in a box—the same pieces that Agatha and I had almost finished assembling together—were almost as shattering as the time, years later, when I stumbled upon paperwork documenting how Peter Cassell had actually charged Ma rent for housing me there.

That Christmas, if we could have called it that, I set out in search of a new home base, and with nothing to lose, I defiantly went down to Dudley Station and brought back a surprise for Agatha. Peter stood in absolute shock as I single-handedly dragged the tree up the stairs and erected and decorated it, all the while humming Christmas carols. Ma was so happy. The miracle that followed was that Peter let us have our holiday.

Together, Ma and I placed the festively wrapped gifts under the glorious pine. While we were both having so much fun, I noticed that she was visibly weary. My concern was that she no longer had the one person to whom Agatha always turned for true counsel.

In the foregoing years, Aunt Marion had succumbed to the onset of Alzheimer's and had moved to a nursing home. Ever since my arrival in Boston at age nine, no matter where I lived, I gravitated back to Aunt Marion and Uncle Al's gray gingerbread house in Roxbury on Montrose Street.

I wanted some of that soulful food that she and Ma, and all the Wooten women, baked, shucked, stirred, and frosted. I wanted to taste her signature lemon meringue pie, to know she still retained secrets for baking that delicate crust out of lard and love, and to know she was there to answer the door with life's most essential welcoming, "Come on in, sugar, and take a load off." I needed my Agatha, or the image of her. Disappointedly, I tucked a note in Aunt Marion's screen door and moved on.

Toward the end of Aunt Marion's days, Agatha honored me by asking if I would accompany her to the nursing home, an old Roxbury house converted for convalescent care. We arrived to see Marion seated on the edge of her bed, lost. Diffused light streamed through the gable, offering the only inspiration in an otherwise depressing scenario, until I was blessed by the chance to witness two remarkable souls trying to reconnect.

There was no glossing over Marion's absence or what remained of her trapped in a shriveled, corporal form—a shadow of the virtuoso I witnessed playing the organ in a downtown Boston church not so many years earlier. She kept repeating, "I want to go home, Sis. I want to go home." Agatha calmed her frail older sister by wrapping her arms around her, rocking her. We sat in silence as words were useless.

Agatha and I rose to leave. I reached out to Aunt Marion to kiss her for the last time, my lips touching her cold-cream-soft cheek. She looked at me and smiled that reassuring smile that had always told me that everything would be all right. Agatha led us out, then turned back to say, "Don't worry, Sis, I'll be back."

I wanted to fix it. I wanted to fix the hole that had formed in Ma's life with the loss of her closest sister, to free her from Peter, to ward off the uncertainties of age and changing circumstances. I promised myself that some day I would, but in the meantime, I needed to get myself to terra firma—which turned out to be in Framingham, Massachusetts, a world away though only twenty westward miles from downtown Boston.

It must have been a metaphysical call for Sylvia Silverman to have been so perfectly placed in my path at the most necessary time. She was

everything that I might have asked for at the time and then some—
given how amazingly she prepared me for my life to come.

Sylvia was unselfish and instinctual—loving to the nth degree. Unwavering in her support, in her authentic being, in the sacrifices that
she made for family, in the connection she maintained to her own
dreams—allowing them to evolve as she nurtured the dreams of others. Sylvia not only gave me the confidence that I would need to compete for acceptance into the most prestigious international ballet
schools and professional companies but also provided me with an introduction to privilege and all that it encompassed—travel, culture,
restaurants, cars, current affairs, social etiquette. These were all a part
of her world and by association would become part of mine. Instilling
in me the value of responsibility that comes with privilege, Sylvia
added to what I already knew about the need for financial organization
and independence—especially for women, regardless of marital status. As my last foster mother before emancipation, no one could have
prepared me more soundly for weathering that monuzmental change
of status than Sylvia Silverman.

In the mid-1970s when I first began staying overnight and sometimes through the weekends at the Silvermans' home, at the invitation
of their daughter Robyn—my ballet buddy "Robs"—Framingham
was a mostly upscale enclave, a mix of old Boston wealth and the nouveau riche then flocking to the suburbs in so-called white flight spurred
on by the busing crisis. Little did I know at the time that my ancestor,
Warren Collins, was buried at the local cemetary. After living in the
projects, Framingham was like going to the moon. The town was filled
with both older and newer houses, some on smaller scales, others on
expansive wooded estates, nestled next to gristmills and modern suburban mansions, along with smatterings of tennis courts, swimming
pools, and the latest-model cars everywhere. Lawns and yards were
kept meticulously manicured by oversized lawn mowers that we would
have driven as cars in Maine.

The feeling of being in a foreign land stopped whenever I entered the Silvermans' comfortable two-story home on Maple Street. The more I visited, the more I understood where Robs had learned the fearlessness and confidence that she brought to her dancing, and I also could see that her incredibly giving nature was an inherited trait from Sylvia. A feeling of inclusiveness dominated the household, thanks to the two of them and the acceptance I also received from Robyn's sister, Jill, and brother, Michael. Maurice Silverman—or "Slivey" as he was known—Robyn's smart, hardworking dad, may have initially been less embracing of my presence, but at the same time was genuinely concerned for my welfare.

On a weekend evening when I was staying overnight at the Silvermans', Robs picked up on my distracted state of mind. I rarely told anyone about anything in my private life, but I felt a safety in confessing some of what was going on at what I was calling home. Robyn immediately offered, "You should come stay with us." That would be incredible, I thought, but how would I tell Agatha? How could I leave her again?

Bracing myself for disappointment, we hurried downstairs to the kitchen where Sylvia heard Robyn out and, with a look identical to her daughter's, agreed, saying, "Vicki, we'd love to have you move in with us." No hesitation, no deliberation. Robyn—a younger version of Sylvia with her long neck, chiseled face, and flawless alabaster skin—smiled at me with a "see, I told you so" look in her eyes. Standing there in her suburban, modern kitchen with all the latest conveniences, Sylvia smiled in welcome, looking to me like an early Italian Renaissance woman painted by Botticelli.

When he was later informed, Mr. Silverman may have had some reservations about me moving in but dutifully complied with his wife's and his daughter's wishes. And so Mr. Silverman went to Roxbury to meet with Agatha to discuss the financial and logistic arrangements and to collect my belongings. Never liking the "cut of his jib," as they say in Maine, Peter stood in the background wringing his hands, blinking through his bifocals and grinning. I hated leaving Ma alone because that's really what it had become. Mr. Silverman struck up a conversation with Peter, mentioning how his family had once lived not far from his very house and how much the neighborhood had changed.

Maurice Silverman ran a very successful linen and drapery business in Somerville, Massachusetts, that had been owned by Sylvia's family, the Pasik brothers, and was passed on to him after he was so fortunate as to have made her his wife. The Silverman home was tastefully appointed in every way, with early American oak antiques and Sylvia's prize collection of antique American blue glass. Her own watercolor paintings adorned the walls. My favorite was of a flamenco dancer, much different from the Saergent but still somehow familiar. It hung next to the fireplace near which Margot Fonteyn graced the cover of a large art book that was set on an elegant glass coffee table.

For the first time that I could recall, I finally had my own room, furnished with a cream desk set, matching designer bedspread and curtains, and wall-to-wall shag carpeting.

Early in the same summer that I'd moved into the Silvermans, I came across a photograph in their den of a young black girl in pigtails, reminding me more of myself than anyone in the Silverman family. How was she a part of this white Jewish suburban household and so meaningful to the tight nucleus that she had won a place on Mr. Silverman's mantle? Who was she?

Before long I would meet her. She was the daughter of Mr. Silverman's sister and the comedian Richard Pryor. Her name was Elizabeth, and she was not much more than eight years old, and one of the most beautiful, angelic children I had ever seen. I was face-to-face with the person, younger than myself, who had broken the ice and paved the way for me to have a relationship with the man of the manor. Mr. Silverman adored her. Did I remind him of her when she was gone? Maybe. And maybe that was part of why he tolerated my stay. I had to hold onto that.

Robs insisted that whatever was hers, including her family, could be mine, too. I wanted to offer her the same. I had a family of friends, much different from what she was accustomed to, that I wanted to share. In that process, I learned that not all friends could be friends to all. I did, however, cross-pollinate some friendships, such as with Jackie Legister. Jackie and I had continued to be close, stopping in at Paul's Mall, our favorite jazz club, or a popular Jamaican hangout in Cambridge now and then. Since the three of us attended the Cambridge School of Ballet together, we had that common bond, too. It was like one big slumber party.

The difference in backgrounds fell away more and more, a process helped by Robyn and Sylvia who included me in the family observances of all the holidays. We lit candles by the stove on Friday nights as the sun set on the eve of the Jewish Sabbath. I listened to prayers recited in Hebrew before feasts celebrating Rosh Hashanah, fasted on Yom Kippur, fried latkes and lit the menorah for Hanukkah, cooked for days to prepare a seder for Passover, and when a loved one passed away, I joined the family in sitting shiva, the traditional mourning rites. The rhythm and melodies of the prayers had a familiarity and solemn beauty that allowed me to connect and to follow along, which spurred a realization that true soul is omnipresent—on a farm, in the 'hood, and anywhere that the spirit lives.

Tradition, heritage, and the importance of family were definitely pronounced in the Silverman household, but the main ingredient that nurtured me during my year there was how Sylvia infused ballet into the very air that we breathed—through literature, music, discussion, and food.

Sylvia had trained to become a ballet dancer but had chosen to become an educator instead, in part to be able to devote time to her husband and children. Did she have any regrets? If so, she did not share them with me. My sense was that even if she could have gone back and done things differently, she would not have changed any of the decisions she had made.

One of two girls born to the Pasik family, Sylvia was absolutely doted upon and raised in an atmosphere that combined the work ethic of New England and that of her Jewish immigrant family whose roots went back to Palestine. With a winning recipe of love and encouragement, her parents supported her in pursuing whatever she loved to do—all the essentials that would make her successful. Indeed, like Agatha, Sylvia was a pro at everything she touched—dance, painting, raising and educating children, antique collecting, her prized passion for breeding bichons frises, and throwing bashes for traditional holidays. For one of many celebrations, Sylvia enlisted me and Robyn to act as hostesses—providing us with uniforms and all—and then gave detailed instruction for serving.

My handwritten notes of this event, inspired by the Emily Post of Framingham, include some of the following highlights:

- Always serve from the left, clear from the right.
- Before guests are seated—cheese, caviar, bread, and silver will be on table.
- Broil chicken livers on cookie sheet—approx. 10 min.—napkins will be accompanied with basket pans (always keep ice bucket filled).
- Jell-O appetizer will be served on a bed of lettuce with ring of pinapple, and Jell-O mold atop that—this will be on table before guests are seated.
- Shrimp oderv (crossed it out, couldn't spell it) will be served while guests are seated. It will consist of four pieces of shrimp also on a bed of lettuce with special sauce in center.
- Chicken will need heating maybe until sauce bubbles—put in platter of pineapple chunks, cherries with sauce over it—with clamper. Rice will also be served at that immediate time. One (Robyn) will serve chicken while one (me) serves the rice.

• Tea and coffee will be served along with cream, sugar, and Sweet'n Low.
• Cookies, brownies, and tarts will be served after medium saucers and forks and spoons are placed. Immediately cake, chocolate cake, and saucers will be brought.

Sylvia might have been a composite portrait of all the women who had raised me until this point in time—with the grounding and stability that Bertha Taylor had provided; the boundless energy to embrace life to the fullest that she shared with Agatha Armstead; her honoring of the many faces of womanhood that were so strong in the Wooten and Armstead aunts; the same kind of devotion to ballet, the arts, and teaching that Sylvia and Esther Brooks had in common; and the spectacular beauty mixed with fearlessness that both she and Rosa Turner embodied.

Many significant, tangible gifts were to come from Sylvia, yet the most important was a level of empowerment that I had never known. Without saying it in so many words, she provided a reminder that I had been given everything I needed from multiple sources in order to flourish in the world. But it was now up to me as to how I would apply what I had received to chart my own course.

Backing up the message that I was ready to compete on a higher level was Carol Jordan, who had begun to talk more seriously with me about my plans after high school, promising me not that I would get into a top ballet school and professional company in New York, but that I would face the task of choosing which one. There were many to consider elsewhere as well as in New York, but there were really two that topped the list. Would it be George Balanchine's School of American Ballet and the New York City Ballet? Or would it be Lucia Chase's American Ballet Theatre School and Company?

But first I needed to transfer to a high school more centrally located. I began researching schools in the Boston area and found Shaw Preparatory School. I contacted my intrepid social worker, Linda Webb, and informed her of my next venture. I explained that I had found a high school that would award me 50 percent of my tuition if I could find someone to match the other half.

Together we undertook an Agatha Armstead-like campaign with the Department of Human Services in Augusta, Maine, appealing to my only legal institutional parents to pay the remainder of my tuition. Though my first series of written requests were denied on the grounds that it had simply never been done before, Linda was able to have an exception granted for one year.

The powerful feeling I experienced from this victory was only tempered by the realization that I had to now live up to the confidence being placed in me. In fact, I had to do it in half the time, mainly because there were no guarantees that the Bureau of Social Welfare in Maine would be willing to make the exception for me the following year. This worked in my favor since Robyn and I had just had a taste of New York that summer and I was raring to return. This all came about quite by happenstance.

Robyn Silverman's summer had already been planned out by her mother: she would go to New York City for three weeks in the summer of 1975 in order to take advantage of classes at the American Ballet Theatre School with her sister, Jill. It was soon announced, however, that due to an injury, Jill had to stay behind and have surgery. Rather than cancel, Mr. and Mrs. Silverman proposed that I take Jill's place for the three-week summer program with Robyn at ABT—public classes offered to intermediate and advanced students taught by a stellar faculty—all expenses paid. Wow! Only later did I realize that attending this summer program was common practice for children of privilege, a rite of passage because it was an opportunity to be seen by ABT's decision makers for placement and scholarships for the following year, an advantage only the affluent could possibly afford.

In the weeks of anticipation leading up to our departure, I could not keep my heart in my chest. Taking off for New York with Robs, my transportation, accommodations, tuition, clothing all provided, to study at ABT—it didn't get any better than that!

Part of what made this so meaningful was that I wouldn't be doing it alone, but with someone who deeply shared the same dreams and hopes that I had. We counted the days. Being kindred spirits and greatly admiring each other's abilities, we usually avoided the inevitable competition that comes with being driven competitors. We both had different challenges. Weight was an issue for every dancer, whether it was a problem or not. Food and body issues became extreme in our adolescent lives, as is common for most teenagers, yet with dancers the sense of control can become all the more heightened. Ballet was inevitably a harsh way to become acquainted with one's female self. We all battled against our natural development, stunting, repressing the flow of womanly evolution.

These concerns did not elude me, even with a balletic body. Robyn, though a natural beauty with an enviable instep and arch, had to work hard at her turnout. She did so with athleticism, intelligence, and a daunting force of will. The one thing about our anatomies that we could not manipulate were our robust derrieres. All the tucking under in the world could not disguise what clearly was our ancestral inheritance.

Our diets could be alarming. I went along with the program with my own restrictive diet of a poached egg on dry toast, a grapefruit for lunch, and "air pudding and wind sauce" for dinner. We knew the exact caloric calculations for whatever meager morsels we reluctantly allowed to pass our lips at dinner. Anything exceeding the quota of eight hundred calories was punishable by running laps outdoors around Maple Street in the dark—hysterically burning off the last bites of a brownie.

I prepared and practiced for our trip, defying gravity and cutting the air with pirouettes. This time period and the following school year before graduation were marked by a hunger for a life of independence through dance that would have me balancing my existence on five toes at a time, attempting to take flight in imitation of gossamer wings in one movement, and making fists with another.

A confidence about myself emerged. I felt the line of dance innately. Before nightly prayers, I jogged in place on the shag carpet, adding a series of sit-ups. Exhausted, I fell asleep in a Russian split, dreaming about New York City—all on a grapefruit, a poached egg and toast, and something too minuscule to recall.

Impossible though it seemed, our three weeks in New York City were more glorious than anything I had dreamt. Unchaperoned, we traveled together daily from our lodgings at the Katharine House, a Ladies Christian Union establishment that offered rooms at 118 West Thirteenth Street. The minute we were situated in our rooms, I had to venture out, and it didn't take long to realize that I was finally home. Yep, this was it—with all of the indifference, the warring smells, Balducci's, host to multitudes—orphans and kings. I would melt into a lasting sense of connection to this city, forever thankful that I had lived a life that would confirm my belonging here.

Those three weeks passed much too quickly. Aside from the city itself, what I experienced and witnessed at ABT's public classes was electrifying. The classical technique was beyond superlative, built on the foundation I already had—on a very different level of competition. This was an awakening, a sighting of where I wanted to be, where I wanted to belong. I had my work cut out for me and couldn't wait to return.

⁓

When I returned to Cambridge it was with total focus to prepare myself to return to New York that following spring, just before high school graduation, for auditions on April 13, 1976, and to win a full scholarship with the American Ballet Theatre School. Maybe even, as the training program provided, to join the smaller company, Ballet Repertory Company, and eventually, the *big* company—with Baryshnikov, among others.

Robyn was right in step with me in her own aspirations. I was hopeful for both of us. Always chosen to demonstrate combinations in class as the kind of attentive dancer who could reverse steps at the drop of a hat, Robs had everything to support her desire, along with the stamina and abandon. We could live together in New York, travel the world as company members. My optimism was boundless. Even the State of Maine, thanks to Linda Webb's assistance in securing me a bus ticket, was part of the team. My social worker's good luck note was so cheerful, how could I not be confident? She wrote, "After all your years of hard work, you certainly deserve this chance. Let me know what happens."

By the time Robyn and I disembarked from the Greyhound bus at the Port Authority, in the heart of Manhattan, anxiety had set in.

In the mammoth studio on Sixty-first Street at Columbus Circle, we were given audition numbers to pin to the fronts of our leotards and divided into groups. Mine was C12, a number that didn't correspond to Robyn's. That was the first separation between us, a meaningless one, to be sure, but still disconcerting. A row of judges sat at the front of the studio against massive mirrors.

After the barre work, groups were ushered into formations and led through a battery of combinations. Unceremoniously and very rapidly, dancers were eliminated and excused. After moving successfully out of the early rounds, I was shocked and disheartened to see Robyn gathering her things. She had been eliminated.

I was crushed for her yet knew that I was still standing in one of the most coveted schools in the world, competing against international contenders, because of Robyn's unflappable loyalty as a friend. As a competitor, I came to win and would not allow guilt to stand in the way. While I was asked to return on April 15, 1976, for the final round of elimination, Robyn spent time on her own, contending with her disappointment in her own way and time.

When the second portion of my audition began, I knew I wasn't walking into that studio alone. In spirit, I was flanked by Esther and Carol, Rosalind and Tatiana, Billy Wilson and Agatha, Bertha and Laura, Barbara, Sylvia, Rosa, and Linda Webb . . . they all were there with me. Young aspiring dancers on either side of me were excused.

Then the legendary Russian pianist Valia stopped playing the upright. The audition was over. A small group of dancers, myself included, remained, frozen in our stances, uncertain. I had everything riding on this decision. Various judges, made up of the crème de la crème of ballet royalty, pointed, then went back to their huddle, then pointed again and began whispering. Finally the deliberations were over. Artistic director Leon Danielian stood without the assistance of his cane, walked toward me with a distinctive limp, took my face into his hands and said, "You've won." He took my face into his hands and kissed me in a European way. A quick peck on both cheeks.

Hard work had paid off. I wanted to shout to Esther and all my mentors and fosterers right there and then: *We did it!*

One among this select group, I looked at my fellow dancers excitedly. None of us could repress our euphoria, as everyone spontaneously hugged each other, too exhausted to leap for joy, victoriously drenched as we curtsied before the judges and speedily exited the studio.

There was no one who wanted that scholarship as much as I did, for different reasons perhaps, other than Robyn Silverman. My reality broke it down for me yet again, reminding me of that tough mantra— *Be counted and don't ask why.*

Robyn and I made the long trek back to Framingham on Greyhound. We didn't sit together. How could I bridge the surreal chasm suddenly formed between us? Mr. and Mrs. Silverman met us at the station, clearly challenged as how best to comfort Robyn and congratulate me. The dream long cherished for their daughter had fallen to me, afforded as the result of their fostering. Bittersweet hugs were exchanged between Sylvia and me, few words were spoken, and a somber return to Maple Street ensued. I had to stem my excitement. And I did. That was so, even when a letter soon arrived from American Ballet Theatre School confirming that the summer session would begin Monday morning, July 5, and continue through August 28. I tried not to make a fuss with the flurry of correspondence necessary for my arrangements, quietly writing

my social worker to request assistance for caseload number 19267-C—
that was me—in any way possible from the State of Maine, Department
of Human Services, Bureau of Social Welfare, led by Commissioner
David E. Smith. I hoped that Linda Webb and her manager, Richard
Totten, would present my appeal to the right bureaucrat. It was a long
shot, but I had to try. I had nothing and everything to lose if I didn't.

I graduated in the spring of 1976 from Boston's Shaw Preparatory
High School. I completed both my junior and senior academic requirements in one year and I was chosen to be the graduating class salutato-
rian. The speech that I gave incorporated themes of gratitude and
pride in how far we had all come, with a challenge to my fellow gradu-
ates to strive to unimagined heights along our different journeys
ahead.

Looking back at the speech that I handwrote, now a fading piece of
my history, it is interesting to observe how formed my feelings and attitudes about life already were. This, too, was credit to all those who
had helped raise me to this point. What I most wanted to share was
that success wasn't the end goal, but that the feeling of progressing
through life mattered most, through individuality, expression of self,
and the power of an artistic outlet:

> I have found that being able to express inner feelings and to be
> unique is far superior than to just follow—never expanding one's
> personality to what it could be. I look to the bright side of things
> and find that a book or a career has an opening and closing, and
> by that understanding this feeling of excitement fills my heart
> knowing that my first page has been turned.

None of my extended family of fosterers attended my graduation,
which took place four days after my seventeenth birthday, on May 14,
1976, except for the one person without whom the milestone never
would have been reached—Agatha Armstead. As I stood at the lec-
tern, with second-highest honors, delivering the salutatory commence-

ment speech, I had no problem finding her ever-shrinking frame in the crowd. Diminutive as she was, her megawatt smile beamed with well-earned pride.

Ma had foreseen many pinnacles that she urged me to climb, including this day, so many years earlier, perhaps from the very day she came to Gray to get me, a crying, confused toddler, and brought me home to Forest Edge.

Though the ceremony conflicted with the Silvermans' schedule, they had given me the graduation gift of a lifetime, one that was further validation of all that Agatha had done to raise me, and one that had first been handed to me the previous summer when, through a set of seemingly unrelated circumstances, my fate was determined.

Following the auditions, Robyn and I remained sisters, cheering each other on in every respect. After high school she would be college bound, destined to be an academic star, following in her mother's footsteps, Robyn became a teacher, now on her second master's in education and psychology. Not surprisingly, given the example set by Sylvia, Robyn would become the kind of mother to her own two children that you would wish for every child.

Sylvia Silverman and I had also cemented a lasting foster mother/daughter bond, for which I was forever grateful. The wheels were set in motion.

When the day arrived for my departure to New York, it seemed everyone in the Silverman household was elsewhere while I loaded up the waiting van in the driveway—until just before it was time for me to walk out the door. Then Mr. Silverman—who had been watching television—came out of his den and handed me a check.

"Good luck, Vicki," my last foster father said, the one who showed me how to cook matzo brei that I loved to have as a breakfast treat. Mr. Silverman did not comment on his unexpected gift, the size of which I had never received into my own hands from anyone in my life, over $300. He cautioned me, "Open a bank account as soon as you get to New York." Then he added, "Never go below that amount."

It was to be my only financial security until I could find a job. Having just turned seventeen years old, I had a year left to receive institutional support. Otherwise, I was on my own. I was on the Foster Care Emancipation Clock and it was ticking, big-time. I was about to be a statistic, one of the twenty to twenty-five thousand children released into adulthood at eighteen. I had a head start. In what was the most affection we showed to each other during my entire stay, I embraced Mr. Silverman and accepted love with this most unexpected, never forgotten gift.

There was never a question as to whether Sylvia knew what her generosity to me had meant and would continue to mean. Of everything that she gave to me, what I would always treasure most was the tacit acknowledgment she conveyed that I had been a gift in her life as well.

SEVEN

VALENTINA PEREYASLAVEC & PAULINA RUVINSKA DICHTER

For every artistic dreamer willing to do the hard work and courageously walk through the doors of Carnegie Hall or Lincoln Center—or any other artistic venue—that is only the first step. Everything changes when you're in New York City, the ultimate proving grounds. The big show. A supreme reality check for the naïve and the uninitiated. Whether you will rise to the top or not depends on so much.

From the start I saw that hard work was a given. Everybody worked hard in the Big Apple. Cabdrivers, Nathan's hot dog concessionaires, scam artists in Times Square, all artists. It wasn't just talent or luck that made things happen, you had to have connections, and those connections had to think you were talented. You had to bring it all: guts, stamina, professional beauty, determination, and many things not in your control—random occurrences, Lana Turner moments, those circumstantial split-second choices that had no true or false classification but that, once made, could radically alter your path.

For me, the ability to use everything in my arsenal was to be of vital importance over the next six years, while my major lesson was that I had to be willing to fall, which I did not like to do. That meant literally, professionally and personally. No one was exempt from enduring applications of harsh constructive criticism. Sometimes taking silent umbrage was my only outlet. I made mistakes. Disappointment was inevitable. But what I was about to discover was my resilience, the ability to brush off and get back up again. And to do it with panache!

Though my guides along this learning curve were many and varied, I was most influenced by two inimitable grande dames—prima ballerina, choreographer, and legendary ballet teacher Valentina Pereyaslavec and piano virtuoso Paulina Ruvinska Dichter. They were the grandest of grande dames.

Although they had much in common and both contributed to my evolution as an artist and as a human being, they lived in different worlds and entered my life at different junctures, like complementary yet individualized bookends. The first of the two to appear on my horizon was Madame Pereyaslavec, whose name alone was enough to send reverberations of anxiety through me when I learned that I would be studying with her.

I didn't know how to pronounce her name but would soon learn. Madame, nearly seventy years old and petite, was a kinesthetic powerhouse—a vibrating entity, influencing everyone she touched. She was never without her felt fedora and walking stick, unassuming loose navy blue pants, and a cardigan.

Valentina Pereyaslavec was one of the most sought after living ballet teachers and coaches of this era, a prima to the primas. Her master class was so famous among ballet luminaries that it was known simply by its time—"the 11:30." The same year that I arrived at ABT, Valentina was celebrating her twenty-fifth anniversary with the school and as company teacher—at age sixty-nine. Whether her students were members of ABT or in the school, or were visiting principal dancers from other companies, she was universally exalted by an endless list that made up the who's who of ballet—from Lupe Serrano to Erik Bruhn, Carla Fracci to Ivan Nagy, Anton Dolin to Merle Park,

Lynn Seymour to Rudolph Nureyev and one of her most celebrated pupils, Margot Fonteyn.

Fonteyn—one of my early idols—was said to schedule special stopovers in New York whenever she was touring anywhere in the world and had been first introduced to Valentina Pereyaslavec by a colleague who arrived in the United States from Russia in the early 1960s. That certain celebrated artist was described by Valentina in a *Dance* magazine profile of her, in which she recalled the young male dancer, unlike any she had ever seen, who arrived in her class unannounced. What captivated her beyond his masculine beauty, his poetic and nobly expressive face, was the astonishing concentration and control in his work. After class, he introduced himself as Rudolph Nureyev. Rudi, or Rudichka—as she knew him from then on—became a regular in class whenever he was in town. For me, this was historic, to see him in all his majesty. Standing at the barre with a knit hat on to retain body heat, he followed along like everyone else. He described Valentina as one "possessed by the muse, a priestess of dance."

A similarly familiar quote from Margot Fonteyn—whom Valentina coached, just as she did Nureyev, for their historically acclaimed 1976 ballet film of *Swan Lake*—was "If you can survive Madame's barre, you can survive anything."

I couldn't have said it better. Double rond de jambe à la seconde en l'air en demi-pointe was one of her favorite exercises. She believed that holding the leg at ninety degrees on half pointe, applying a circular motion from the knee down, for extended periods of time built strength and it did. She thought nothing of choreographing an adagio that applied a derivative of this position from a grand plié simultaneously adding en tournant.

Valentina was from the Ukraine, where she was born in 1907 in Yalta, before traveling to Moscow at the age of nine to train at the Imperial School of Ballet. She later spent three years studying in Leningrad under none other than Agrippa Vaganova. Valentina's reign on stage in theater and opera as a prima ballerina lasted twenty-two years, ending not by her own decision but by the outbreak of World War II.

Though Madame never spoke of what her experience had been during the devastation of the next seven years—certainly never in class, nor during the treasured conversations I had with her in private—I have to believe that what she witnessed would haunt her forever.

What little I do know is that she was sent to work in a factory in Germany, a fate far more preferable than that which met so many in the arts, Jews and non-Jews, condemned to concentration camps. Hitler released his infamous "List of Degenerates, Jews, Bolshevists, and other Undesirable Geniuses." The single most powerful threat to the Third Reich was apparently not an enemy armed force but creative freedom, thus requiring the murder of all forms of individual thought or expression. Hitler's list of undesirables included the names of the twentieth century's greatest thinkers: Albert Einstein, Sigmund Freud, Thomas Mann, Pablo Picasso, Marc Chagall, Berthold Brecht, Kurt Weill, Billy Wilder, and Josephine Baker.

However Valentina Pereyaslavec survived, Madame must have found empowerment from whatever lived inside of her—the power of art to mount the ultimate resistance against tyranny. Her experience under communist regimes must have fed that intensity. It was assumed that was the reason she so loathed the color red and that students were banished from class for making the error of wearing even a hint of it.

Passion and having an inner wellspring to defy limitations was how she later described the difference between a good performance and a great one.

"Many dancers beautiful," she said in her broken yet melodic English, almost dismissively, during one of the first classes that I took with her as we began our pliés at the barre. "But many beautiful dancers the same. Only artist *inside* can make role great." That inner work had to happen away from class and in rehearsals, Madame insisted.

She compelled us, through the first exercise of the day, crying, screaming, beseechingly, "Pleeeee—" her face distorted, hands reaching out to the class, drawing it out, never finishing the word, making it a combination of *please* and *plié*, teaching with a go-for-broke approach.

She would scamper across the studio floor in tiny black-heeled shoes, in bourrée fashion, to make the slightest correction. "Po-po in," she commanded, as I attempted to conceal my derriere, which wasn't going anywhere. She moved on to a fellow student, barking, "Don't sleep, lady!"

For any of us to aspire to ascend to the ranks of corps de ballet of the apprentice company of American Ballet Theatre, the main company, possibly becoming soloists and ultimately principal dancers—a daunting hierarchy—we had to fully inhabit our roles and allow them to inhabit us. That was an ongoing theme in Pereyaslavec's teaching, as was the importance she placed on sequencing and not rushing movement. Every developé had to unfold and unfurl higher; full relevé (rising on to pointe) without a clear demi-relevé first was met with a "No good, lady" or, worse, a look of absolute repulsion. There was no room for slackers, and she could smell 'em a mile away. I loved her tenacity.

On one occasion in class, she demanded that I close my fifth positon, "Heel kiss toe, toe kiss heel!" Miss Jordan's drilled placement lessons back in Cambridge were not lost on me. In a split-second decision, I replied with a verbal answer. Unheard of. Dancers were supposed to talk with their bodies, not their mouths. That rule changed. As much as I respected Madame Pereyaslavec, and God knows I did, I was all I had, I was my own meal ticket, and I wasn't about to bust my kneecaps before I got into the big leagues. Common sense dictated that I couldn't compromise my instrument on a request, not even for the teacher who taught Margot Fonteyn.

As the incomparable Valia began playing, I raised my hand and said, "I'm sorry, Madame, but holding the position hurts my knees." The entire class stood dumbfounded at the incongruousness of the moment. Her eyes had a wildness in them, then ever so slightly, she curled the ends of her lips; I smiled back in the same way.

Without missing a beat, she carried on with class and never, ever asked me to close my fifth position again. Here were the exacting lessons, essential for survival of the fittest, preservation, and technique.

Pereyaslavec stood behind me and tapped her walking stick to remind me that my leg could go higher, elements that added to the drama and would be an asset to me as a dancer. As Madame watched me in all phases of my technical development, she also seemed to have the unnerving ability to read below the surface, as though she could perceive so much more about my life and circumstances than anyone could have told her.

Maybe she was harkening back in her mind to her own experiences after World War II was over, when she found herself in a camp for displaced persons of Ukrainian descent and started to live again by offering to teach ballet lessons to children among the refugees. Within a short time, Valentina put together a group of students there at the camp to form a notably well-trained youth company who went on to perform extensively under the sponsorship of the United Nations Relief and Rehabilitation Agency.

Maybe there was something about me, a scholarship student, that reminded Madame of her arrival in the United States in 1949, alone, with nothing more than the grand sum of eleven dollars in her pocket. At the age of forty-two, Valentina began her American odyssey as a factory worker in Philadelphia, before leaving soon thereafter for a ballet teaching job in New York City. By 1951, Madame Valentina Pereyaslavec had made her way to her home for the next thirty years at ABT.

Whatever it was that spurred her to take me aside after class just before Christmas 1976, Madame didn't say, except that she may have noticed the condition of my ballet slippers and pointe shoes and must have surmised that I had limited resources.

By now I had adapted many of Agatha's methods for extending the lives of my ballet shoes—washing them with Comet, drying them on the radiator, frequently recycling ribbons, and using floor varnish to reinforce the shank and box of the pointe shoes. No matter how diligent I was, they had to be replaced periodically.

This was one of those times, and that was my first thought when Madame told me without asking, "You come to office now."

Saying nothing, I acquiesced, following her toward her private office. I doubled my steps to keep up with her astonishingly rapid, smooth gait, not sure what was coming next. Madame waved me in. "Now," she began in a tone so serious I wondered if I was in some sort of trouble. Then she reached into her big pocketbook and pulled out an envelope. "You buy new shoes; appearance important," Madame said in a deep, soft tone I had never heard come out of her before.

Inside the envelope was a crisp twenty-dollar bill to purchase a pair of new Freed ballet slippers. My words of gratitude were simple: "Thank you, Madame."

She said sweetly, "No cry, no cry, lady." Then, becoming stern again, Madame cautioned, "You tell nobody or I get in trouble. Secret, yes?"

I could not imagine a woman of this formidable strength fearing trouble from anyone. I swore to her, emphatically, that I would not say anything to anyone. She nodded, then waved me off.

Two days later I came to class with my new ballet slippers. Madame stole an approving glance as she gave me a correction. I couldn't wait for class to be over. Following *reverence* at the end of the scholarship class, I took Madame a bunch of daisies. Very touched, she told me I shouldn't have spent the money on her. I pasted the empty envelope into my expanding scrapbook with a caption about how fortunate I was to have her interest in me.

Valentina Pereyaslavec probably suspected correctly that I had financial concerns that went beyond the need for the refurbishment of ballet supplies. But for the time being, I was doing my utmost to keep my life folded in the smallest of ways, a well-kept secret.

⁓

I had completed my first summer in New York City at the ABT School. It didn't take long to discover that the checks from the renamed Maine

Department of Health and Human Services were nowhere near enough to support me in New York, not to mention the fact that they were chronically late in coming. The only thing I could depend on were regular letters and Toll-House cookies from Agatha, with peppy asides, reminding me that the cookout was coming up and letting me know: "I stayed up until 10 o'clock last night watching Mary Tyler Moore in Russia with the Bolshoi Ballet. It was marvelous."

Aside from these financial worries and late checks during this, my last year on the State's clock, I loved the independence of my new terrain, where fitting in by being like everyone else was less important than being unique. Nobody cared where you were from or who your parents were or weren't, but rather why you were there and what you could do. Being unfettered from the word *foster,* creating my own persona and living in New York City was brilliant. It was a first stab at opening doors that I could have never dreamed about.

There were many nights I sat by the Lincoln Center Fountain, scoping out Park Avenue couples sipping champagne during intermission, hoping someone would become so enamored with their date that they'd lose interest in the ballet. One night I saw a couple do just that. I watched as they tossed their ticket stubs to the ground and hail a taxi. I managed to glide past ushers into one of a pair of plush ruby orchestra seats, oblivious to the snobbish highbrow crowd around me, so that I could witness the second half of Cynthia Gregory's Sleeping Beauty. Amazing!

It was thrilling to be in New York City as simply one of many pursuing the American dream, of which I would be reminded every time I happened by the patina-covered thirty-foot replica of the Statue of Liberty on Sixty-fourth Street. After discovering it, I thought of her as another sort of mother—not as flashy as her bigger sister out in the bay—but one who nonetheless welcomed all, tolerated all, and especially gave freedom and opportunity to all.

Next door to my residence was a jazz club, with a name like the Half Moon or something similar, where I made my way as often as I could. With red lipstick, heels, and my best vintage dress, I passed muster for the doorman at the club, an African American sequoia of a man, who let me in with a grunt and an upward tilt of his chin. At nearly five foot seven I still had the face of someone younger than my age, but I put an edge in my stroll and nobody was the wiser.

Inside, ensconced in live music, nursing a beer in a whisper of light and noshing on a fistful of peanuts, I recognized some of the regulars—a Vietnam vet, an old man, and the bartender. Having my fill of torch songs and conversation, I headed out and tiptoed back into my five-by-twelve room, undressed for bed and fell into a Russian split—legs pressed against the institution green painted wall. Fantasizing about Baryshnikov, I recited the rosary as I fell asleep.

In November, Lauren Turner wanted to see what all the fuss was about in New York City. She asked if she could crash in my room at the Katharine House for a few days while she checked things out as she pursued a singing and modeling career. There would be consequences if I got caught harboring someone in my room. It was strictly prohibited. Katharine House was run by a Mrs. Martin, who was more like a warden than a resident manager. Needless to say, it was going to be very precarious, at best, to keep Lauren under wraps.

After a lot of back and forth she convinced me to let her stay. Against my better judgment, I snuck Lauren into my cubicle, and soon was busted, with grounds for me to be kicked out.

The Katharine House was already battling with me and the State of Maine over the late rent payments, with long-standing threats of eviction. And when I returned from a trip to Boston to visit Agatha, following Christmas break, on a late January evening, around midnight, the night clerk said, "Don't bother going upstairs. All of your things have been removed." Not believing her, I went upstairs and found that all of my belongings were gone and the room reeked of disinfectant. I knew this was final. I stormed the office, demanding to know where my things were. The clerk snidely replied, "You'll get them when we receive the rent. We kept warning you to get those checks to us sooner." There was no use explaining how welfare worked to the robot sitting at the desk. With that, she informed me that I was now trespassing and to leave the premises immediately.

"Leave the premises?" I asked her. "Where the heck am I supposed to go at this hour?" Her response was worse than the previous, "I don't care where you go, but you can't stay here." I refused to leave. "The police are on their way," she gloated. I didn't believe her, retorting, "And you call yourselves the Ladies Christian Union?" I was mad, seventeen, and about to be arrested for late rent. Where were my guardian angels?

Blue and red lights swirled outside, and I hid behind one of the double doors in the cafeteria. With what little I could see through space between the door hinges and the wall, I watched the burly officers talking to the night clerk. Before this turned into a bigger fiasco than it already was, I surrendered myself.

Because I was still a minor at seventeen, they threatened juvenile detention. I begged that they hear me out. My heart pounding, mouth dry, feeling backed into corner, I tried to do the right thing and pled my case, explaining as fast as the words could form in my mouth, trying not to stutter, "Officer, I'm a full scholarship recipient at American Ballet Theatre School. It's the best school in the world."

"So?"

After providing the five-minute version of my story, I listened as the more compassionate officer said, "I'm sorry, but you're a vagrant and a minor and so you'll have to come with us to the station." It didn't even help when I told them that if I wasn't in class in the morning, it could jeopardize my scholarship. "Sorry."

They granted me my request to make a phone call. When my neighbor upstairs, Laurie Weir, picked up the phone, she immediately flew downstairs and came with me to the station.

Sitting in the back of a black-and-white was a huge wake-up call. As I looked at all the homeless people and the prostitutes, many of them so young, I thought how cold they must be. I was so close to being on the street. Something in me shifted, rose up. Emancipation was less than five months away and I had better get some kind of game plan together. I had worked too hard and had come too far to be classified as a vagrant and thrown into juvenile detention.

At the station, the officers, now more informed about my status than before, understood that I was a ward of the State of Maine; they also took into consideration that I had crossed four state lines to study ballet. Apparently not in the mood for bad publicity or the mound of inevitable paperwork that they would have to do with social services, they came up with a perfectly acceptable offer. If I could prove that I had a secure place to stay, I would be released.

Survival wheels turned in me like they never had before. Laurie Weir called her older sister who lived in Greenwich Village and the plan was set in motion. The officers confirmed the arrangement and gave me a ride. Of course, I was always grateful to Laurie's sister, a perfect stranger, who on the spot made a decision that made all the difference in my life and to the two New York police officers who decided to let me go.

It occurred to me later that this happens every day. Children frightened beyond their own comprehension make rash decisions based on confusion and fear, not facing the crisis head-on but running from it, perhaps because no one ever told them that confronting problems was an option.

I stayed for two weeks at the whimsical Greenwich Village apartment, regrouping, bringing my new social worker, Patrick Moynihan, up to speed, and getting my life together. I moved on again, this time staying in a series of seedy hotel rooms before landing a room at the Hotel Barbizon for Women on the East Side. Lauren Turner became my roommate there. She had determined to make her mark in Manhattan by entering into a Miss Black America pageant. To help pay the rent she worked for Eastern Airlines at LaGuardia Airport. God, please let her win, I kept praying. It was apparent to both of us that the tides were changing. The geeky girl from Maine was making her way in the big city. It would take Lauren some getting used to.

In early 1977 I auditioned to be, and booked my first tour as, a professional member of ABT's second company. I was over the moon. The two-week tour was salaried, with a per diem on the road, rehearsal and performance shoes, and a stipend. No one at ABT had any idea about my near homeless straits and surviving on iron-grilled cheese sandwiches, right in the middle of the good life: Bloomingdales, Madison Avenue, attentive lines of chauffeur-driven town cars. Pedigreed pooches out for a spin with their hired dog walkers. Nannies pushing elegant baby prams.

The challenges kept on coming. I could rarely convince any establishment to accept the timetable of the welfare checks, and when I was unable to make my rent at the Barbizon Hotel, the keyhole was rudely plugged. I decided to supplement my stipend from the State of Maine with a part-time job. Going yet one more rung down on the rent ladder, Lauren and I moved into another seedy hotel on Broadway.

We rented a room with an elderly European couple. Both with cases of agoraphobia and other Howard Hughes-esque obsessive-compulsive habits. We didn't stay long.

At my wit's end one afternoon as I walked up and down the streets of the Upper West Side, I was drawn to a soulful building on Seventy-first Street. No doorman, simple, nondescript. Rich with some kind of history, I was sure, though I couldn't tell much—in spite of the fact that there were no blinds on the windows. I rang the manager's bell.

"I'm here to see the apartment for rent," I said into the intercom. Positive thinking.

"We're not advertising," replied a woman's voice. "How did you know?"

Impressed when I told her that it was because the blinds weren't hung, the manager/owner's sister invited me in and showed me around the small available space that seemed like a luxury palace after where I had been. We had a brief conversation and she offered me the unit. Then came the hitch—I was underage. Quickly, I proposed that my roommate, Lauren, who was eighteen, would sign for me.

I managed to furnish my first real apartment in New York City with orphaned items left on the street and in Dumpsters. New York then and later had the best thrown-away treasure I had ever seen. This was part of my education in the development of a very strong sense of irony. I fell in love with irony, the most potent coping skill for keeping a smile on my face no matter what happened inside or around me.

Ironically, it turned out the building I was inhabiting was owned by author James Baldwin, whose importance as one of America's greatest living black writers I wouldn't really know until later. Whenever we met, he was phenomenally gentle. His eyes regularly looked like they were crying, for reasons I did not know how to ask him about.

Another irony was that even though I was strapped, pinching every penny and living from check to check, still a dependent of the State of Maine's DHHS, dreading the date of May 10, 1977, with every encroaching week, before the weather started to warm up I learned that I had landed print work with *Seventeen* magazine and would be working with photographers Bruce Weber and Patrick Demarchelier, and possibly traveling to dreamed-about locations. Things were looking up.

All of this was happening at the same time that my new social worker, Patrick Moynihan, another dedicated advocate, wrote to remind me to sign paperwork as I was turning eighteen in May. As if I needed any reminders.

The professional opportunities that were starting to arrive were encouraging. They were also more reasons to keep myself on a strict diet.

From an early age, food and eating were chaotic for me, not originally connected to body image. Whatever my core being was trying to accept, I believe that in the confusion of losing two mothers before the age of three, one thing was certain—there was a communion between loss and physical hunger. Over the years, I would *not eat* in order to feel, or eat *not to feel*. It wouldn't be until well into my adulthood that I could learn how to feed myself for the first time without guilt or shame.

At Forest Edge, Agatha, amazing cook that she was, never understood why I ate like a bird—long before I had begun to dance. I recalled images, sitting alone at the red Formica kitchen table staring at a plate of cold food. Bacon had to have every vestige of fat removed, which I did via a dissection process using scientific precision. Documented well by my social workers and doctors, I refused to eat what I didn't like. I controlled that part of my life.

Fortunately, I loved food from the earth. Raw everything. I loved Agatha's winter shakes—made from evaporated milk, an egg, and vanilla extract poured over fresh-fallen snow—to keep weight on.

Once I outgrew those earlier, finicky habits, eating wasn't a problem until I made the decision to compete in the major leagues of ballet. That summer program had opened my eyes to the idealized aesthetic that the top dancers had to represent, and in preparation for the ABT auditions, I had dieted all year long, telling myself that I was supporting Robyn, but really gaining a sense of my own food and body control by taking in a very minimal eight hundred calories a day.

Upon arrival at ABT—weighing a proud 105 pounds on my fairly tall frame—I was promptly informed that I'd have to lose more weight. That I was heavy. As much as I had riding on my scholarship, I didn't want to seem insubordinate, but how could I eat less than nothing?

Ironically, I noticed that some of the other scholarship dancers ate much more than I did and had no weight to lose. In their perfectly pulled-up buns, not a hair out of place, they were so lavishly carefree in the way they bought boxes of pastries and ate several in one sitting. How was that possible?

No answers were forthcoming until one night in the dorm when

I heard the most thunderous growl coming from the communal bathroom down the hall. I leaned my head out my door but saw no one.

The next day at lunch, the bun heads were at it again. Loading up
their plates with pastries, ice cream, soda, chocolate syrup, and nuts.
You name it. Needing to know, I asked directly, "How are you con-
suming all this food and losing weight at the same time?"

The three dancers, holding their overladen trays in front of them,
their oversized heads disproportionate to their bodies, alien even,
stopped dead in their tracks, looked at me in disbelief, and moved on.

I was dead serious. What was their secret? Somebody had better
tell me.

Finally one of them said, "I'll show you." With that she led me upstairs and we proceeded down the hall into a lavatory. Then she showed
me, plunging her fingers down her throat. "That's how," she said,
matter-of-factly, demonstration over.

I stared at her in simultaneous disgust and amazement.

"It's the only way. Besides, you can eat whatever you want."

The next morning I gave it a try. Hideous though it was, I felt that
I'd been initiated into the clandestine club and didn't always have to
starve myself thin in those instances when, like them, I could eat what
I wanted and not gain weight. From that moment on, we neither discussed nor admitted to its practices.

There was nothing ironic to me when it was made clear that at
ninety-five pounds, I was still classified as not thin enough.

Not until years later did I permanently break through the impossible beauty images imposed on me. With trepidation, I sought help
with this and found a support group of courageous spiritual women in
a St. Louis suburb. I was shown how to feed myself, one mouthful at a
time—and I would finally emerge from the long night of deprivation,
weak at first, but eventually able to nurture and take responsibility for
myself in a healthy way.

But back during my late teens and twenties, these patterns contributed a mighty sword of Damocles that hung over me, tempering the pride I ought to have enjoyed from numerous successes.

Tangled up in all this were the physical symptoms of the excessive, uncontrollable perspiration of my hands and feet. To my credit, it was in these years that I began to research the condition by finding what scientific information was available. Eventually I learned that my malady had a name: hyperhidrosis. Its causes were genetic, an anomaly according to medical doctrine, and in no way connected to physical activity. Some believed hyperhidrosis was caused by an overactive sympathy gland. Hence, to correct it would require a sympathectomy.

My version of hyperhidrosis—palmar and plantar (of the hands and feet) was one of the more common variations. I learned that most cases, like mine, began in childhood or early adolescence and, to my great dismay, not only would persist throughout one's life but might become worse. I read of cases that resulted in extreme limitation of professional options. It amazed me that I had coped as well as I had, avoiding contact, devising ways to take my tests at school by keeping an extra piece of paper under my writing hand.

Dr. George Lipkin of New York University Medical gave me my first glimmer of hope for recovery in my twenties. For the first time I could begin assorted treatments and have a conversation with someone about the isolation.

He reminded me of Mr. Rogers on TV and shared in a warm, but matter-of-fact kind of way different scenarios worse than mine, which helped me get perspective as I rowed a rudderless boat. Dr. Lipkin told me that there were those who were unemployable, a nun who wanted so badly to touch, those whose affliction was so great that they became totally reclusive, and some, I fear, who took their own lives out of sheer shame and loneliness.

Paralyzed by the disorder, one man gave up his political career not because he couldn't get the votes but because he would lose due to a questionable handshake. Hands told a story; they mattered in this world and no one knew that more than I did. I didn't want to fall out of the race.

Few methods of treatment existed. Medications had either proven not effective or had caused such other symptoms as muscular paralysis. Surgeries to date were either so drastic as to require the removal of sweat glands or were in the experimental stages. The only glimmer of hope to be found was the use of a complicated, expensive contraption that involved the application of low-level electrical current to one's extremities while submerging them in an electrolyte solution—a process that had met with mixed reports; some said that it significantly reduced symptoms while others reported the opposite. Riding on that glimmer, I determined to set aside every cent that I could to be able afford the machinery as soon as possible.

In the meantime, I scoured the yellow pages, and found a chiropractor who advertised that he could cure my malady. He turned out to be a quack, and shortly thereafter, I read in the *Village Voice* that he had been arrested.

It would be a long process to understand why the shame of hyperhidrosis drove me to self-medicate. Hard as it was, I chose life and pushed on, secretly reading self-help books and magazines and showing up for dreaded appointments. I thought if I could only fix this one problem, everything else would be perfect. But there's never just one thing.

Over time I had to accept that I had to do *all* of the work and there were no shortcuts. The work was crushing and painful—and I wanted to quit, and I did quit, and then I'd begin again, with the intercession of certain guardians, one of whom was one of my oldest and most trusted friends and fosterers, Margie Cortez, who wrote me words I could remember on the tough days:

When you are ready to talk, I'll listen—until then, you are in my thoughts and prayers—I love you because of who you really are, not be-

cause of or due to any circumstances that have happened in your life; all
trials and blessings have a greater purpose—follow your heart Vic.

For seventeen years, I took to wearing gloves to hide the potential of symptoms erupting without warning in social settings, cultivating something of a fashion statement with my glove collection that was in keeping with my other penchant for vintage clothes and hats. In the dance and theater worlds, no one seemed to think anything other than that perhaps I was quaintly old-fashioned and ladylike. A grande dame in training.

On the last day of my legal unemancipated youth, I resolved to move out at my earliest chance, allowing Lauren to keep the apartment. I was a fighter, but I was learning to pick my battles.

That night I sat in my bedroom, painted the same royal blue as our dinner table at Forest Edge, on the renovated mattress that I had months before dragged in from the cold, with the open window allowing in cool spring air and the sounds of giggling girls on the street mixed with New York City traffic, as I watched the digital clock given to me by the practical Mr. Silverman. Those unrelenting, uncaring red neon numbers flickered by. Tears streamed down my face.

Midnight struck. I was eighteen. Eighteen. Legal. Emancipated. Old. Too old to be the daughter of the State of Maine under the financial care of the Department of Health and Human Services. Too old for my late though steady checks, or for supervision by my social worker, or for the subsidy of my ballet scholarship. Maybe too old for *Seventeen* magazine after all. Too old for foster parents. An adoption. Just plain old at eighteen.

On February 5, a Tuesday, the blizzard of 1978 bullied its way into Manhattan like Raymond Armstead going ninety miles an hour up Route 95 North.

What began as a nor'easter in New England, creating unprecedented carnage in the wake of its hurricane strength winds at seventy-nine miles per hour, had blanketed New York City in twenty-seven inches of snow in twenty-four hours, making it the worst winter in 105 years. Snowdrifts crested the tops of parked cars—which I observed from my window after being awakened by my alarm clock's chirping. Mainer that I was, it never occurred to me that class at ABT that day might not be held as usual and on time.

After all, it was only snow, I reminded myself as I bundled up, grabbed my ballet bag, and headed out. Besides, there was talk that I was in contention for my first film role—dancing, of course, in the corps de ballet in the upcoming movie version of *Hair*. Weather was definitely not going to stand in my way of being in the right place at the right time, wherever and whenever the opportunities were going to come.

A wave of familiarity met me outside on the street as I set off on foot for the studio at Columbus Circle. It was so reminiscent of Forest Edge after a major snowstorm, except that this was New York City. All sense of hustle and bustle had been slowed, to create a cityscape that was uniquely quiet. No traffic. No hurries to get anywhere because there weren't many places to go. There were sights rarely seen—grown men in the street revisiting their long-forgotten youth by throwing snowballs like happy children, cross-country skiers skittering along the snow-laden sidewalks, the regular walkers out on sleds, even one of the ubiquitous NYC joggers in snowshoes. We greeted one another like members of a select club, applauding each other's respective decision to get up and go someplace in the face of what appeared to otherwise be a city snowed to a standstill.

Standing still wasn't an option for me. Not for a second would I have ever taken for granted the station to which I had risen, now as one of twenty carefully selected dancers, getting ready to tour in the fall with the second company, being groomed to compete for the next tier—the main company. Only a handful would make the grade. Out of that group of six or seven, the likelihood was that only one or two might eventually be crowned as a prima ballerina. Already I had seen hopes dim for several who started out with me almost two years earlier, while witnessing the elevation of others who had always stood out.

Susan Jaffe was one such fellow member of Ballet Rep, as we abbreviated the title of the company. We had met at the auditions and had gotten to know each other when we arrived that summer, sealing a permanent friendship after that. Before coming to ABT, Susan had lost her mother quite tragically but rarely acknowledged that she was in any kind of pain or mourning, allowing those feelings to live through her ballet, powering her to astounding heights in her artistry. If anyone had predicted in 1978 that she would be the one prima ballerina to come out of our class, I might have concurred; La Jaffe, as she became known, had an aura early on.

Even though I was given a solo or two, there was a familial comfort and security to being a member of the corps that I almost preferred to being in the limelight.

Belonging at any level to this royal lineage was what mattered, just the prestige of rubbing shoulders with the likes of Natalia Makarova and Mikhail Baryshnikov—who would soon take over the directorship of ABT. What mattered was the privilege of being taught and directed by ABT faculty like my champion, Valentina Pereyaslavec, and another important influence on me, the extraordinary Patricia Wilde. Canadian-born, another force of nature and former prima ballerina, Wilde, always in a pastel leotard and chiffon skirt, was a bolt of lightning as a teacher and choreographer, challenging us all to defy our physical boundaries. Balanchine once referred to Wilde as his strongest dancer because her speed, precision, and ballon (bounce or height in jumps) were peerless. She understood and imparted the aspect of ballet that is all about drama, all about holding the attention of the audience in suspension of disbelief—secrets that became all the more meaningful as a I segued into an acting career.

On the day of the great blizzard of 1978, I allowed myself to feel proud of the privilege of belonging to this world, to know that I was breathing the same rarefied air as so many greats, having the chance to watch through rounded Plexiglas windows in observations of classes and rehearsals, learning from the mastery of everyone from Carla Fracci, Gelsey Kirkland, Fernando Bujones, Antoinette Sibley, Cynthia Gregory, Alicia Alonzo, and, notably, African American Mel Tomlinson.

I was proud to be in a lineage of those dancers, like Tomlinson, who had broken down the racist bias that had operated in the ballet world for decades. It hadn't been until the 1950s that blacks were allowed onto the stages of the major ballet troupes in the United States, making it necessary before then to study privately with white teachers or in nonprofessional segregated settings. That was until 1937, when Harlem's American Negro Ballet opened its doors, followed in the 1940s when the First Negro Classic Ballet was founded in Los Angeles.

It took the incomparable Janet Collins to shatter the color barrier in 1951 when she debuted as a prima ballerina with the Metropolitan Opera, doing for African Americans in classical ballet what Marian Anderson soon did as an opera singer. To follow in the footsteps of Collins—known for designing and even sewing her own costumes, thanks to her training as both a visual and dance artist—that was the star I kept reaching for.

There was one other unforgettable member of this lineage whose path had crossed mine in the crowded halls in between classes early in my tenure at ABT. Incredibly striking, though not tall, with hair twisted imperfectly into a chignon, her dark, sad eyes poured out a luminous beauty that was at odds with her face that was masked in pancake powder, like a member of the seventeenth-century royal court.

There in the hallway, she gave me a piece of advice, unsolicited but welcomed. In an unusually soft, low voice as she studied me closely, she said, "You're a beautiful dancer, but you'll have to work very, very hard."

I nodded in recognition, smiling but also sighing as she moved on, disappearing into the mass of dancers that thronged the corridors between studios.

Her name was Raven Wilkinson. After being forced to leave the United States in order to dance, Raven had eventually joined the Ballet Russe de Monte Carlo as its first black ballerina in 1954. When she returned to America to perform, her progress was interrupted when she was touring in the South and the KKK was said to have marched onto the stage in the middle of rehearsals, demanding that she be turned over to them. None of her fellow company members said a word, allowing her to stay hidden until they could all leave town. With subsequent threats, however, Raven was let go for fear that a boycott of the troupe would happen because of the presence of a black dancer.

Humbled that she had taken the time to stop me, I could never take lightly the doors that had been opened by Raven Wilkinson and those ballet dancers of color who came before me.

That was why I was so determined to arrive at my destination that February morning, not for a second anticipating that it would only be me and the elevator operator, a proud blue-black Jamaican whose patois never failed to warm me as he grinned and said, "Girrrl, da place closed, can't ya see we we're avin' a blizzard? What 'cha doin' up in dis wedd'ah?"

"Same as you," I replied.

He looked over his glasses, snapped his suspenders, and agreed, saying, "Ye'ere now girl, I take ya up so ya can see fa ya'self."

Standing alone in the center of the studio that was unlit, gray, still—as a rat scurried into safe hiding from our feline mascot—two contradictory feelings arose in me. The dance/fight that ballet had always been was now a duel between my need to be rooted and a growing need for motion, travel, exploration. Europe in 1979 had become my mantra. But doing anything to unsettle the taut wire of dental floss on which I was balancing was out of the question.

After all, at almost nineteen, I had managed on my own, helped by an ABT living stipend, supported emotionally by what had really become my family; so the thought of this not being my home forever sent pangs of anxiety through me. Then again, I was starting to see that "forever" didn't exist, and, whether I embraced change or not, it was heading my way.

All I could do was to trudge on home through the snow, stopping first to cast a glance back at the Metropolitan Opera House and wonder if I could actually see the fantastic reds and yellows of the Marc Chagall murals through the frosted glass of the lobby. I took another moment simply to admire the simple architectural power of Lincoln Center—standing there in immortal defiance of the weather, a cathedral with many chapels for honoring all creation. The mystical work of Marc Chagall, gracing the lobby of the Metropolitan Opera, did more than hang there—it pulled me in.

In the great blizzard of 1978 it was hard to imagine that years later I'd fly to France to see Chagall's masterpiece in the form of a ceiling mural at the Opéra National de Paris, originally founded by Louis XIV in 1669 as Academie Royale de Musique et de Danse. The opera house that stands today was designed by famed French architect Charles Garnier and was commissioned by Napoléon III in 1862.

On my own tour, I would stand in the face of history in a private suite decorated in crimson red. Poised at the loftiest tier of the opera house, I would never forget looking up at a swirl of color and nature that the seventy-seven-year-old Chagall painted when I was only four years old living on a farm in Maine.

Between touring with the Ballet Repertory Company and then on circuits performing with other ballet companies that allowed me to earn money but mainly fed my hunger for travel and adventure, I went through extended periods where a Manhattan address wasn't necessary.

"Why worry?" asked Paulina Ruvinska Dichter, the grandest dame of them all, as we sat in the living room of her Riverside Drive apartment. I was welcome, she reminded me, to stay on her green 1960s sofa anytime that I was in town, in between apartments, jobs, or boyfriends.

The year was 1981 and I had already been through several of all the above.

"Tell me," Paulina said, a virtuoso listener as well as a pianist revered by the elite of the international music world. As I began a quick recap before dinner, not necessary to do because there was never anything that needed to be rushed with Paulina, I allowed my eyes to wander through the spacious apartment that was a veritable art museum. From the moment that we had met after being introduced by mutual friends in the art world, we clicked immediately and cultivated one of the closest and most enduring relationships that I had with any of the women who raised me.

My visits with Paulina were like nothing I'd ever experienced or would again. Her art collection was vast, amassed over the years in her travels with her husband, Chester Dichter, who was no longer alive. Not one but two grand pianos presided over the living room, used both for practice and the steady stream of private students who came and went at many hours.

As I told her where I'd been, my attention returned frequently to a dominant piece of art at the entrance to the living room—a black, smooth owl that stood three feet high and set a tone of mystery, signifying the presence of wisdom, strength, and beauty. All qualities that Paulina commanded.

We laughed about my adventures three years earlier in the apartment that I had shared with four other dancers.

When I first heard about an opening at Mayfair Towers, on West Seventy-second Street, a security building with a doorman and a chandelier in the lobby, Shelley Winters on my floor, all next door to the Dakota, my response was, "Are you kidding me?" The Dakota was where Roberta Flack lived, not to mention that it was the famous address of Rudolf Nureyev, Yoko Ono, and John Lennon—for what would be his last year of life.

These were the high-flying disco party days of the late 1970s, and I wasn't going to miss out. I had to say yes and didn't have a dime. Had to scratch, beg, and borrow my way to keep that roof over my head.

We made the most of it, ballet by day and disco by night. Definitely underaged, we went to Studio 54 often enough to be on a first-name basis with Mark the gatekeeper and where I hit the dance floor with the likes of Pelé. The really big excesses of the '80s hadn't kicked in yet, but there was a lot of contraband and hanky-panky.

The wonder days in that apartment came to an end when my room-mates started booking contracts with various domestic and international ballet companies, leaving for assorted foreign ports of call. This was when I made one of those decisions that I spent years second-guessing, only to later conclude that I hadn't made a mistake so much as I had come to a fork in the road.

I was offered the opportunity to work with choreographer Twyla Tharp on the feature film of *Hair,* which was being directed by Milos Forman and costumed by Ann Roth. But the shooting dates conflicted with the ballet *Little Improvisations,* which I'd already committed to, with the Juilliard School of Dance and legendary choreographer Antony Tudor. With Tudor's blessing, I found a wonderful dancer as a replacement, freeing myself to work on the film.

The moviemaking process was thrilling, as was the experience of dancing in a corps of eight dancers, hand-selected by choreographer Twyla Tharp, an Einstein of a modern dancer who always wore tennis shoes to dance in, and who held an expression that matched the seriousness of her focus and intensity. Twyla later paid me an immense compliment by including me in a workshop she presented, another exposure to dance so different from the pure classical training that most shaped me.

When I returned from filming, I discovered that my replacement for Tudor's *Little Improvisations* had failed to show up because Forman's secretary forgot to tell her that she'd gotten the job. And I took the hit. I was naïve, obviously, and learned a hard lesson that with ambition comes responsibility. From then on, I would be very meticulous in attending to details in all professional arrangements, an excellent policy. If I had everything to do over again, that would be the piece of advice that I wish someone had given me. Unfortunately, without it, my career at ABT was effectively ended.

I decided to audition for Ballet Hispanico, uptown on Eighty-ninth Street and Amsterdam Avenue. The studios were located next door to horse stables. I had gone from witnessing Nureyev to navigating horse dung—taken with a sense of humor. Here I was smack-dab in the middle of Manhattan and back on the farm at the same time.

Artistic Director Tina Ramirez, an olive-skinned beauty born in Venezuela, the daughter of a Mexican bullfighter, inherited her teaching inclinations from her mother, an educator of Puerto Rican descent. Whether it was her ancestry or not, she had a hot temper, which I loved to watch when she became angry without apology, then return her focus for the benefit of what she loved most—children and dance. Tina lifted everyone to a high standard, never failing to remind all of us, "Without discipline, you have nothing."

Although she suffered from a severe back injury in her thirties, her heel work was impeccable and at lightning speed, evoking a sense of vertigo. Watching her was like being transported to the front seat of a bullring, excitement personified, harkening me back to my favorite John Singer Sargent painting. Possessed no doubt of her father's drama, Tina's nostrils flared, her eyes seductive—all to a diabolical riff with what some consider the most sophisticated of percussion instruments, her castanets.

Being a part of Tina's family introduced me to another way of expression, another voice through dance, as she guided me toward becoming a soloist and learning the art of flamenco, introducing me to my soulful self. This was all a departure from ballet—moving my body to the choreographic rhythms of Geoffrey Holder and Talley Beatty, meeting the graceful Carmen De Lavallade, and performing at the Copacabana, connecting to Afro-Hispanic rhythms with Ballet Hispanico.

During my time with Ballet Hispanico, Tina contributed to my dance heritage, passing on what she knew from studying with the incomparable Spanish dance teacher Lola Bravo, even after Tina had taken Broadway by storm and tours took her across North America and to Cuba and Spain before she commenced her forty years of teaching.

Tina Ramirez was the perfect mentor at the perfect time, for which I became increasingly grateful over the years, showing me that just as there are many languages to speak, so too, there are many ways to dance, to communicate, to celebrate.

Those were some of the learning experiences I could share with Paulina Ruvinska and appreciate how she empathized so heartily, knowing as I did of her long and laureled career. There was still regret on my part about my departure from ABT.

"This is the life of an artist," she reassured me. "We evolve. Mistakes are part of growing."

I wasn't so sure but leaned in attentively as Paulina went on to regale me with accounts of numerous ups and downs, all of which she promised me had made her stronger in the end. Her point was that sometimes we learn more from our mistakes than from our victories. If she really believed that—known as she was for her indomitable power, masterful technique, and incredible range of repertoire—then I had to take that on faith.

Almost seventy years old, Paulina was born and raised in New York in the musical, intellectual atmosphere that flourished in her own home. A child prodigy, she made her professional debut at the age of seven in a performance with the Detroit Symphony but then waited another sixteen years before giving her first major concert in New York at Town Hall—taking the music audiences by storm, so much so that for the next ten years her annual recital was a much anticipated cultural event.

In her thirties, however, Paulina had taken time off from performing. "The best thing I ever did," she insisted, affirming my decision to
take time off from ballet after the fiasco that caused so many doors to
close for me.

In her forties, Paulina Ruvinska picked up right were she had left
off and was more acclaimed than ever. Whether she was practicing in
her living room or performing for a sold-out crowd at Carnegie Hall,
she channeled music as though from the mind of the composer, playing
some of the most challenging Bach transcriptions with an effortless-
ness that made what she did seem almost easy.

Was it really effortless? Paulina smiled. An echo could be heard in
my mind of what Raven Wilkinson had said to me: "You'll have to
work very, very hard."

From a Russian Jewish family background, Paulina knew about
overcoming prejudice and transcending limitations. As she spoke, a
Miró hanging on the wall behind her, her message to me was to allow
myself to season as a human being, to live a full life and laugh about it,
which could only elevate my art. And, she added, "Don't underesti-
mate yourself."

Remembering what my first experiences away from ballet were, I
wasn't sure I agreed. After deciding to give up dancing or it deciding
to give up on me, I took a job as a live-in au pair in the employ of a
society couple, which involved being a round-the-clock housekeeper
and babysitter, all for the princely salary of one hundred dollars a
month. After one morning of having to fend off the husband who came
in to where I slept with the children, I had to then deal with the wife's
jealous retribution, as well as her imperious questions about whether
I had washed the floor.

"Yes, I did," I told my soon-to-be-former employer in a final episode of inquisition.

Bonwit Teller hatbox on her wrist, she snarled right back, asking,
"By hand?"

That was the end of that job. Nothing left to do but to pack up my belongings, load a dolly, and roll it right down Seventy-second Street, past James Baldwin's building and onto Broadway, not sure where I was going next but drawing on faith for guidance at being able to find new digs in the Big Apple.

Some of this was familiar territory to Paulina from previous conversations but she knew very little of what had happened over the past two years.

Basically, I explained, trying for irony, after getting settled in a place to stay, "I went from the fire to the frying pan."

What began as a passionate affair with a friend of Milos Forman's, whom I affectionately, and later not so affectionately, called the Cinematographer, had turned into an all-consuming nightmare. There had been those initial whirlwind moments—this dashing, successful fellow in the arts and in film who approached me on the street when I was window shopping on Fifth Avenue, then a romantic date ice-skating at Rockefeller Plaza. At twenty years old, I had lived in the convent of academic and professional ballet a long time and wasn't yet worldly wise, a virgin still. Emotional intimacy was a completely foreign concept. There were still so many parts of myself that I kept cloaked, like my hands in protective gloves.

The Cinematographer was clearly smitten and I was definitely scared. Before things developed, I departed for San Francisco, where the promise of adventure and opportunities had beckoned.

Not much adventure or opportunity cropped up in the Bay Area, where I boarded with a club owner and his girlfriends, getting by on affordable junk food and splurging on a ticket to see myself in the movie *Hair* in an otherwise empty movie theater. Where was everybody?

I returned to NYC after asking the Cinematographer to meet me at the airport. When I arrived with my one black trunk, I informed him, with my heart beating wildly, "I'm moving in," which was what seemed to be my only option at that time. I compromised myself for basic food and shelter.

Two years later, some of which was turbulent, and many ports of call afterward, my desire to see Europe in 1979 had been far exceeded—even if I had been on a tight leash.

Highlights from my visits to Czechoslovakia, where I learned more Czech than I ever thought possible, included witnessing arrangements to clandestinely acquire family photography belonging to Milos Forman that had been left behind during the invasion of Prague Spring of '68. There was also a memorable trek through the lush Czech forests to gather Lisichky—fox mushrooms—meant to be served with freshly hunted deer. In a throwback to my New England youth, I thought perhaps of screaming to warn the hapless deer. Instead, I watched hunters from the village gut and tie the carcass to a tree limb, which I helped carry down from the mountain into the village for a feast. Two days of celebrations by the villagers proceeded with beer and stories flowing as a local accordion player accompanied fanciful tales of Slavic royalty. Having not seen a brown face since World War II, they treated me as a celebrity.

The more I saw of the world beyond my corner of it, the more I wanted to see. One of our most memorable trips was when the Cinematographer and I vacationed in Saint-Domingue/Haiti. We stayed at Habitation Leclerc, a converted colonial estate owned by dancer Katherine Dunham. Once occupied by Pauline Bonaparte and General Charles Leclerc during the Haitian Revolution, it sat atop an aquifer, nestled in Marssaint, a neighborhood just outside of Port-au-Prince. We drove into the heart of the countryside over washed-out mountain roads, past historic battlefields and monuments, and through sudden rainstorms. The soul of the country spoke to me, making me feel a strong connection. (Many years later, I would return to that rich history filming *Feast of All Saints*, written by the brilliant Anne Rice. Since energy so often follows thought, that would be fitting as I had so much wanted to return to one of the most beautiful places on the planet.)

During my trip there with the Cinematographer, we seemingly stumbled upon a guarded hotel, complete with an aviary. Inside the lobby, a woman with her back to me was giving the kitchen staff instructions. All I could see of her was her coarse waist-length black hair. As I approached her, she turned. Her beauty was blinding. Her name was Lahaina, and she would curiously turn up in my future in a very different capacity. But at that time, she and her husband were gracious hosts, whisking us for the day to their private island, attending to our wants and needs.

Lahaina was lonely in her gilded cage, even with the company of her daughter, and hated to see me go. As we were saying our good-byes, she implored us to return, promising, "The next time you come back, I'll have my leopard cubs."

My travels certainly fed the passion for photography that had been instilled in me at an early age by Agatha and my ever-ready Brownie camera to capture moments that would otherwise be lost. It so happened that in the same building where the Cinematographer and I lived, I'd met a fascinating female photographer named Sina Essary.

We had met one morning on the elevator and she asked if I would pose for her, to which I answered, "Sure," little imagining until I entered her penthouse apartment and saw some of her work what a phenomenon she was. Sina apparently had three apartments—one to live in, one for her studio, and entirely separate quarters for her Persian cats.

It was my first portrait shoot, created from stunning shadows and light that felt true to my existence. What most fascinated me was that she made a living as a medical assistant, not full-time as the prodigious photographer that she was. Sina didn't seem to mind in the least, as though it was enough for her to do her art, even preferable to create images that pleased her rather than having to live up to the market's expectation. Still, I wondered how she supported herself in such a well-appointed lifestyle. Few clues arose until one visit when Sina, with tears in her eyes, told me that she was a widow. Describing in detail how much she had loved her husband, she went on to recall the day when she sat next to him and witnessed him being gunned down by hitmen. He was Joey Gallo, a mobster known in most New York circles.

Not that my situation had any direct parallels, but it was instructive to meet Sina and realize that being dependent on a man for financial support under any circumstances was dangerous. This was another wake-up call for me at a time when the Cinematographer was trying increasingly to isolate me, very much like a concubine. Finally I realized I needed to take control of my life and end the relationship.

This fairly recent chapter was all news to an alarmed Paulina, though I reassured her that what had seemed to be a detour had provided me with many lessons that were now helping me back on course.

To find myself and my balance again, I had gone back to studying ballet—both at Carnegie Hall, where, for the first time, I paid for classes, loving every minute of being in that hallowed space, and also in Harlem with Arthur Mitchell through a scholarship I had received. To pay the bills, I took a job in a department store, managing fairly well.

Paulina asked me probing questions, as was her habit, without being invasive. What was it really, she wanted to know, that would make me happy?

No one had ever asked me that question. My dream of being a prima ballerina was just that—a dream. To become a ballerina required that strength a dancer finds just above her pelvic bone, forsaking all else; I couldn't do it twice. I had kept that part of myself for my very survival. The life I lived outside, walking up Broadway to my next audition. Why not? It was an open call and I needed the cash. My training gave me the appearance of having a fistful of dollars, when in actuality I had little more than a subway token.

I was Odette/Odile on and off the stage, executing thirty-two fou-ettés every day I woke up; it was a way of life. The idea of being a bal-lerina had been such a part of my being that it was automatic to say so. But I had finally figured out that it wasn't really what I wanted to be at all. I did just want to be a part of the corps de ballet, the spit and glue of a family that danced. I wondered if maybe I could pour my life into something else artistic? Was there something else out there? The first thing that came into my mind, at that moment, sitting in Paulina's ex-pansive living room that overlooked the Hudson, was that I had won-dered what it would be like to connect to the family that I first came from, most of whom I didn't know. It felt important to see my mother, Dorothy, and to locate my brothers. It was time.

Paulina Ruvinska cheered me on, as usual, telling me that before we had dinner she wanted to give me something and then presented me with three gifts: a Japanese cloth cloche, a 1930s perfume bottle, and a twenty-dollar bill that she retrieved from her brassiere.

"I can't," I pleaded, insisting that she had done too much. It was ironic that I had been jet-setting all over the world not so long ago, but now could really use the carfare.

"Yes, you can," she insisted more vociferously. "Give an older woman her pleasure."

What was it about her that created such a defined aura of sensual-ity? Certainly it was how she revealed herself, enhancing her soulful eyes with black eyeliner, keeping her red lipstick smoothly applied at all times, and never shying away from showing her décolletage in her array of plunging necklines accented by multiple necklaces.

As every great grande dame should, Paulina had a handful of pas-sions that were separate from her calling, three passions to be specific—art, Italy, and beauty.

I hoped that she didn't mind if I had those three passions as well, I joked.

"Not at all," she replied thoughtfully.

In the nearly two decades that followed this night, we would stay in frequent contact. In 1998, when she was eighty-six years old, Paulina hadn't responded to letters for long enough that I worried horribly about her. I called "Skane," a term of endearment for a man I loved and secretly dated, Wynton Marsalis, whom I met at the Hollywood Bowl through jazz impresario George Wein. I had desperately wanted to introduce him to Paulina but hadn't been able to do so. I loved that Paulina—who knew jazz luminaries like pianist Teddy Wilson—was of the opinion that what made Wynton so great was his classical prowess.

From California, I called Wynton in New York and asked for him to personally go and check on her. He did so, whereupon the doorman informed him that she had died—which he explained to me when he called to say, "Vicki, she's gone."

There was such an inheritance of passion and resilience that this grande dame had bequeathed me and that I wanted to thank her for one last time. Her vitality, however, stayed with me always through letters like these—

Vicki, dear,

How sweet of you to send the Valentine Day's message—it arrived with green enclosure . . . you are probably the most reliable "repayer" in the whole art world . . . and the only one who acknowledges debts . . . Teddy Wilson may do the Chester Dichter Memorial Festival Concert. Wouldn't it be great if he could pull it off?! . . . Ted is now in Germany concertizing . . . (concertizing?) and he'll be in touch. And I'm to be in a Off-Broadway play, by David Wolfman. So, life moves on—

Bless you and all my love, darling
—Paulina

Dear Vicki,

Just played a most successful recital in Rome and also gave a one and half hour lecture at the Marymount Int. School, on music and demonstrations, kids from eight to nineteen loved it. Danny, my son, was

delighted and so were the other teachers—Back after Easter—
Carnegie Recital Hall again on May 12—Save that evening.

Love,
Paulina

That concert left me with a magnificent memory of the indomitable
Paulina Ruvinska Dichter. But more than anything the most priceless
gift given to me by Paulina was in a question she posed at the end of
one of our long talks.

No one had ever asked me this, so she took me by surprise when
she leaned in and said with great curiousity, "Vicki, do you know that
you are beautiful?"

An awkwardness overcame me.

"Vicki," Paulina repeated, in all seriousness, "take the time to look
at yourself and know that you are all that you need to be, just as you
are."

EIGHT

DOROTHY & AGATHA

There were a handful of important reasons I left New York City in the early 1980s and returned to Boston and vicinity, each framed by earlier events that I should explain before describing the whirlwind in which I was soon immersed.

As early as June 1978, one month into emancipation, I sat down and wrote out a check in the amount of ten dollars, payable to the Cambridge School of Ballet. This was the last of my *Seventeen* modeling earnings. I had just made my first charitable contribution. Henceforth, I would consider myself a patron of the arts, and when I had a chance to do the same on behalf of the National Association for the Advancement of Colored People, the feeling of being able to contribute to the leading organization in the area of civil rights was equally amazing. What better way to honor every woman who had raised me than to pay it forward, as it were, in one form or another?

Earlier that spring I had sent a repeated request in an exchange of phone calls and letters with my social worker, Patrick Moynihan—who had been exceedingly helpful already in the many particulars related to my case—asking, please, that the State of Maine write a letter of commendation to Agatha Armstead for her exemplary contribution as a foster mother.

Patrick Moynihan did his best but wearily explained that his superiors were concerned that it would set an unfair precedent. Their position was "It hasn't been done before."

Those had become fighting words for me. "That's not how we do it." "We don't do it that way." "It'll never happen." I was relentless. I was a daughter of Maine, born under the sign of "I lead."

Needless to say, Agatha was soon sent the commendation, signed by the governor, to my lasting gratitude, and her infinite surprise. Modest as she was, after she called to say how thrilled the letter had made her, Ma switched quickly to the topic of how I was doing, asking, "Did you get my Toll-House cookies?"

Our conversations were always truncated, not only because she didn't believe in wasting money on the phone bill when a well-composed, newsy, thoughtful letter was much more preferable, but also because Peter Cassell was probably standing over her shoulder with a stopwatch.

The ability to give a little something back, both to the Cambridge School of Ballet and to help give Agatha long overdue recognition, had started me thinking early on about the idea of one day teaching ballet to inner-city kids. Part of the ethic of having the caliber of training that I had received is to eventually pass it on. Also one of the things I learned in 1981 when I took my first clerical job in New York City was that typing wasn't going to be my calling in life.

The job had come through my wonderful friend Colleen Atwood— the multiple-Oscar-winning Hollywood costume designer then in the nascence of her career. Colleen and I had been introduced by another dancer friend, Kimberly Von Brandenstein. Colleen had worked with Kim's mother, Patrizia Von Brandenstein, also an award-wining costume designer, on such films as *Ragtime* and *Amadeus*. When I needed somewhere to live, it was Kim who reminded me that I had met Colleen before and suggested I get in touch with her.

I recalled a dark-haired woman of tremendous focus taking direction from Patrizia. A wide worktable in front of them was covered with accent ribbon and flowers, materials they were using for period hats for *Ragtime*. Exuding calm, Colleen seemed not to flinch under the crunch of the deadline, the same calm with which she greeted me at her door, knowing I was having a crunch of nowhere to stay, welcoming me in with a wide smile.

A grande dame in the making already, with her signature brilliant style, Colleen had decorated the room that she had to offer me—complete with a daybed and kitchenette—with fabulous fabric to camouflage cracking plaster. Sharing her decorating secrets with me, Colleen was a maestro in her treatment of cloth and garments. I studied how carefully she folded and preserved her extensive knit collection in a large cedar chest, how she cared for delicate articles of clothing, how she examined and compared vintage lace, buttons, and beads.

Her generosity during this time could never be measured. At a critical point in her career when she was studying for the oppressively difficult test to get into the union, Colleen energized and motivated me to tackle the next challenges of finding the independence that I was looking for. A staunch advocate of a hot bath at the end of every day, she was also enormously supportive, giving me space to regroup, and was interested and intrigued in the research that I had undertaken to find my family that I knew so little about.

During this time, my attempts to contact Dorothy were to no avail, mainly because of her sister Lillian. Even so, I was able to collect more Bevan-Sawyer-Collins genealogy that helped me see the ancient roots and ties to the past, giving me that connection I sought.

I followed some clues that led me to Normal Rowell Sr. When he answered the phone, it felt strange to talk to the person whose name I carried but who was of no blood relation to me. Of my three brothers, David was the most forthcoming. It meant the world to me when he made the effort to meet in person by riding his Harley to Manhattan as soon as he could. We connected through our different stories and experiences, not quite putting all the puzzle pieces together but allowing me to be grounded in the reality of how we ended up where we did.

Colleen never pushed but encouraged me to find employment, not only for income but also for structure and a sense of purpose, responsibility, self-esteem. All of those things were to be lasting requirements to which I would become addicted, although when the temp agency landed me a secretarial position with the New York State Council on the Arts, I could see that my stay there might be short term. Colleen and I celebrated her admittance into the costumers' union together and my being gainfully employed. She never, not once, made me feel like I was a burden. She always encouraged me not to give up, no matter how inexplicable or ridiculous my new job seemed. Many of the organizational skills, in fact, would help me on numerous fronts to come.

It had been almost a year as I heard myself promising Colleen that she could have her room back, knowing that it was time for me to move on, but not sure where I was headed. The destination suddenly became clear when three distinct reasons became cause for me to leave New York.

Out of the blue, almost, I had received one offer to teach ballet in Pawtucket, Rhode Island, and another job offer from Elma Lewis in Roxbury, Massachusetts. The third reason was that Agatha was dying.

⁓

For the next two, almost three years, my return to Boston was to grace me with a graduate education in what we commonly call reality. These lessons came from big events—life and death passages—and from smaller, everyday moments. At the same time, they were crash courses in the beauty and power of mystery that continued to color my experiences. Tests of faith, they reaffirmed that there weren't always clear-cut explanations to why things happened, but that it was important to accept and trust the generosity of the universe.

This was an emphatic lesson that came out of the actual moving process, which involved, as always, painstakingly wrapping every single one of my earthly belongings to be shipped from New York to my new address on Dwight Street in Boston. I choreographed and coordinated my travel to make sure I was there before the moving truck arrived. But after waiting for hours on the stoop—no truck in sight—with panic and sorrow welling, I was sure that almost everything had been lost for good.

Finally the truck showed. Relieved beyond words, I presented a check.

MOVER: Sorry, lady, we don't take checks, cash only!

Not missing a beat, he got back into the truck and readied to drive off.

ME: Where are you taking my belongings?
MOVER: The nearest Dumpster I can find.

I anguished over the sight of the movers driving away, my belongings routed for demolition. I begged them to come back, screaming in the middle of Dwight Street, throwing my coffee mug after them. They had everything tangible that mattered to me: the collection of rocks once loved by Robert Armstead Sr., used pairs of pointe shoes and ballet slippers, my hat collection, photos, my two scrapbooks, correspondence from all of my mothers, linen and lace, my priceless book and doll collections, a set of mismatched dishes found in New York City trash. I stood there wailing for God and the whole world to see. They kept driving farther and farther away with my life.

Suddenly, a sharp pain shot through my chest that sent me to the ground, something that had happened throughout my childhood whenever I was extremely traumatized. I took shallow breaths to ease the discomfort. When a hand reached down to pull me to my feet, I looked up to see the kindly, weathered face of Mr. C., as I would call him, a neighbor I'd just met who lived in an apartment above mine. He listened as I told him what had happened. Without giving me any advice, his calm worldly manner helped me think about what resources I had for retrieving my things.

Both Uncle Richie and Uncle Roger Armstead were there for me when I reached out. What exactly they said or did, I never knew, except that their influence was brought to bear on the moving company to return everything to me at once. Without too much of a delay, all of my belongings were soon delivered and to my amazement everything was intact.

During the rest of the time that I lived on Dwight Street, Mr. C. continued to be a positive, grounding force. He never judged or told on me even when he knew that I was tapping the building's electricity source in the basement through a series of extension cords I'd set up. This was when the utilities company had cut me off for nonpayment, after my fuel assistance application had been denied. As a ballet teacher on a tight budget, I frequently lacked for money. Mr. C. must have known that I wasn't eating much and fed me on more than one occasion, sometimes in the company of his friend, a retired prostitute who was going blind. As we ate, Mr. C. kept me spellbound with his stories as he took deep drags from his filterless cigarettes.

At what turned out to be our last visit, it dawned on me that all these stories he had been sharing with me each entailed some aspect of surviving the hardest knocks. They were being told for my benefit. Toward the end of my visit, he, the soothsayer, turned to his friend, Miss Penny, the blind oracle, and then back at me.

"Vicki," he said, "you're gonna have twelve lives, you know?"

"That's right; better listen to him," Miss Penny murmured in agreement.

"Each is gonna be real different from the next." Mr. C. added, "You don't have to worry. You just gotta be prepared."

"Preparation's for free, baby girl," said Miss Penny.

This was definitely food for thought. After I left that day, I wanted to visit again to hear and learn more, but the next time I ran into Mr. C., he informed me that he was moving out. He gave no reason other than he was "Going to where work is."

Not knowing that his mantra was an oar I would use more and more in years to come, I did feel myself torn between the reasons that I'd come to Boston—to fulfill a dream by teaching ballet in the inner city and to be close to Agatha in this hard time of her life—and where the work increasingly was going to be for me: New York.

With all the challenges of this period, not everything had been disastrous since I'd arrived. One irony—there it was again—was that the minute I left New York for Boston, I was called back for auditions. It probably did wonders for Agatha to witness the turn that my road was starting to take toward acting, knowing how many doors that dance had opened for me. She had always been very specific in advising me not to say that I wanted to be a dancer. That was because, she said, "They won't know what kind of dancer you mean." Instead, she told me, I should say that I wanted to be on the stage, to perform. The idea that I had something to offer by way of entertaining and inspiring was never, in her teaching, strictly limited to ballet.

This was all apparent in early 1983 when I received a call in Boston that I was wanted in New York to audition for Francis Ford Coppola's *The Cotton Club*. There was a small catch: I had to sing for the audition. Agatha, ailing though she was, insisted on playing piano and coaching me for the audition. Somehow she got it into her head that I should sing "Amazing Grace."

To help defray the costs of traveling to New York and staying there, I contacted benefactors such as Mr. Bernard Frank, an executive investment broker for Smith Barney at the time, and his wife, Bossie.

Mr. Frank was more than generous, securing a place for me to stay. I promised that I would allow him to invest my money once I started making some. And though that was a long way off, that's exactly what I did.

I arrived at the address that had been provided for me. It was a real palace. The Helmsley Palace, to be exact. Wow! Gilded this and marbled that. Pure luxury. Mr. and Mrs. Frank really outdid themselves and room service to boot. There was no question now—I had better book the job to make good on our arrangement.

As it was Agatha's philosophy that a woman ought to always dress to the nines when traveling, I arrived in style—in black lace-up shoes with black tights, gray-striped lederhosen, my 1940s Persian lamb coat, and, to complete the look, an oversized vintage black beret with copper sequins. You couldn't tell me I didn't belong. I was prepared, not only with my appearance, but when I checked in and presented my well-traveled passport and my Social Security card.

The next day I headed off to Astoria Studios wearing two pair of gloves. With a treatment for hyperhidosis that I had begun, this was necessary. The undergarment gloves were plastic, lined with aluminum chloride, while the outer gloves were fashionable, concealing my private chemistry kit. It seemed like a lifetime ago that I first stepped onto these stages for *Hair*, but here I was again for another round. Nearly running into tap greats Henry LeTange and Frank Hatchett, I made my way to a makeshift dressing room to change and waited for my name to be called. Then a door opened and in I went. Sitting behind a table was none other than dancer extraordinaire Gregory Hines. He beckoned me to come in with a wave of his long graceful arm and a smile. The accompanist asked what I would be singing and in what key.

I replied, " 'Amazing Grace' in C."

There was an exchange of looks as the intro began to play. Once that interminable torture was over for us all, I was asked to prepare for my dance number. I quickly changed my shoes and gave my taped music selection to an assistant. I performed a tarantella. Spinning, leaping, beats, tour jeté after tour jeté I finished to the knee!

There was no applause. In fact, they all were in complete disbelief.

GREGORY HINES: "Nice dancer, but can you tap?"
ME: "Ah, no."

Feeling completely dejected, I returned to the Helmsley Palace and decided to treat myself to a beer. The bartender looked at me and said, " I know what you're up to; not in here." At first, I had no idea what he meant. I assured him I was staying at the hotel and presented my room key. He still refused me. To this day I wonder what lady of the evening would be wearing lederhosen and a 1940s Persian lamb coat. He was reprimanded and gave a me a backhanded apology. I proceeded to write Leona Helmsley a letter describing the incident. To my surprise, she responded with an invitation to me to stay at any of her fine establishments. I carried her letter with me like it was a passport. At a later date, I took Leona up on her offer and when leaving the hotel and I was presented with a bill, I whipped out her letter.

The manager sniffed and explained, "Mrs. Helmsley meant you were welcome to stay at her hotel any time, not comp your expenses."

These were politely called "incidentals." The devil was in the details. Of course, that was the way of the world. Nothing was to be taken just literally. Soon enough, I would learn to read between the lines and even what was not on the page.

Looking back, it's easy to see that the disappointments and mistakes were fantastic forms of preparation. They were funny, too. There was the time in Boston in this period when I took a day off from teaching ballet to attend my first antique auction—at the DeCordova Museum in Lexington, Massachusetts. I was completely overdressed in full Edwardian regalia, accented with velvet leg-o'-mutton sleeves, a hoopskirt, and a Victorian hat to top it off. Nearly passing out from the heat, I used my paddle to fan myself and inadvertently won the bid. All of this, including the chair, would have to fit back into my friend Barry Savenor's Subaru I arrived in. I would be paying for that nineteenth-century chair by teaching at three different ballet schools throughout Massachusetts for some time. I still have the chair.

In these years, I often thought of that handful of visits that Agatha had arranged for me to see my mother when I was growing up. That image of the two of them standing arm in arm outside the Howard Johnson's near the Trailways station and waving at me when I was fifteen years old had come to haunt me. At twenty-four, while I didn't have Dorothy's records as I later would, I knew enough to recognize her valor in the face of so many obstacles to make sure that I was happy and loved. Those were the words that she wrote to me in letters that were surprisingly coherent, thoughtfully written, very cheerful, and loving.

Whereas in my youth it had been too unbearable to contemplate what her suffering had really been, I now felt the need to know, and I began my own painful, extended process of gathering the facts. What I eventually established from her records was that for short periods of time, she could be disarmingly lucid and high functioning, but after her six children were born, starting in the mid-1960s, she was being institutionalized for intervals of between four and six months a year, and in the 1970s for yearlong stays. Dorothy's diagnosis of paranoid schizophrenia was the one constant amid the ever-changing regimen of medications that she would inevitably stop taking whenever she was released to her own care. Her reasons, she told doctors, were that the pills blurred her vision, and that they didn't help. I was sure that they blurred her heart, too, and her ability to recall happy memories.

Toward the late 1970s, Dorothy had been supporting herself with Social Security and food stamps, living in a rooming house in Bath. But she was not feeling safe, she explained to her psychiatrist at the Augusta Mental Health Institute. It was true that something was trying to kill her, but it was in the cancerous cells that were working their way through her insides.

This same something was also spreading through Agatha, and I became increasingly aware that her condition was worsening.

My solace and structure came from being at the ballet barre, in a new capacity. I discovered that I loved teaching ballet with a passion and loved teaching children. Working for the Elma Lewis School of the Arts was an honor. Elma was in her eighties, the grande dame of the arts whose school in Roxbury had set standards for inner-city programs all over the country. She was also a much admired costumer, seamstress, and character. She wore a large gray oversized bun atop her head, a wig, anchored with a few bobby pins, and she had the habit of looking over her thick bifocals in such a way that she always seemed skeptical, even though she was quite the opposite in temperament.

There was also something both tough and motherly about Elma that was just what I needed when both of my mothers were ailing. Work helped take the edge off my sense of powerlessness to stop the natural cycles of life that include death.

In retrospect, my disdain for Peter helped me cope after Agatha died in the winter of 1982. When she was in the hospital, Peter told me that I should move out because it wasn't proper for a young girl to be living in the house, especially after Agatha was no longer there.

Peter Cassell and Raymond Armstead could never accept the relationship Agatha and I had—neither of them understanding the love for music and dance that she and I shared, both of them resenting our bond that transcended biology and legal standing. Directly after the funeral, Raymond paid me a visit at the parlor floor apartment in the South End that I shared with a few mice.

I heard the knock at the door, and looked through the frosted glass to see Raymond's pitbull frame standing next to his wife, Francine. Still in a state of shock, I opened the door and Raymond brushed past me and went straight to my mantel, removing the one thing on it. It was the one keepsake that Agatha had given to me when she was alive—a photo of her at around the age of eighteen, similar almost to a daguerreotype, framed in faded red velvet with gold trim and folded into a leather black box with a single latch. Needless to say, it was my most beloved treasure because it held Ma's energy and intentions and was meant to stay with me.

Clutching it in his hands, Raymond looked dead at me and said, "This belongs with blood." With that, he turned and left, Francine following behind him. We never spoke again.

Several years before, much to my despair, Agatha had sold Forest Edge to Raymond for next to nothing. Shortly after that the house was burned to the ground, the cause of which was never proven. Still, I knew it would help to heal my heart to get on a bus and stand in awe, not of the charred remains of what was once my home but to come to the understanding that home was from within. Once I arrived, I closed my eyes and could see and breathe in the edge of heaven. I could hear Agatha saying, "Just received the lilacs. They came in a carton taller than me. I will plant them as soon as I get to Maine." She still existed right there with me. I realized that Ma had created a universe of memories that would sustain me forever.

Between the fire that destroyed the Cambridge School of Ballet and the one that burned down the two-hundred-year-old farmhouse at Forest Edge, even with the shock and loss, I had learned that it was possible to emerge out of the ashes, and I would again.

I took solace in the loving condolence cards from many in my inner circle, like the card from Colleen Atwood that was a reproduction of *Ballet Rehearsal* by Edgar Degas, a painting from the collection of the Boston Museum of Fine Arts. Colleen wrote:

> *The news of your mother's death made me very sad; but we know that the pain she was going through must have been so terrible—It is good you were close by and a comfort to her.*
>
> *Your life and beauty must go on and she will always be with you— Please don't hesitate to call me and don't worry about things—You know by now that you are loved by God and your friends, so be comforted.*

Of course, there were other family members of Ma's, as well as my sisters, who were grieving themselves, yet were considerate and comforting to me, many of them who had paid tribute in life to Agatha by helping to foster me.

Uncle Richie and I were brought even closer in the loss of his mother. In later years, after he and Aunt Laura divorced, following his retirement, he returned to Forest Edge to his trailer on the two acres that Ma had bequeathed to him.

We would talk about her greatest gift of all for cultivating everything—how she taught the most seasoned local farmers her secrets for the perfect potato harvest and how to grow melons, squash, even peanuts and other produce not always suited to the weather in New England.

Decades later, Richie would confess that he could still see Ma all the time, long after she was gone, always up on the hill, hoeing her garden. No one was more grateful for being Agatha's last child than I was. I was in the very early stages of grief over Ma when I received a letter from Dorothy, as though she was tied to me by that invisible cord mothers have to their children, and knew that I needed some cheering. Dated February 1, 1983, she wrote:

Dear Vicki,
Wasn't sure whether your address was Dwight Street or Dwighnt
Street, write and tell me for sure. Tell me about Agatha's (Cathe-
rine's) funeral service. Has Sheree gone back to Germany and how's
Lori and baby? Write soon. Is your apartment warm? Time for the
mailman.

> *Love,*
> *Mama xxxooo*
> *Tell the girls to write me—*
> *Bye with love & lots of it—*
> *Give me Sheree &Lori's addresses.*

Dorothy's letter reminded me of something that had happened in Rox-bury when my sisters and I were living with Agatha that first year I attended the Cambridge School of Ballet. In what was an aberrational act on my part one afternoon when Agatha was out, I went to have a look in the rear of her closet—knowing that was where she kept her oversized black pocketbook, a makeshift briefcase. Still hearing the music of *Dark Shadows* that we had been watching, I expected light-ning to strike at any moment for going into the other room in the first place. Drawn curtains that partitioned her room from the rest of the apartment were to be considered locked doors. But I had a certainty there was something in her pocketbook that I was meant to see, what-ever the consequence.

In the midst of files, papers, letters, and old bills, I found a let-ter from Dorothy. I read it, frenzied, following her handwriting that took up the front and the back and the entire border of the page. Every space was used. It was dizzying. Then, I froze, read-ing what she said was my father's name. My validation, that two people, each of whom had names, had created me, a father and a mother, was there in black and white, literally. After folding the let-ter, exactly as I found it, I returned it to its dark vault and never touched it again.

That memory was part of the motivation for going to Maine with David in the hopes of seeing Dorothy before she succumbed to her illness. Again, I was toughened up by my outrage that her sister Lillian wouldn't permit me see my mother, even on her deathbed, so that I could give her the acknowledgment and love she so richly deserved. When David alerted me those few months later that Dorothy had died, I was once more grateful for my indignation and determination to claim my right to be present at her viewing.

Upon my departure from Maine, I had made the decision to never again be denied permission to visit Dorothy, deciding I could visit her any time that I pleased at the cemetery.

The Collins family unwittingly gave me the gift of something to hold on to in the rough days ahead, in the form of the verse one of Dorothy's sisters selected for inclusion on the printed programs that were prepared for her funeral service. Those words were very important for me to read some weeks later, when, in a fit of exhaustion, sorrow, and loneliness, in grand dame fashion, I would dress up in my most elegant vintage ball gown with a hoopskirt, pin up my hair under a black antique funeral hat, and apply the reddest lipstick I owned. My would-be poison, in the form of some aspirin and lots of beer, knocked me out good, leaving me with a royal headache and very much alive the next morning. In preparing to return to the art of living, that passage from Dorothy's funeral program was appropos:

> *God hath not promised*
> *Skies always blue,*
> *Flower strewn pathways*
> *All our lives through;*
> *God hath not promised*
> *Sun without rain,*
> *Joy without sorrow,*

Peace without pain.
But God hath promised
Strength for the day,
Rest for the labor,
Light for the way.
Grace for the trials,
Help from above,
Unfailing sympathy
Undying love . . .

In the weeks and months after Dorothy died, almost a year after Agatha's death the previous Christmas, I thought about the rites of passage, and what a privilege it had been, even as I watched her decline, helping her rise and meet the day, assisting her in whatever small ways she would allow me, remembering how she tended me and my sisters in our vulnerable states of life, thankful to reciprocate for as long as I was given. It was Agatha who had taught me that death was not an end but a transition, preparing me from an early age as a daughter of Maine to respect the stages of life. In theory, I had understood the loss that was pending, but even so I still had to learn that Agatha was mortal. Weak and tiny, spending more hours in her bed than out of it, Ma remained positive, continuing to offer up her tribulations, promising to rally any day—just going through a bad spell.

I hated seeing her in pain, and I cherished every second, not knowing if it would be the last, not wanting to leave anything unsaid.

Then there was that one morning before Christmas, when Agatha couldn't get out of bed. I called the ambulance and rode with her to the hospital. The family gathered around her, knowing as I did that we would never see the likes of her again. After everyone left, I lifted up the blanket and kissed one of her feet, and then tucked her back in for the sleep she had prayed for, for a whole lifetime.

If I can take any solace from the loss of these two women in so short a breadth of time, it is that the happenings of my life allowed me the privilege of attending their departures—whether it was being able to see Dorothy one last time at her viewing or to be at Agatha's hospital bedside when she finally closed her eyes.

It was a privilege to have been the daughter of both my mothers.

PART THREE

SISTERS

(1983—PRESENT)

*There is no royal flower-strewn path to success. And if there is,
I have not found it for if I have accomplished anything in life
it is because I have been willing to work hard.*

MADAM C. J. WALKER

NINE

MILLIE SPENCER &
IRENE KEARNEY

New York City doesn't give many contenders a second chance.

That was something I didn't need to be told as I returned to Manhattan in the passenger seat of a rented VW hippie van, minus the curtains, driven by a hired mover.

It occurred to me en route that unlike my first foray almost a decade earlier, my reasons for wanting to make my pilgrimage back to New York City were entirely different. There was the necessity of physically removing myself from an entanglement with a man who fed, clothed, and housed me—like so many young girls who continue to enter compromising relationships after emancipation from foster care. We need to eat, and to have someone to hold, even if it's dangerous. This one had become life threatening. After years of reading signs that had been consistently pointing to opportunities for me to pursue a career as an actress, I had decided to take the major risk required of me to make a real go of it.

A sense of urgency filled me. Though I had been officially on my own for almost eight years, the finality of burying two mothers made that reality all the more apparent. Gone were the days of Ma's extras to tide me over—five-, ten-, and twenty-dollar bills safely kept between rib and dish towel. During this very ride, I made a pledge that I would not relive the embarrassment of being kicked out more frequently than I wanted to admit for not having the rent. With each of those incidents, something turned inside of me every time I found myself with no place to call home.

At twenty-six years old the single most important driving force I had was the quest to be the proprietor of my own home, for permanence. I made a silent pact with myself as we cruised closer to New York City—that if it was the last thing I would ever do, I would one day have to pay property taxes.

I would never forget that promise, even to the point that I would henceforth always go to the bank to make my own deposits and oftentimes personally pay my property taxes. This commitment would bear out some years later when I was able to hand over a large down payment toward the purchase of my first and only house; I would respond to a banker who would advise me of the tax advantages of doing it differently. Not wanting to tell my life story or why I preferred to handle my business my way, I insisted on showing up regularly to do my banking. To the question, "Don't you have someone to do that for you?" I would respond, "Whether I do or don't is beside the point. It gives me great pleasure making my own deposits simply because I can."

Of course, going to the bank was a practice originally inspired by Agatha who started me with my own savings account at the Rochester Trust Bank in New Hampshire at the age of six. So no matter how busy I might become, how many alternate methods there would be of sending payments, or whether or not someone else was available to do it for me, the act of doing it myself would be my way of honoring how I was raised and the home I would eventually create, for my children, foster and adopted children I mentored, and the child in me.

That day loomed far into the future with this move back to New York. I had spent all of my savings on first and last months' rent and a security deposit for an East Side fifth-floor walk-up apartment on Eighty-ninth Street, leaving to my name three hundred dollars for the driver/mover and an apple. Knowing that the apple represented dinner later that night and breakfast the next day, I took careful small bites, relishing the excitement of where I was headed and the true wealth of experience and love carrying me forward. Remembering how I had worried that the last movers had taken my things from me, this trip was validation of how miraculously, even after evictions and the threatened loss of my belongings, every cherished treasure and the ephemera of my life were still with me.

Those same boxes, along with many others, were in the back of the VW van returning to New York, absorbing every pothole along the way. Also in tow was a vermillion love seat, purchased at the Salvation Army, and a tin-top table with four chairs.

Gingerly taking my fifth small bite of apple, I couldn't help smiling as the eternally glorious, indomitable New York skyline came into view. Before I knew it, night had fallen and we were rolling to a stop in front of the apartment building. Wasting no time, we began the chore of unloading items that required heavy lifting to go up five flights of stairs and down the hall to my apartment, only to discover on the first trip that the key didn't work. I panicked.

The weight of every previous eviction washed over me. I pounded the door so hard the key cut my palm.

A disgruntled neighbor in curlers peeked out through a door with the chain still attached. In a distinctive Polish accent she said, "Quiet! It's late."

To which I replied in my best Polish, picked up from living in the East Village years earlier, *"Dobrow naughts,"* as a way of wishing her good-night and I'm sorry. Inconvenienced and confused, she shut the door.

That would be the extent of our neighborly relationship with the exception of one day later on when we passed in the hall and she said with in her deep Eastern European cadence, "You work hard like me, *must* remember, buy one piece good jewelry each year so you not forget."

The mover and I continued to rattle the key. Finally, it worked and I opened the door to another adventure. After multiple trips up and down the stairs late into the night I thanked the mover and gave him his payment in cash. The second I closed the door, I realized that I'd forgotten my apple in the van. With lightning speed I flew down the stairs and caught the mover. "Wait, wait . . . my apple!"

"You didn't want that old thing. I tossed it."

I trudged back up the stairs. By this point in my life I had learned to acclimate to different sleeping surfaces and scents held in someone else's couch pillow or bedding. I would begin my search for a mattress in the morning. Still, in the empty silence of 2:00 A.M., interrupted by the sound of someone using the communal lavatory down the hall, I needed to eat in the worst way. Tentatively, I opened the old refrigerator in the apartment, which reminded me of Agatha's pink Kelvinator she painted yellow to match her curtains. Inside I discovered a half-eaten bag of walnuts of unknown vintage and in the freezer a near-empty carton of frost-encrusted strawberry ice cream. The lesson learned was to leave something behind, no matter how small, no matter how old, by accident or on purpose—something for the cleaning lady at the hotel, something for the powder-room attendant, something for the next hopeful anybody.

Delirious with hunger I closed my eyes, depending on Stanislavsky's sensory recall that came very easily to me. I dug into the hard dessert conjuring up the flavor of homemade ice cream Agatha used to make from wild strawberries in Maine. I recalled the rich nutty taste of walnuts that I helped her crack for Toll-House cookies lifetimes ago as I crunched down on the stale ones that were in my mouth. That was wealth, all of that, permeating my senses as I sat atop a piece of plywood that covered my bathtub on four metal lions' feet in the kitchenette. Exhausted, I reflected upon the fact that my life would never be a linear one.

Unlike ballet, which was the dream that I had sought, acting was a profession that actually found me. The suggestion that I act had come in August of 1978 during a period marked by a social whirl that brought me into contact with none other than Sammy Davis Jr., a black man who proudly embraced Judaism and who became one of the most important entertainers to set foot on any stage or in front of any camera. The ultimate icon, there was no one like him. Sammy was transcendent, human yet not earthbound. He could sing, dance, act, make you laugh or cry, and hold you captive effortlessly. In one of those flash-bulb moments between seconds, I was invited by a member of Sammy's entourage to see him in *Sammy Stops the World*, a musical revival of Anthony Newley's *Stop the World, I Want to Get Off* at Lincoln Center. I was ecstatic! It surpassed every expectation. I attended an after-party, where I met the incomparable "Mr. Entertainment" himself. Also in the room was a prominent photographer formerly with *Life* magazine who asked me, "Are you an actress?"

"Not in a movie star kind of way . . . it's a long story," I replied.

"Well, you should get yourself an agent. You could work."

Not bothering to explain, the next day he proceeded to arrange an appointment for me to meet Millie Spencer and Irene Kearney, a top-flight management duo whose office was in the Ed Sullivan Building on Broadway.

Somewhat nervous and a tad dubious, I waited for the rickety elevator to clang down to the bottom floor. Before pushing back the metal accordion door and stepping inside, I took a deep breath, remembering what the retired *Life* magazine photographer, whom I only knew as George, said, "I vouch for them as two of the most honest women I have ever met. They are truly respected for their integrity and tenacity on behalf of their clients." As the elevator climbed slowly toward the seventh floor, I felt the presence of Agatha and the June Taylor Dancers with me. I felt their strength and spirit.

Inside the dimly lit suite, a cloud of cigarette smoke diffused what little light there was. I walked into a small vestibule before entering into an even smaller office that consisted mainly of two desks and a tiny refrigerator.

Two seasoned professionals were in evidence, both talking on telephones, as they gestured for me to sit down on a folding chair. As they continued their dueling conversations, using terms that were foreign to me, I noted the walls, covered with framed, miniature-sized posters of Broadway shows, and painted no descriptive color other than drab, and file cabinets on the verge of explosion.

The women both wore oversized 1970s glasses and polyester leisure suits. Both talked at lightning speed into heavy black telephones that looked to be as old as the elevator I rode up on. One of them, who turned out to be Millie Spencer, had a kind, motherly persona, like Mrs. Claus. The other was Irene Kearney, who looked tough as nails, with a malleable face on the verge of imploding over some theatrical production mishap. She took an emphatic drag on her cigarette. With each new piece of information, showing tremendous focus, she suddenly erupted into laughter that turned into coughing that became serious. Finally she was done.

"Hello," Irene said in sync with her gesture of hanging up the phone and stubbing out her cigarette in the ashtray. She welcomed me with a brief smile, advising, "We'll wait until Millie gets off the phone."

Clearly, this meant that Millie was in charge.

Indeed, the moment Millie clunked down the receiver, she rose from her '60s Sealy swivel chair and came around her desk to give me a hug. The warmth of her genuine greeting was all the more appreciated by me because she hadn't tried to shake my hand.

Dizzy from Irene's secondhand smoke and chilly from the blast of an old air conditioner, I could see that these two women could finish each other's sentences. They were a team and that was obviously what made them tick. Irene drew up contracts and balanced the books. Millie was the purveyor of contacts and ever the mentor to Irene.

I liked them at once. They appeared to be interested in me. When they asked about a headshot and resume, I stammered something to the effect that I was in *Fiddler on the Roof* and *Yankee Doodle Dandy*. They were impressed until I told them the producers were nuns at St. Patrick's School in Boston.

MILLIE: Do you sing, dear?

ME: No.

IRENE: Have you been on Broadway?

ME: No.

MILLIE: Off-off Broadway?

After I said no again, Millie asked as nicely as she could, "Well, can you at least dance?" to which I answered, "Yes!"

Millie and Irene exchanged glances, showing relief that finally we were getting somewhere. Irene asked, "Where did you hoff?"

"Hoff," I asked.

"Tap," an impatient Irene stated.

"Oh, I don't tap; I'm a ballet dancer."

"A belly dancer, how interesting." Irene remarked.

With fierce pride, I said, "Not belly, ballet."

They simultaneously dropped their pens and stared at me. All that could be heard was the wheezing of the old air conditioner.

With that, Spencer & Kearney decided to take me on, patiently encouraging me every step of the way, literally feeding me at times, as well. Occasionally, I asked Irene for an advance, but rarely got a different response than "Can't do that, sweetie, but go into the fridge and help yourself to half of my bologna sandwich."

Born in New Jersey, they both were blue-collar, working-class Irish American women. Millie had learned the ropes of career management for her son, John Spencer, who had been a child star on Broadway and became a recognizable name in television. Millie got her feet wet as a stage mother to protect her son and in the process discovered she was terrific at protecting talent in general. Irene, on the other hand, had a son whom she struggled with, often giving him office work to keep him occupied and out of trouble. Rarely did either of them speak of their personal lives outside of the business at hand.

As a result, I chose not to reveal much of what had been my special circumstances as a foster child. In the world of ballet, mine was a secret not always easy to keep, but in the world of acting I was an unknown, anonymous. It was completely liberating. At the same time, there was so much to learn. Ballet required expressing and executing everything with body and facial expression; acting, however, employed not only the body but even more so the voice. Dialogue had to be retained, providing an opportunity for me to utilize my memorization skills from years of learning choreography. Acting required choices that lent themselves to an array of styles as varied as the repertoire from Fokine's *Les Sylphides* to Twyla Tharp's *The Catherine Wheel*. I realized I could transition into another performance art as a professional, using the enormous amount of mental and physical discipline that had gone into becoming a dancer. What was profoundly synonymous about both professions was the necessity of élan, heat, the divine principle of life in man—soul.

I knew how to tap into the purest part of myself without distraction. I held onto my belief that if I could channel the discipline I'd attained through ballet and apply it to acting—or designing, costuming, writing, gardening, musical scoring—my creativity was limitless. That was the greatest gift and lesson of all. I just needed to keep my imagination buoyant. I learned that hunger somehow made the art in my soul click and clarified where it was going and what I was doing.

Another advantage I possessed, both from growing up in the foster care system and from auditioning in ballet circles, was the painful ability to digest and compartmentalize, taking the most constructive parts of rejection. Giving myself credit for that and knowing I had to begin a second career if I was going to eat, I adopted the approach that Millie and Irene took. Making no promises to themselves or me, they believed that if I went to every audition they sent me on, I would eventually land something.

By observing the ironclad professionalism of Spencer & Kearney, I learned lasting business principles that would serve me in good stead for many years to come. This began early on when my managers improved my salary after becoming aghast that *Seventeen* magazine was compensating me with less than scale, a term for the standard professional minimum.

Millie and Irene embraced my potential, continually reinforcing the idea that I was a valued client. Their stance, like that of most patient gardeners, was that a slow and steady tending would give way to the greatest blossoming. That philosophy wouldn't always be shared by the show business machinery of New York and Hollywood, which loves to boost overnight stars into the stratosphere only to have them fall precipitously when their younger replacements are hatched.

I wanted what Millie and Irene wanted for me: consistent work, financial stability, and a creative foothold. Once that compass setting was dialed in, I began to believe that I would become gainfully employed. One of my first jobs was starring in an AT&T commercial opposite fellow struggling actress LaChanze. Years later, we would celebrate backstage over her acclaimed Tony Award–winning portrayal of Celie in the Broadway production of *The Color Purple*, reflecting on our resilience and the power of motherhood.

I worked side by side with Spencer & Kearney during those halcyon days when I was doing it all—living next door to the Dakota, partying at Studio 54, touring with ABT II, formerly the Ballet Repertory Company, even seeing commercial residuals for the first time. I was in the chips!

After I'd stopped in one day to pick up a check, Millie and Irene raised a subject that had never come up before. Without preamble, Millie said, "We want you to think about a stage name."

I replied, "Okay, what about Vicki Lynn? After all, Lynn is my middle name."

"No," scowled Irene, "that's too country-western."

"How about Victoria?" I offered, feeling a little embarrassed after having suggested it. Victoria, to me, was a lofty name. One associated with a faraway continent that I was connected to by faceless ancestors. Victoria Falls, running between Zimbabwe and Zambia with its unbridled power and Lake Victoria, shared by Kenya, Tanzania, and Uganda with its massive placid grandeur, connecting people or keeping them apart. Water, I knew, had the ability to shape and mold. I had faith that my new name would carve a way for me through life, the way water carves stone with slow and steady persistence.

Irene twisted her face into an inscrutable look of deliberation before she finally said in a no-nonsense manner, "Victoria it is. I like it."

Both of their phones began to ring and I rose to leave with a cool affection. They weren't dictatorial, nor were they coddlers any more than they were grande dames. They were mentors, no-frills sisters, part of my team.

That woman-to-woman sensibility among colleagues and friends, long-standing and new, would form the through line of the next league of women who raised me. Millie and Irene were emblematic of every sister in these years. They trusted me as much as I trusted them.

For the years I was back in Boston taking public transportation across New England, teaching ballet classes, I never missed a New York audition. Four hours each way. Once again, the Spencer & Kearney team had been inordinately patient, even as they aggressively implored me to return to New York City. After Millie's usual pep talk and discussing how soon I could get myself back to town, it was Irene's turn for some pragmatic advice. If I really wanted to make it as an actress, she quipped matter-of-factly, "You're gonna have to let the dancing thing go; you can't do both."

But letting the "dancing thing" go was like letting go of my family. The ballet studio was the single most consistent home I had known since the age of nine. Yet I had to go where the work was. So, at twenty-six years old, I decided to roll the dice, figuring I had better odds of creating a lasting career as an actress than I would a ballet dancer. To ignore that would have been to my own detriment. So I let the dancing thing go.

That's how I ended up returning to New York with that lavish feast of *le pomme* that had to last until the next day, or until I could find some money. Millie and Irene had secured several auditions: "Georgette the Chaufferette," an under five, and a L'Eggs commercial not needing my face, only my legs, and a coveted audition to portray Bill Cosby's daughter in *Leonard Part 6*, a film for Columbia Pictures.

I booked it. I booked all of it. There were no words to describe what it meant to prevail over the vicissitudes of my life. While *Leonard Part 6* was a commercial and critical disaster—an utter flop—I didn't care. I had been in a movie with Moses Gunn, Tom Courtenay, Joe Don Baker, the indomitable Jane Fonda, and of course Bill Cosby, who inspired me profoundly. Millie and Irene had promised that the cachet of having played Bill Cosby's daughter in anything would prove to be a pivotal credit on my empty resume. They were right; I now had a theatrical credential.

Slowly I began to build some financial stability. This also provided for the needs of my dichotomous life. I was finally able to afford treatments for my hyperhidrosis. Out of everything I would try, nothing had significantly eased the malady except for one incredibly medieval device and regimen that my improving finances and time allowed me to try, one that required me to spend great lengths of time in near monastic solitude. My nighttime ritual would begin by setting my clothes out for the next day with matching gloves. Next, I commenced applying pure aluminum chloride to my hands and feet, then placed them into plastic bags. I bound my wrists and ankles to a suffocating degree with rubber bands, my pores absorbing the chemicals, reducing the sweating. Under my pillow, I would voluntarily reach for my luminous plastic bead rosary, feeling each diminutive oval through the plastic, slowly drifting to sleep as I recited one Hail Mary after another, in meditation, as I had since I was ten. This was my sacramental rite, an acknowledgment of the sins committed by my mother, Dorothy, and henceforth me. I would do penance and pray for absolution.

In the early morning, I would remove the filmy plastic bags, revealing grayed, shriveled hands and feet, not believing they belonged to my body. I continued my ritual by filling four plastic trays with three centimeters of water each, placing two on the table and two on the floor. With all wires in place, I set the alarm clock for twenty minutes and turned the dial to classical music; Ottorino Respighi's "Pines of

Rome" played in the background. This was the same clock given to me by Mr. Silverman when I was sixteen.

With my index finger, I scooped a dollop of petroleum jelly and outlined a horseshoe on the back of my hand and across my wrist, so as to lessen the inevitable burns. I sat, completely naked, in front of a metal box called an iontophoresis machine. Setting the intensity of the electric current, I slowly immersed my hands and feet into the trays of positively and negatively charged water. As the current passed through, minerals within the water mysteriously impeded my sweating for a finite four hours every day. Feeling the voltage, every muscle tensed. In my own private war, I battled with mind over body yet together, both elements writhed in unison, reaching toward a final end. I hungered for the simple social interaction of touching another person, to feel the flesh of another without the psychological torture of being deemed a misfit.

In the next twenty minutes, I would talk to God, sing, cuss, wail, twitch, and beg for mercy for the procedure to be over. When it finally was, the process of removing one hand to turn the machine off always resulted in a mild electric shock. I reflexively collapsed in the chair, relieved and grateful that it was over for now.

In that precious window, my typical day began. So as not to lose time, I quickly slipped on my preset clothes draped over the chair. As an added precaution, I poured a tablespoon of aluminum chloride in the palm of my hand and distributed it as though it were lotion, slipped on the plastic sheaths disguised by fashionable gloves. All meetings, social gatherings, anything that had to do with shaking hands would have to happen in the confines of those four hours. It was truly a Cinderella existence.

For a time I endured this austere way of living. But after keeping this up for such an extended time, as my hands prematurely aged, I wondered how much longer I could hang on.

Fate answered that question none too soon, delivering Tom, the Marlboro Man, to my front door. Wearing a possum-lined leather coat, Tom flew up five flights of stairs, showing off his machismo with a gift of a massive boom box on his shoulder. Before long, I discovered that this blue-eyed light-haired Celtic rogue loved every imperfect misfit inch of me.

Everything he did was Texan-esque, humongous, gargantuan. BIG! From leasing the loudest Eldorado Cadillac in yellow to ordering Magnum-sized everything. Slightly perspiring, looking like John Travolta in *Saturday Night Fever* with his shirt unbuttoned one too many buttons, he set the box down on the surface of my tub and said, "Everybody needs tunes."

I rarely invited others over out of a embarrassment. But Tom just came unannounced and gave me no choice. Once inside, he never showed one modicum of disapproval. It could have been a palace. It just didn't matter to him. I decided right there and then that I would eventually marry this man not just because of a boom box but because I believed he really cared about me. Love had nothing to do with it; it had everything to do with acceptance.

A year later, we moved into a studio apartment on the Upper West Side. Tom wanted me to meet his mother, Harriet, a retired nurse and mother of five. Tom, the oldest child, told me one story after another as we drove to her home, coincidentally in Maine. I was intrigued to meet this woman, originally from New Jersey, who was working in an emergency room when her adolescent son, Tom, was rushed in covered with blood after running through a plate-glass door. I marveled at the fortitude Harriet must have possessed to function under such duress. We liked each other instantly. Harriet was nothing like I had imagined. She had a full head of short cropped white hair and was standing in the breezeway, waiting in anticipation. I breathed a sigh of relief. It was the unspoken word, what we didn't say, that we understood between us as women.

Harriet's mother, Millie Hruska Worley, a razor-sharp businesswoman with a theatrical likeness to Mae West, owned a home in the prominent community of Rumson, New Jersey. Millie had lofty plans for her daughter, grooming her to be a debutante and exposing her to the best of the best. But at seventeen, Harriet chose a simpler path, falling in love and marrying an Irishman who worked in a cannery.

One of the things I could appreciate in my adulthood about being a former foster child was that there was no family to answer to or seek approval from. Unlike Harriet having to rebel or worrying about not living up to expectations, I never had any of those limitations. I sometimes witnessed affluent friends twist themselves into pretzels trying to meet every demand that was put upon them, resulting in stress and unhappiness. Where they had the security, they did not have the freedom to explore who they really were; rather, it was dictated to them. There was a familial protocol, a mandate to uphold the distinguished pedigree, forcing them to give up their artistic dreams—if they were to be a part of the inheritance. Many of my trust fund friends confided that they were kept from doing what they really wanted to do and keeping what company they truly wanted to keep.

Harriet and I talked about such observations, sitting for hours by her potbellied stove as snow fell outside, just the two of us, doing puzzles, knitting, and just shooting the breeze. I asked her, "How did you go from the pressures of working in the emergency room and raising five children to an old house in rural Maine?"

"Easy," she replied, and chalked it up to knowing what was right for her at the time.

After I had dreaded meeting the Scottish matriarch, my preconceived ideas turned out to be wrong. I didn't want to have to morph into another pleasing personality, an old habit from growing up as a ward of the state. I didn't want to adapt to meet anyone's approval. To my utter surprise, she couldn't have been more warm and accepting.

I would always appreciate her support that came during a rough period with Tom, after I had become pregnant with my daughter who I would name for Maya Plisetskaya, as I had promised myself so many years earlier. Harriet thought we should get married, although she understood my reservations about Tom when suddenly he went AWOL, a pattern that would continue. No explanations, no clues. He simply vanished into thin air. I had to keep on going.

Just before I really started to worry, a call came in from my manager, Millie Spencer, letting me know about a commercial audition starring Bill Cosby and famed percussionist Tito Puente. They needed dancers. You guessed it. There I was kicking up my heels to Tito's soulful rhythms with Maya in my belly.

When acting jobs appeared to be scarce, I went looking for whatever I could find, not selective, proud of my experience. I had worked as a wardrobe mistress, a dancer, a waitress, a lighting fixture salesperson, a vintage clothing vendor, an au pair, a model, a secretary, a Park Avenue Virginia Slims leaflet giveaway girl. I was that invisible person standing at every corner across America with a board strapped on the front and back of my body, hoping that out of the throngs of people passing me, someone would take my annoying leaflet or sample and wouldn't toss it in the trash until they turned the corner.

Later I would look into the eyes of my former self on Park Avenue, take the leaflet, and say thank you. It was a living for me and who are we to judge how a person tries to support herself? I never subscribed to segregating effort. If you tried, it counted. It all mattered.

With that attitude I promptly secured a temp job as a secretary for Sabena Airlines and got fired. Immediately following, I became an executive secretary at Chase Manhattan Bank for the Broker Dealer Division in the Wall Street district. Even when my boss, Douglas Anderson, stated without amendment, "You're a terrible typist," as I braced myself for the inevitable, he continued, "but your personality is good for office morale; you have leadership skills. Now learn how to type." He actually saw beyond my pregnancy and limited office skills. He was willing to give me a chance and that's all I needed.

To support myself and my child on the way, I had to have this job, even though I knew it would be baptism by fire to learn what it would take to keep my desk in the most famous financial district in the world.

But who would teach me? As usual, the answer didn't come the way I expected.

Stepping off the Staten Island Ferry with purpose, a blond pompadour, spike heels, and a skirt way too short and too tight was Anne Marie, my soon-to-be mentor, saving grace, and future office buddy. She taught me how to type and how to operate the latest high-tech equipment of the era. Snapping gum like nobody's business, Anne Marie's fingers undulated at lightning speed, like she was Rachmaninoff himself. How could I ever learn to do that? Practice, practice, and more practice. Not that I ever tickled the computer keys like she did, but I got good enough to make a living and keep my job.

Still unable to make rent and not willing to wait for another shoe to drop, I turned to Sarah Neece, my former ballet mistress with Contemporary Ballet Company of New York, a company in which I had danced and toured in my post ABT years. Without reservation, she took me in to live with her in one of the most enchanting spaces in all of Manhattan. Secretly tucked behind an apartment building facing Fourteenth Street sat a Hansel and Gretel carriage house, complete with its own private garden entrance. This became my home for a brief and magical period during my pregnancy.

As a quote attributed to Lewis Mumford has it, "Let us confess it, the human situation is always desperate." I needed a lifeline. In a time of crisis, Sarah was there for me, creating a haven in her home that I would commemorate by sending her two dozen yellow roses every Christmas henceforth. This ritual was born over a decade and a half ago when I stayed with her, as she and I walked home together from our respective jobs and noticed a solitary street florist, who then tried to sell us his last two bunches of roses. Challenging times would not permit me to purchase Sarah a Christmas gift that year, but I knew she loved flowers—another common thread of the many women who raised me—and I told the near frozen florist, "I'll take both bunches."

When we got back to Sarah's carriage house, she filled her bathtub a quarter of the way with tepid water and after clipping the ends of the stems she gently placed the Candelabra roses into the bath. I'd never seen anything like this before. Such care and tenderness for cheap roses bought on a street corner.

I asked Sarah, "Why all the ceremony?"

She answered, "Just watch."

Very slowly, the revived blooms began to gain strength. I was in awe at what a simple act of kindness could produce, even for a flower, even for me. The two dozen roses sat in a place of honor in front of her leaded-glass window. Continuing in the holiday spirit, we hung her infamous Texan chili pepper Christmas lights, setting fresh pine saplings purchased from the Union Square farmer's market throughout the carriage house. Listening to Ella Fitzgerald, we reminisced about our friend David Cuevas, a painfully beautiful American Ballet Theater dancer who had succumbed to AIDS. By the late 1980s so many of our cherished friends had fallen or were about to. A natural moment of silence followed with just Ella's voice echoing what was in our souls.

Flowers typically adorned the interior of Sarah's home, which was chock-full of heirlooms, furniture, silver, books, and deer hide fur throws—vestiges of the family wealth and privilege that she had inherited from her father's tremendous success as a tract housing developer after World War II. Jack Neece built houses from San Diego to Los Angeles until the 1950s. When Sarah was eight, her mother suddenly died, and she was soon sent to boarding school. Eight years later, Sarah's father died, leaving her and her brother orphans.

Describing her boarding-school experiences, she once told me, "I was raised by cocker spaniels, 'get home by dark,' and just enough toast." After graduating from Sarah Lawrence College, she went to work as an apprentice at LaJolla Playhouse in San Diego during the summer of 1963, starting out as a dresser to the stars. I was enraptured by the stories Sarah told of her life outside of ballet; before this stay, I'd only known her as my benevolent ballet mistress. More and more I understood that when a body stands before you, that's not all there is to it.

She had worked for everyone from Ginger Rogers to Howard Duff when she was asked to interview for none other than Paramount Studio's London import, by way of Alabama, Tallulah Bankhead. I remember how transfixed I was as a child when I saw her in Hitchcock's *Lifeboat*. That voice, that hair, that sensuality. After Sarah's interview with Ms. Bankhead, there was a poignant silence before she was informed that the job was hers. The two hit it off instantaneously.

At 6:30 Tallulah would arrive at the theater and was quite talkative, but once the clock struck 7:00, she uttered not one more word and you better not ask her a question that required an answer. They worked in complete silence, only communicating with their eyes. Not a hair on Tallulah's head was ever out of place and for good reason. On the eve of opening night for *Milk Train*, Tallulah asked Sarah—whom she renamed "Sally"—to wash her hair. Sarah, eager to do well, said, "Sure," then she realized the shampoo wasn't shampoo at all, it was Energine lighter fluid. Tallulah explained that when she saturated her hair with the flammable liquid, before it evaporated, she could style her tresses into her signature page boy wave to perfection.

At the vanity, Sarah held a candle snuffer over a flame and melted the wax. Tallulah would dip her orange stick and expertly stroke each lash, giving it a bead at the end. Every night Sarah would stand in the wings and watch with amazement at what she called "zinger moments."

It was no secret that Tallulah was a smoker; in fact, she smoked right down to her fingertips, often burning the flesh so badly, she couldn't use her fingers at all. It was little known that each evening, backstage, Sarah placed a glove in her beloved Tallulah's mouth to muffle her cries from the acute pain she felt while rings were removed during costume changes.

"That's where the real learning began, *on the road*," Sarah recalled. On tour, she met the likes of Tennessee Williams, David Merrick, Tab Hunter, Bobby Dean Hooks, Conrad Rooks, Marion Fields, director Tom Richardson, and composer Rodion Shchedrin. Sarah, once wanting to be an actress, thought twice about the profession and decided, "If this could happen to Tallulah, as strong as I knew she was . . . what would become of me?" So Sarah pursued a career in classical ballet. I don't know if that was an easier road, but it was her choice to try.

It occurred to me that we each were finishing in the profession the other began.

Propped up on her hand-carved daybed, I watched one of her Burmese cats, Ditty-Boo, scamper and play with the cascading ribbons of her pointe shoes drying on the radiator. A service tray sat on my lap at a distance with my ever-growing stomach preceding it. Sarah served her signature pork chops and spinach soufflé, then fed a movie of old Hollywood vintage into her VCR, a film I inevitably fell asleep watching.

My sleep was a deep sleep, the kind of sleep that when my head hit the pillow it was the very last thing I could have done for the day. Sarah provided that safe zone where it was okay to fall asleep, in which I didn't have to be or do anything other than rest. In the morning, she would tell me what I missed as we both set off for work—me to Wall Street and her to the ballet studio.

The best gift she endowed to me was the certainty that I would survive this passage. After all, she reminded me, "Nothing is more intimidating than doing a double pirouette onstage at the Met!" Sarah was right about that. I had nothing but respect and admiration for this Texan, who intrepidly changed the course of her life and saved mine.

Sarah Neece was transformational in allowing me to grow, to nurture myself while preparing to bring a new life into the world, and to save enough money to rent my own apartment. Just as it was time to fly the coop, Tom resurfaced, wanting to make up for lost time, determined to prove himself.

I was ambivalent. I had already begun to think about moving to California, where the signs were starting to point, and had nearly reconciled myself to single parenthood. Tom's mother wrote me a persuasive letter, insisting:

Living in California is not necessary, if you want to stay in New York.
Surely, if you love each other, you can work it out. I, if anyone, know
how Tom can be, but I know he loves you and if it's possible he will do
what he has to do to keep you.

So, with Harriet's encouragement, at nine months pregnant, I put my
hand in Tom's and took the train with him to city hall. I wore a floral
muumuu; my feet were too swollen for anything but white Keds. The
train screeched its way toward the justice of the peace, carrying a
would-be bride and groom and an unsuspecting Iranian couple who
would be our witnesses. We returned the favor.

⁓

My relationship with Tom's mother deepened after I gave birth to my
daughter, Maya, in 1989 at Lenox Hill Hospital in New York City. While
recuperating, I contracted staphylococcus, causing such extreme illness
that I was written up in a medical journal. For nearly one month I remained in the hospital while my infant daughter went home with Tom
and her grandmother. I was devastated by the turn of events as there
was not a second during my pregnancy that I didn't enjoy motherhood.
There was an enormous opportunity waiting in the balance for me to
break the cycle of abandonment once and for all. Oddly enough there
was a parallel, a reenactment of what had happened to me and Dorothy.
Who could explain an anomaly recurring in two generations? No one.
My breasts fully engorged with mother's milk, desperately wanting to
feed my baby, I had to come to terms of the seriousness of my condition
and that it would prevent me from nursing completely. The silver lining
was that this circumstance allowed father and daughter to bond at such a
primal level that no matter what ups and downs Tom and I would have in
the future, their father-daughter relationship was forever secure.

Blankly staring out of the hospital window at a brick wall, pumping
my milk, I knew a nurse would collect and discard, I decided to take a

sip of my own elixir. I was utterly shocked by its sweet taste and more so by its effect. I became the baby. At thirty years of age, I tasted my own mother's milk and in that process finished what Dorothy would have done if she could have. There was never a second during my pregnancy that I experienced fear about becoming a mother. The women who had raised me gave the best possible preparation for being handed the torch. I realized Tom came into my life for the purpose of giving me life through motherhood.

Under a doctor's strict supervision I was finally discharged from the hospital and allowed to return to our studio apartment, more cramped than ever with six-foot-two Tom, a newborn, baby accoutrements, a mother-in-law, and a hospice refrigerator stocked with antibiotics. Still on portable intravenous fluids and atrophied, I bonded with Maya. I was able to nurture her as well as myself with Harriet's maternal guidance. Parenthood anchored me.

Accepting that life was never perfect and rarely manifested according to my own or other people's preconceptions, I felt happier than anyone could understand to finally be a part of a family, to be a Mrs. Somebody. That happiness was multiplied exponentially by Maya, who was, according to everyone (in addition to me), the most gorgeous baby girl in the world. Born under the water sign Cancer, gentle and nurturing, Maya, was an old soul. Only one other time would I feel this kind of love and that would be with the arrival six years later of my son, Jasper. My children would teach me and raise me and later share their childhoods, supplanting the one I had lost.

Even emerging from natal waters, Maya had the features of my mother's English lineage with what I saw as ancient African wisdom rooted in her by her maternal grandfather. Looking into her mystic blue eyes, I tried to fathom who this miraculous soul was. I would very often recall the words of an otherwise innocuous woman who approached me on the street when I was pregnant and said, "The child on the way will bring you good luck."

With Maya asleep in one arm, I reach for the phone with the other. It's Spencer & Kearney. Irene says, "There's an audition for *The Cosby Show*. Oh, by the way, how's motherhood?"

This of course meant, Was I ready to work and had I trimmed down from the one hundred and sixty plus pounds I had weighed? The request had come from Bill Cosby himself, who hadn't forgotten my situation.

After booking the job, there I was, on my way to rehearsal at Astoria Studios in Queens, where the show was produced—the very same location where a decade earlier I had shot that surreal dream sequence as a dancer in my ill-fated film debut in *Hair* and my even less successful audition for *The Cotton Club*. Not for the first time in my life, I experienced the truth of the adage "You can run a hundred miles and end up at your front door." No matter what had happened in the interim, that first intoxicating glimpse behind the scenes of moviemaking had never left me. I was excited about the coincidence, otherwise calm and confident, though there was a vague gnawing in the back of my mind that I had forgotten something in the flurry of getting ready that morning.

All went seamlessly for most of the rehearsal until Mr. Cosby said that he had a note to give me, before asking for my hand as he reached out his toward me.

That's when I remembered what it was. Oh my God. My gloves—I had forgotten them. I had no gloves. The dreaded moment had come. During my pregnancy, I had to let go of the entire hyperhidrosis ritual. As I had done so many times before, I did the inappropriate but face-saving substitution for a handshake, offering a hug. Anything to avoid hand-to-hand contact. My arms were swung out wide in hug preparation for Mr. Cosby.

"No, no," Mr. Cosby said, "your hand." He extended his hand to me a second time.

This time, I put my hand in his. I had developed a special way of cupping my hand, hollowing out the palm so as to diminish its grotesque nature.

As he held it for the duration of his note, I could not hear anything he said. My senses could only register the sight of his lips moving and then the cool air that came between his hand and mine—revealing my long-held secret.

He looked at me, clearly puzzled, then said out loud as he wiped his hand against the marble table, "Snails . . . she has snails for hands."

There was nothing I could do to cover as I shrank into myself and bowed my head in shame. Trying to be constructive, Bill advised me to take more acting lessons if I was that nervous, to which I could only nod and mutter a thank you.

That dreaded moment had come and gone. Though I survived, I prayed that I could one day explain my circumstances to Mr. Cosby. My consolation was the fact that my work on the show was part of the catapult that would bring me and my family out to Los Angeles, where a stable acting career would begin. But I couldn't bear the thought of ever going through anything like that again.

I had to do something.

⁓

Before saying good-bye to the Big Apple, Tom and I drove to Maine with Maya for her first visit with her paternal great-grandmother, Millicent Hruska Worley. Millie, as everyone lovingly called her, had a thiry-acre estate. One thing was for sure: Millie had worked hard for everything she had, including Millie's, her popular bar in upscale Rumson, New Jersey. The well-attended bar was a popular watering hole for a wide range of customers, well-to-do New Yorkers, politicians, and even a few cads.

One particular evening, when an inebriated customer got familiar with Millie, she looked him dead in the eye and said, "Do that again, and I'll cut your balls off and shove them down your throat." She was no shrinking violet. I loved the dichotomy of Millie: Annie Oakley one moment, Emily Post the next.

Loving everything that had to do with a Rolls-Royce, diamonds, furs, art, and strong influential men, the thrice-divorced Millie married an Exxon executive. This platinum blonde was irrefutably a grande dame who loved theater in every sense. Even her country kitchen was fitted with an imposing crystal chandelier. A gal after my own heart, she and I got along famously. Millie doted on Maya and could not get over the remarkable resemblance her great-granddaughter and her daughter Harriet shared. Millie had an attic space filled to the gills with truly remarkable costumes. Buried beneath the elaborate evening gowns, fur stoles, shoes, purses, capes, and, of course, jewelry was a box of photographs she found. Inside it was a picture of Harriet as a baby that bore such a striking resemblance to Maya that whenever people saw it they inquired, "Is that Maya?" The only thing that gave the photograph away was its age.

Millie was thrilled that I appreciated all her knickknacks and keepsakes. She gave me permission to decorate and rearrange whenever I came to visit. Though she wanted Maya to have some of her history, that wouldn't come to pass until after her death some years later when we had moved to Los Angeles.

As families can be mysterious in their actions, at that point I made a simple inquiry about Millie's estate and asked if Maya might have some remembrance of her great-grandmother. My reply was an inheritance of six Tiffany demitasse spoons. Upon further investigation, I learned there would be a little-known public auction.

After some intense sleuthing, I rose early on a Saturday morning to make my first bid by phone on a short list of Millie's antiques that, for some unknown reason, Harriet put up for auction without notifying anyone, not even her family. It meant everything to me to salvage these few heirlooms that held Millie's legacy for my daughter. As I had been denied any tangible fragment of my mother's history, Maya would not suffer this fate. It was unconscionable that Millie's prized nineteenth-century candelabra, silver-engraved trumpet vase, inlaid trays, and ubiquitous flask would be lost to strangers forever. Not on my watch, if I could help it. The auction began. My heart pounding, I bid fiercely, completely at the mercy of the liaison on the other end of the phone. I could hear the volley of counterbids in the background. Putting no limit on my determination to secure Maya's keepsakes, I won everything I bid on. The last and most important item of Millie's lot were her candelabra. A hush fell over the room as the auctioneer described their exquisite beauty. I transported myself back to Millie's dining room, filled with china, crystal, and silver, and accented with a Japanese garden scene. I carefully set the candelabra on an ebony credenza, admiring their fragile grace.

On the other end of the receiver I heard, "Ms. Rowell, I need your opening bid." The flurry of activity was over as quickly as it started. I not only won back the candelabra but also was victorious at breaking another cycle. If I could show up for my mother at her private funeral, then surely I could show up for my daughter and what was inherently her birthright.

New in Hollywood and living in a motel with a newborn, I waited for Tom to truck across country in a U-Haul with everything we owned. Upon his arrival, as he downed a beer, I asked, "Where are my antiques, my desk and dresser?" He replied, "You didn't want that old junk. I left it in New York." Drama! We gave drama a whole new meaning. A gig in daytime drama would be a cinch.

Landing a series regular role on *The Young and the Restless* was a stroke of lasting fortune. The truth of the matter was, having a day job gave me structure and a consistent income. It also gave me the security of medical and dental insurance for my family and me. When I received my first *Young and Restless*/SONY/Bell Television check, I smiled. I knew, just as energy could beget energy, that work itself was a magnet, begetting more opportunities. My first spring in California was full of fertile promise, set against the backdrop of palm trees with no water towers to destruct my view. There were endless days without rain, none with snow. New sights and smells were everywhere, from the tropical mix of greenery to the rich fragrance of a canopy of violet blossoms I found myself under one afternoon. But as to my ultimate success or failure in Hollywood, I knew that it was going to be determined by whether or not I could overcome one major stumbling block. Out of all the lessons I learned from Spencer & Kearney, there was one thing they couldn't teach me to do that was an absolute necessity in Los Angeles: *drive*.

I was thirty-one years old and had avoided learning how to drive all this time because of the fact that Agatha had been forbidden to drive by her husband, Robert. I had to get a grip and realize that the ban had been on her driving, not mine, and that had been a half century ago in Maine, not 1990 in the tropical climate of Hollywood.

In a last-ditch effort to avoid the inevitable, I resorted to hiring a chauffeur to get me around town for auditions and anything else that required driving. This was no ordinary driver. Her name was Lahaina Kamilah Coquelin, formerly married to New York City's revolutionary night club entrepreneur of Le Club, Cheetah, Hippopotamus fame, Olivier Coquelin. The same gorgeous woman who had wanted to show me her leopard cubs when I visited Haiti many lifetimes ago, Lahaina was indisputably the most beautiful woman in the world and had been the toast of New York, after apparently bewitching Olivier.

She had almond eyes so large they were almost alien. Her skin had a hue of obsidian stone and not a single imperfection. Her aura was completely serene, like a child without a care in the world. Though she had once been trapped in her gilded cage, or so it had seemed to me, she had gone through a bitter divorce, leaving her without her posh Manhattan penthouse, two Yorkshire terriers, the Picasso, and the surreal opulence that had been her reality with Olivier Coquelin. Vestiges that she kept reminiscent of that period were an enormous diamond ring, an heirloom brooch, once belonging to her mother-in-law and that I could speculate was nineteenth-century or older, and a portrait of herself sitting in a chair flanked by full-grown leopards—no longer cubs.

Transplanted to Los Angeles and needing a car, she left her diamond ring as collateral for a used Toyota Corrolla. She needed an income and so, in exchange for a fee, she accepted my offer as a pseudodriver for the time being. Remarkably, there was never a hint of superiority or resentment from her. We both knew we now needed each other and had come a long way from speedboats, escargot, and big cats. Lahaina needed cash and I needed wheels. It worked.

Lahaina drove me to auditions and meetings and showed me how to understand the complexities of getting around L.A. freeways and back-streets. She taught me how to read the "yellow pages of maps," *The Thomas Guide*. As an aspiring actress herself, she knew the lay of the land, what opportunities to count on, which ones to avoid.

I couldn't have had a better teacher. Before long, facing down my fear, I forced myself to learn to drive, something that turned out to be not at all mysterious, and was ultimately an empowering, liberating experience. Rolling on at my own pace, in the slower right lane of the freeway, I now understood the driving metaphor that defined life in Southern California. The reputation for laid-back and casual that Hollywood was supposed to have in comparison to New York was deceptive. In truth, everyone was even more in a rush to make it into the fast lane than anyone I'd seen in New York. The only thing we did faster in NYC was walk and talk. Sure, fast and flashy could be fun, but I preferred the speed limit for now. I looked at traffic like a huge corps de ballet, the freeway being its stage.

For reasons that had less to do with my success and more to do with the part of Tom's world and life that I knew little about, he continued to go missing in action more often than not. His multifaceted legal and financial complications mushroomed from one day to the next. It failed to amuse me that nothing on the soap opera on which I acted by day could ever approach the drama that was unfolding in my personal life by nightfall. With my skill for keeping secrets, not one person at work had an inkling as to what was transpiring on the home front: settling legal disputes and raising a baby.

After testifying in court, I knew, as he did, that a divorce was immanent. Either way, I couldn't afford Tom, emotionally or financially. Because he had accepted all of me, hyperhidosis and all, and because we shared a child together meant that I would always care for him, no matter what. When Tom eventually got back on his feet, he structured his life around being a committed father and making Maya a top priority.

All that happened in the span of a year. I came home from work one evening, said goodnight to the sitter, and collapsed in Tom's left-behind baby blue crushed velvet La-Z-Boy. I flipped on the television and absentmindedly listened to the evening news while folding laundry. Consequently, what I heard next resulted in my dropping the laundry as I raced for a pad and paper. I scribbled the information as fast as I could about preeminent neurologist Dr. Martin Cooper's hyperhidrosis procedure, then called the television station to no avail.

At first, my efforts to be seen by Dr. Cooper were for naught. His office insisted that the waiting list was at least six months long, not to mention that the risks outweighed the potential. How could I have explained to a stranger that vanity meant little or nothing when you desired human touch? What I did explain was that the opportunity to have a consultation with Dr. Cooper would be the chance of a lifetime. I was granted my request.

The moment I walked into the examining room, I made my decision, trusting the essence of Martin Cooper implicitly. He wanted me to be very sure, first by making me understand the procedure, which required me to sit perpendicular under anesthesia while holes would be drilled into my temples and two rods inserted to maintain complete immobility. A lung would then be navigated in order to sever a nerve through my back that controlled the hyperhidrosis.

Obviously undaunted by the disclosure of these particulars, I told Dr. Cooper that I wanted to schedule the surgery as soon as possible. Dr. Cooper again reminded me of the risks, especially the possibility of facial paralysis. He continued, explaining that I would be in intensive care for one week and that the pain would be so intense I would need to be on a morphine drip.

Holding back tears, not revealing my foster past, I simply said, "I am thirty-one years old, and all of my life I have been afraid to touch people and allow them to touch me back."

Before surgery I wrote the letter to Bill Cosby that had been in my heart to write for some time, first telling him about my recent work with Whoopi Goldberg and Will Smith, among others, then going to note:

> *In our last phone conversation you referred to something I believe that occurred the last time I appeared on the show. If you recall I had horribly sweaty hands and thank God you didn't want to hold my feet . . . I was terribly embarrassed because of it and felt that you made mention of acting classes not for technique but to enhance possibly my confidence. I don't perspire due to lack of confidence but due to a disorder I've had all of my life called hyperhidrosis, which is an abnormality caused by a nerve (ganglion) in the spinal region.*
>
> *Over the years I have tried just about everything on the market with only marginal results. I knew of the surgery, but to find a neurosurgeon who specializes in this disorder was another story. Quite by accident I have found one (Dr. Martin Cooper) and am scheduled for surgery on December 7, 1990, at Cedar-Sinai Hospital.*
>
> *Enclosed is a tape that better describes the procedure and a letter written by a woman who has undergone the surgery.*
>
> *All of the information might seem excessive but I don't want the hyperhidrosis mistaken for lack of confidence. This is something I've told very few people—it is confidential.*
>
> *Looking forward to shaking your hand after December 7.*

When the day for the surgery arrived, Tom joined me out of support and continued to tell me, "I like your hands just the way they are Vic." For a moment I became apprehensive, not of the possibility that some medical mishap might occur, but of its success, its removal of my protective shield.

In the twilight of going under anesthesia, I gently reassured myself that it was time to be touched in a meaningful, fundamental way. Time to break another cycle, time for Victoria to take care of little Vicki by not abandoning the core of her being. No more secrets. No more hiding. I would be all right.

Moments later, or so I imagined, I opened my eyes in recovery, tentative about my new self. With the soothing music of operating room machines clicking away, I wondered how long I'd be allowed to stay in this amazingly serene state of floatation. For now, I would have to enjoy and bask in this feeling, even if it was through a morphine drip, even if I would extend it with the pills that would follow. Even if I would have to face the consequences later.

TEN

THE SISTERS WHO TAUGHT ME

The operation was a complete success. I carefully placed my trusty bottle of aluminum chloride and iontophoresis machine in a box for posterity.

I was emboldened to stretch further and higher than I ever had before, as I came to fiercely love my independence while accepting the inspiration and support that came from my various surrogate sisters. Friends, colleagues, and peers—some had been in my life in earlier eras, and others were new sisters. No matter how low life laid my soul, I never felt abandoned. These grounded women who carried the mantle of their forerunners in my life reminded me often of what Alice Walker wrote in *The Color Purple*, "Is solace anywhere more comforting than that of a sister?"

Demonstrating that love by example, and sometimes by confrontation, they each helped to keep my feet on the ground and eyes on the prize. More important, these sisters were teachers, providing me with life lessons that, in the final analysis, changed my life forever, and saved it.

Part of this was possible because without the protective shield that hyperhidrosis had given me, my relationships deepened. I didn't have to carry all the secrets anymore. I was even able to start sharing more with others about the challenges of growing up as a foster child.

Within months of my return to work after surgery, I did something that I'd been promising myself to do since I was eighteen and had made my first ten-dollar contribution as a patron of the arts—I founded the Rowell Foster Children Positive Plan, a charity focused on providing scholarships in the arts and higher education to foster and adoptive children. For years, I would run the charity out of my home, before obtaining office space in the Department of Children and Family Services building in Los Angeles.

From the beginning of my work on *The Young and the Restless,* the creator, William Bell Sr., and I developed a special bond. We appreciated hard work and working together. After he had done so much to gain my trust, I shared with Bill my love of dance and how helpful having that anchor had been for me when I was growing up in foster care. I never could have imagined his reaction. He ingeniously penned a customized story that wove my passion for ballet and acting all into one. It was the first time that my actual ballet technique proved valuable in an acting capacity. The blending of two performance arts I loved equally into one charged moment. It was atomic! William Bell understood as I did that work was what you made of it wherever you stood.

When Bill Bell asked me to stay on his show, knowing the high attrition rate for daytime actors going off to work only in feature films and/or prime-time television, I promised him I wouldn't leave as long as he was there. Instead, we found ways of allowing me to do it all.

In 1991, for example, I asked Bill if he would consider collaborating with producer Leonard Goldberg, to iron out some sticking points so that I might be able to work opposite Eddie Murphy, in Disney's *The Distinguished Gentleman.* He smiled and said, "Leonard and I are old friends. I'll give him a call."

That was followed by an even bigger request to Bill Bell that required the collaborative effort of then Columbia Broadcasting Systems;

the senior executive director, Jeff Sagansky; the former executive director of ABC Television, Fred Silverman; and the producer Dean Hargrove and VIACOM. The focus for this effort was, in a name, Dick
Van Dyke, the personification of excellence and elegance. I had the
privilege of working with this master of contortion, song, and dance for
eight years on *Diagnosis Murder,* a show loved by a generation of people
who didn't fit into the specifics of America's coveted demographic for
advertising dollars.

When I was pregnant with my son, Jasper, and working on two
shows, Dick surprised me with the gift of a beautiful wooden crib. As
an executive producer, he gave me another gift. It was the nod of approval to stretch not only as an actress but as a writer. Membership in
the Writers Guild of America was on the horizon. I cowrote a script
about what I knew by telling the story of a Chinese dancer leaving
everything behind—an entire family—for a dream. Ballet was more
than dance for so many, whether we lived in America or not. It was a
passport to a better way of life.

From the outset, it was me and the boys hammering out a way to
cohesively make *all* of the work, work! And we did. I would go on to
break television history as the first actor to consecutively perform on
two shows for six years in two different mediums—daytime and prime
time. My incentive? Owning my own home. Unquestionably, this was
my window to lay down tracks, to be autonomous, and to build a financial foundation to become a proprietor just the way Agatha, Ruthie,
Millie, Barbara, Sylvia, Esther, and so many other women had taught
me to do.

The 1923 Italian-villa-style house allowed me, at long last, to permanently unpack all the cherished gifts that I'd been towing behind me
for so many years. Later, through a major renovation, I would restore
the house to its full splendor—in tribute to the influences of the many
women who had raised me. In the meantime, their gifts to me were very
much on display. There was nothing like the feeling of moving in to
stay. There was nothing like knowing I finally had an heirloom to pass

on to my children. Walking out on my terrazzo, I thanked all the women who taught me how to pray as only women know how. I looked at the yard where I could cultivate my own garden and thanked Mother Earth. I'm home, finally, and it's beautiful here.

One of the first social events I hosted at my home was a garden party fund-raiser for the Rowell Foster Children Positive Plan. When I started to put the elements together, since I was still getting my feet wet in the nonprofit arena, I employed the services of political fund-raising veteran Maryann Maloney. As this was to be my first West Coast fund-raising event, my hope was to reach out to Bill Bell. Nervous and not sure what the protocol was to make a financial request and one from a boss who had already given me so much, I had no idea how to begin. Maryann promised to guide me through the process.

Sitting uncomfortably in Bill's well-appointed office on Beverly Boulevard, I told him why I thought the event was important and how it would help foster and adopted children in Los Angeles.

Before any guidance was needed, Bill looked at me with his ice blue eyes and asked, "Do you need fifteen or fifty thousand?"

I nearly fell off my chair. Bill revealed something that I'd never known about him, that his sister, Mary, born with a severe cleft palate, had been a foster child. His mother, Gertrude "Trudy" Bell, had taken an interest in the little girl and provided the funds for the surgery and later adopted Mary.

Of all the connections I had to Bill, this was probably the single most important one. It meant the world that he had decided to tell me about his sister after the years we had known each other, especially in the context of my coming to him with a funding request.

William Bell graciously underwrote my first garden party for the Rowell Foster Children's Positive Plan. Wynton performed, and it was a huge success. The event was attended by Representative Diane Watson, Dick Van Dyke, the Honorable Michael Nash, the Annie E. Casey Foundation director, Douglas Nelson, who would later appoint me as Casey's Family Service's National Spokesperson for Foster Care and

Adoption, people from the Los Angeles Department of Children's and Family Services, and many other celebrities, important representatives, and organizations. How far Agatha had carried me from our mock tea party the first time we met when I was two years old in Gray, Maine.

Through a network of fellow activists and child advocates, I found myself with an expanding sisterhood that brought me the inspiration and education of women like Pat Gempel, one of the founders of HOPE Worldwide, an organization dedicated to global relief. Before getting to know her, I couldn't imagine how she maintained the stamina to take on so much, championing the needs of abandoned and orphaned children in the United States, Africa, Russia, and India, working to support her hospital in Cambodia, along with all of the global relief she did for AIDS through HOPEWorldwide. What drove her? I wondered.

While in Philadelphia, where I had flown to help with her charity event, I received some insight when she invited me to lunch. I knew this was serious because Pat doesn't have time to take people to lunch. We sat in a lovely civilized café at the National Museum of Philadelphia. She, clearly uncomfortable, told me that there was something she wanted to tell me for a long time. In uncharacteristic fashion, tears filled her eyes as she said, "I gave my own daughter up for adoption a long time ago."

Instantly, I loved Pat more. I sat across from her as she wiped her alabaster face with her napkin. Her tears represented so many mothers' tears. There was no embracing, no holding of hands. We just let time pass between us before speaking again. Then I said, "It's all right; I understand," and proceeded to tell her about my own mother.

In the oddest of ways, one person's suffering is another's salvation. Dorothy, in her absence, was teaching me what compassion really meant.

Pat and I got to know each other more through other events, including a Christmas celebration in east Philly, where "the Rev," tactical and proactive, cared enough to care about the forgotten. "The Rev" dressed up as Santa, I as Mrs. Claus, and Pat as herself, in order for the three of us to pass out wrapped gifts. The crowds were so great and families in such need that the police had to be called to maintain order. I would never forget feeling the desperation of hands reaching, reaching, and reaching again, some coming up empty-handed.

When Pat called me one day, not long after I moved into my home, and invited me to accompany her on a trip to Russia, I leapt at the offer, deciding that I would take advantage of time off and take Maya with me. Travel fed me on every level—allowing me to carry on the tradition of the travelers who raised me, like Agatha, Esther, and Paulina—and also was a passion I would instill in my children.

This trip to Russia not only helped me realize a lifelong dream but was eye-opening in terms of how fortunate we are as Americans. ABT prima ballerina Nina Ananiashvili escorted me on a personal tour of the Bolshoi School and the Bolshoi Theatre, after which I was invited to sit at legendary Maya Plisetskaya's vanity. Several rotations of the wheel had come full circle. With incredible joy, I relived my memory of seeing my first full-length ballet performed by the Bolshoi in Boston and of witnessing Maya's heart-stopping performance. Now I could share with my daughter a sense of the greatness for whom she had been named. When we visited Saint Petersburg, seeing the Kirov was another pinnacle for me. So many of my Russian and Eastern European mentors had glided across these stages that I had read and heard about since the age of nine. Amazing.

Before leaving Moscow, Pat Gempel, a woman on a mission, took me and Maya to a circus orphanage she supported just outside of the city. Each child was required to learn a circus act. The children put on a special performance and amazed me with their level of ability. On the drive back to the hotel, an unshakable melancholy came over me, as I looked out the window at the gray buildings set against the gray sky and thought of orphans everywhere, tucked away, forgotten. In that moment, the only redeemable light I could glean was the knowledge that even in a circus orphanage, there was hope in the children's faces for a future.

The power of ballet to transform young lives was a national tradition that went back more than two hundred years to 1773, when the Trusteeship Council of the Moscow Orphanage decided to provide ballet classes for orphans, whom they referred to as inmates. A former dancer with the Saint Petersburg Court Theater Council, Filippo Beccari, volunteered his services as an instructor and exceeded expectations. The children wanted to learn how to dance. Out of his sixty-two pupils, an astonishing twenty-four became soloists. The Moscow Orphanage resoundingly became the mecca of ballet training in Russia and provided dancers to its Ballet Theatre.

Pat, a role model of a surrogate sister, saw for herself how the trip had reinforced my desire to do more to empower children and youth through the arts. She must have known that when she called the next time to ask, "Hey, Vicki, want to go to Africa to visit my AIDS clinic in Abidjan?" that I would find a way to negotiate my work schedule to make it happen. South Africa Airlines, here I come.

With the certainty of African soil under my feet, I eagerly anticipated stepping into the rich history of South Africa. Once settled in my hotel located on the Victoria and Alfred Waterfront inspired by Prince Alfred in the 1800s, I took in the verdant majesty of Cape Town, boasting over fourteen hundred species of plants. The subtle fragrance of the flowers, like the jacaranda, was unforgettable.

Rather than be a typical tourist, I hired a local tour guide, who provided clientele like me an opportunity to experience Cape Town and beyond by foot. I peered into a dilapidated clapboard one-room building where passbooks were once issued to natives of South Africa, granting them permission to work in Cape Town before the end of Apartheid. I emphatically told the dreadlocked tour guide that there had to be a way to preserve the building as a historic landmark.

He replied, "They want to tear it down." We walked farther into the village, where I was welcomed by a host of families into their homes. Each home smelled of burning fuel so pungent I thought I'd pass out. But the warmth that exuded from the women in their individual shanties tending to their families was infectious. Where were their men? I wondered. Where were the fathers of these children? The guide told me that finding jobs in Cape Town was difficult, therefore forcing the men to seek work miles and miles away from home for extended periods of time. Many women suffered the consequences of these long separations, later resulting in contracting HIV. The highest population of people succumbing to AIDS (acquired immunodeficiency syndrome) today are women on the continent of Africa and their sisters in America.

As the sun fell behind Table Mountain, I prayed for tomorrow to come swiftly, as I had reserved a chopper to carry me to Robben Eiland, Dutch for "seal island," also known as Robben Island. In 1991, Robben Island Prison had closed its doors forever but had reopened as a museum under President Nelson Mandela's administration and the South African Natural Heritage Programme. It was something I had to see to understand what Madiba had lived through. I also wanted to get a glimpse of a rare migrant seabird, the Caspian tern, flying free against the South Atlantic Ocean, protected against further extinction. Yes, that would be in keeping with my interests in ecological oases. But the greater purpose was to connect to Mandela, Madiba, through this geography and history.

At dawn, I was awakened by my first mother, Africa. She bathed me with her sunlight and fed me with the fruits of her labor and sent me into the world to see more of what her altruistic beauty had in store. Energized, I ran with her love to the heliport, only to collide with a very frantic American photographer. He immediately asked if I would forfeit my helicopter, whereupon I replied, "It's my last day in Cape Town, and I must see Robben Island." He gave me a blank stare and said, "No one can get on the island today without credentials. Nelson

Mandela and Arnold Schwarzenegger are lighting the torch for the Special Olympics this morning." The photographer had missed the boat that took security and crew earlier and was desperate. I said, "Okay, take it." He and his crew looked at one another, perhaps expecting a different reply, then he turned back to me asking, "Do you know anything about photography?"

Should I err on the side of complete honesty? As I stared at the multiple cameras that swung from their shoulders, outfitted with mile-long lenses staring back at me, why, it was a bit intimidating. But I was a photographer. It may not have been with a Leica but it was all I needed to record time between time. Never lost on me was Agatha's philosophy that if there wasn't a photograph, it never happened. I had been taking pictures since I could remember, and Gordon Parks was my hero. It was my way of keeping a personal diary. So I replied, "A little."

"How about being my assistant? It's the only way you'll get onto Robben Island today."

I was excited beyond words; the historic significance of the day ahead was palpable. Into the chopper we filed, lifted into an uncharted stratosphere. Not only was I going to see Nelson Rolihlahla Mandela, I was going to work side by side with Francesco Scavullo's former protégé, Dee Swanson.

Through a veil of dust churned up by the chopper's whirling blades, I could see the infamous penal facility. We landed. The security was extremely tight. Once I was approved, I joined the photography team and entered what felt more like a sanctuary than a prison. It was very quiet; only the echo of our footsteps could be heard as we followed the guard deeper into the austere prison. Deep-rooted suffering left behind could still be felt. The guard abruptly stopped and slipped the worn key into the lock. The heavy iron door was pushed open. The key was placed in the photographer's hand, and once the guard disappeared, Swanson placed it into mine, for safekeeping, as he and his crew left to scout another part of the prison. I stood there, in the middle of Madiba's cramped cell, alone, motionless, with history in my hand. How did he survive it? I dropped to the cement floor, face up, with my arms and legs outstretched, making angels as I did as a child in the snows of Maine. It was all I could offer up for his suffering.

The moment had arrived. Security plowed through the crowd, warning people to make way. But who could stay back? Mandela was magnetic. Noticeably fatigued, with two attendants steadying his impressive physique, he made his way to the makeshift dais and made his address to the overflowing press corps and guests. How lucky I was to be there.

On the grounds of what had imprisoned his body but not his mind, on his own volition, stood President Nelson Mandela, one of the most celebrated leaders of all time. The evil of apartheid implored each and every one of us to look to ourselves to bring change, no matter what the circumstance. At the end of his passionate address he said, "You have to turn tragedy into triumph."

The applause was deafening. How could I not try harder? With that, he turned and lit the Special Olympics torch with the assistance of Arnold Schwarzenegger, his wife, Maria Shriver, and her brother, Timothy P. Shriver.

I couldn't help but admire the dedication the Kennedy-Shriver family publicly exhibited with the leadership of their mother, Eunice Kennedy Shriver, founder of the Special Olympics, formerly Camp Shriver, in 1962, in tribute to her beloved sister, Rose Marie "Rosemary" Kennedy. American royalty changed the compass in me forever that day, reinforcing the idea that it was important to embrace all of our population, all members of our families, regardless of the disorders, disabilities, or differences that characterized them; it was a major release for me to realize that I didn't have to live in shame over my mother's mental illness.

In talking to Timothy Shriver, who served as executive director of the Special Olympics, I was gratified when he invited me to become more involved and handed me his business card.

In time between time, those moments between moments when miracles happen, Mandela's eyes met mine as he was leaving. With his long arms draped over his attendants' shoulders, he pointed his left index finger to me. I touched it, accepting his energy, saying silently to myself—*Father of all fathers, thank you, thank you for drawing me to this place, nearly ten thousand miles away from what has become my home.*

Mother Africa provided a seat for me at the most splendorous banquet table of all, feasting on forgiveness and remembrance, the fall of apartheid and witnessing the *father of all fathers*, lighting a torch in the name of mental illness. So many victories were celebrated in a single morning, through one remarkable man and the bravery of so many others. I left the island full as I sailed back to the mainland, holding on to Mandela's words with Dorothy in my heart, floating like a jacaranda seed away toward Côte d'Ivoire, Abidjan.

When I arrived in Abidjan, Pat Gempel was there to pick me up, ready and waiting with her no-frills, no-nonsense warmth.

When Pat took me to the market, I was struck by seeing so many familiar faces in Abidjan. I saw my Agatha with a basket on her head, Aunt Barbara and Aunt Joan selling fabric, Uncle Richie with a machete slicing coconuts. All their faces were permanently sealed on the west coast of Africa because that is where their ancestors had originally come from. These were the distant mothers, sisters, aunts of so many of the women who had raised me.

I continued on my journey the next day to Pat's day clinic for AIDS patients. Once there, I was greeted by the Harvard graduate who had given up his illustrious career as a doctor in the States. He led me to a makeshift infirmary where a woman lay prostrate, in absolute stillness. Her effort could only be spent on moving her sunken eyes in acknowledgment of us in the little room where other mothers were waiting to die. I sat next to her and held her hand as the doctor described the need to expand the clinic. As I left with Pat beside me, I asked the doctor what would become of the woman I was with. He replied, "A local nun will take her to a resting place. She will be gone in a week."

Heading back to America, with a heavy but fully determined heart, I took hope and courage from the friend that Pat Gempel had become, and knew that I would look to her for guidance in the balance that must come between caring for others and for ourselves. A friend, a sister, she had helped reunite me with my lost family, giving me the gift that I would always remember of that incomparable voyage, that woman's eyes in the AIDS clinic, the air, the merciful beauty of Mother Africa.

I was back in the Hollywood grind. Culture shock with a capital "C." On those occasions when I ran myself ragged, I would reach out to a core group of my sisters/mentors/advisers. Colleen Atwood was one of them. Colleen, who was on her way to Oscar gold, for *Chicago* and *Memoirs of a Geisha*, and juggling numerous projects while being a dutiful mother, epitomized that fundamental principle I had first learned from Agatha Armstead: Diligence pays off.

Back during the days when she so generously housed me in her New York apartment, I marveled at how Colleen could simultaneously study for her union entrance exam, perfect her design sketches, and beautify our meager surroundings on West Eighty-first Street in Manhattan.

"Vicki," she announced to me one evening, "what do you think is under here?" as she tapped the linoleum underneath her foot. I answered, "The only way to know is to find out."

A beat ahead of me, Colleen led the way as we began peeling and scraping every lick of old linoleum off the floor. Though we caught glimmers, like pieces of a jigsaw puzzle coming together, we really didn't know the answer to just what was beneath until the whole was revealed. Finally, we beheld the gift—beautiful, naturally preserved, planked wood. That's what we had both been trying to establish in our professional lives. A foundation on which to build. Colleen may not have consciously thought up that demonstration for my benefit, but the metaphor was an heirloom passed on to me just like the bestowal of a single piece of nineteenth-century Limoge I proudly display in my home today, ever the reminder to look beneath the surface.

Like Colleen, other sisters who pursued careers in the arts inspired me to raise the bar. Prima ballerina assoluta Susan Jaffe had done so from the moment we became friends in our earliest days at American Ballet Theatre School and Ballet Repertory Company. Susan broke the mold, making it possible to be authentic and individual even within the rigidity of ballet's strict requirements. She accomplished this masterfully by being boldly sensual, adding a touch of earth to her ethereal grace, all the while embodying purity at every level with a sense of humor. I witnessed her evolution, from the pressures of being groomed to be a soloist to becoming an understudy for legendary Gelsey Kirkland. This was compounded by the uncertainty that the call might never come or that it could come at any time.

But the call did come, and Susan rose to meet the challenge. Maybe it was the shattering loss of her mother at a young age that built the alpha resilience to face any monumental circumstance thereafter. That once-in-a-lifetime opportunity to step up to the plate and into the lead role of Clara in Tchaikovsky's *Nutcracker* had arrived. She was partnered by a man who most believed to be the greatest danseur of all time, Mikhail Baryshnikov. She dazzled a critical Lincoln Center audience expecting to see Kirkland. Knowing that fate could manifest such things, how could I not be ready for opportunities when they came my way? Preparation was for free.

Two decades later, we both had aged imperceptibly from that bicentennial year, studying with Madame Pereyaslavec, Leon Danileon, and Patricia Wilde at the American Ballet Theatre School. After an extraordinary twenty-two years as a principal dancer with ABT, Susan would take her final bow, dancing the title role of Giselle at the Metropolitan Opera House in New York City.

I wouldn't have missed her last performance for the world. It signified the beginning and the end of an era. Many curtain calls later, I navigated my way backstage, a place I hadn't been to in as many years as Susan had been dancing professionally. There was Susan among all of her well-wishers and endless bouquets of roses. The surprise on her face was priceless when she saw me. She was the apex, the spire

I would have wanted to reach had I stayed in the classical ballet world, but I had no regrets. Susan, upon retirement from the stage, cofounded the Princeton School of Ballet and Theatre in conjunction with Princeton University. Susan Jaffe, deservedly so, had ascended to become one in the pantheon of great dancers; already leaving a mark on ballet forever.

The career advice that manager Irene Kearney had given to me years earlier about "letting that ballet thing go" had yielded a harvest of success. Still, letting ballet go entirely would have been impossible, like abandoning a child or forgetting my native language. When I first stopped dancing as a way of life, I went through my own mourning process. For many dancers, or athletes for that matter, the sudden loss of self when they no longer live to perform can be akin to facing an abyss of uncertainty. My dear friend, colleague, and sister Kimberly Von Brandenstein, a fellow dancer from my post-ABT years, wrote me in the early 1980s after just starting NYU. She would attain an art degree and, after marrying and becoming the proud mother of twins, would go on to teach art at Princeton University. She captured the times well:

> *I decided in June or July that I had danced my last step professionally. You can imagine how troubling a decision that was for me. I loved to dance so very much. It makes up a lot of me. . . . By not being able to dance last year (due to a back injury) I was forced to broaden my scope and realize that new and wonderful horizons were open to me.*
>
> *Days go by and I wonder about my dear Vicki and the very first time we met . . . our gin and tonics and Morelli's [dance studio] and City Center . . . I smile a bittersweet smile. How I'd love to go back in time three years and do it all again. But, alas, the future awaits us and we still have so much to share! Colleen Atwood tells me of your new ventures (acting).*
>
> *Vicki, my deepest love to you and your well-being. You will always remain one of the brightest stars in the sky!*

Patricia Knight—whose friendship and sisterhood went back to Cambridge and Carol Jordan's insistence on the power of muscle tone—maintained her connection to ballet by taking class for no other reason than it made her feel good to do so. After Patti became an executive at the *Boston Globe,* I happened to tell her how I had never forgotten those years of receiving Christmas gifts from *Globe* Santa, a charity effort undertaken by the *Boston Globe.* As a child, I eagerly looked forward to the presents provided by *Globe* Santa.

Along the way, I found the balance and the peace to embrace that part of me that was and will always be a dancer. Dance would remain la dolce vita, the sweet life. I could use it, be it, anywhere I would go. Ballet was enmeshed in my cells, in my identity, as enduring as the importance of a first love. To honor that, I would take a class periodically, but not in any rigid or scheduled way, and occasionally perform and conduct master classes.

As someone who grew up belonging to many families, early in my acting career I was fortunate to make a handful of lasting friendships—starting with Kasi Lemmons, a colleague and sister who bore an uncanny and striking resemblance to me. Or so had been the rumor back in my early days of acting in New York City when casting directors and fellow actors kept talking about sightings of me that couldn't have happened. From later reports, it seemed that Kasi was constantly being stopped on the street by strangers calling her by my name, almost as frequently as I had a different set of strangers greeting me by her name.

My take on this after a while was that whoever this Kasi Lemmons was, no two people could possibly look that much alike. That was until I arrived at an audition and saw, signing in with the casting assistant, my long-lost twin. We both did double takes. Built similarly, with the same heart-shaped faces, and almost exactly the same coloring, we absolutely could have been related. Just as I pointed at her asking, "Kasi?" she pointed at me, asking, "Victoria?"

From that meeting on, although we were in competition for roles, often taking turns booking them, we established a lasting wonderful friendship based on common bonds that we found went much deeper than our physical likenesses. Kasi had gone through a lot of parallel instability in childhood that included her parents' divorce and being raised primarily by her mother. Interestingly enough, though she was originally from St. Louis, she had grown up in Newton, Massachusetts, and had found an outlet through professional training and performing with a Boston theater school.

As we talked about the many neighborhoods and the different worlds we both inhabited in the Boston area, we were amazed that we had never met before. Just as ballet had been my sole trajectory, Kasi had always been single-minded in her acting focus. But in the early 1990s, as we both bit on the Hollywood lure, Kasi decided to switch gears and to focus on establishing herself as a leading filmmaker—as a screenwriter and director. This didn't come totally out of the blue as she had gone to NYU School of Social Research and had already made an award-winning documentary on homelessness. What took me by surprise was her conscious decision not to pursue acting during the period that she was trying to have the Hollywood boys' club take her filmmaking seriously.

As it happened, I was presented with an opportunity for us to play sisters and thought immediately of Kasi. But when I told her, in essence, that the job was hers, she graciously declined. At first, I was baffled. This was saying no to a plum acting part and excellent pay.

Kasi explained patiently that to prove herself to the establishment and to even attempt to create rich, complicated stories and characters in film, especially women's roles, she had to be seen as doing only that. Once this made sense, I was in awe. Moreover, it affirmed the choice I'd made to let go of the ballet barre and to focus on becoming a working actress. The truth is, as I learned from Kasi, we can't always do everything. Definitely not at the same time.

Kasi's focused approach worked spectacularly when her debut feature film, *Eve's Bayou*, which she wrote and directed, made her the first African American female filmmaker to have a major studio distribute her work. Besides the opportunity that I had to play one of the several fascinating women's roles in the movie, I was so proud of the depth and artistry of Kasi's filmic storytelling.

Whenever I stepped out of the creative lane that I was supposed to stay in, Kasi would also encourage me in a very no-nonsense way. Whether it was tackling a writing project, making a documentary, or upsetting the status quo with undertakings related to my charity, her position was always, "Vicki, you can do this."

Was she going to walk me through it? Whenever she could, Kasi lifted my soul by believing in me. I respected her as an artist, mother, a wife, and as a person. The generosity of her investment in our friendship was all the more poignant because she wouldn't do anything she didn't believe absolutely in.

For the rough patches ahead, I held on to Kasi in every way I could. She was heroic, when I didn't always feel heroic.

I would never have to work a day in my life if I had a nickel for every time I heard my sisters wistfully wish they could just talk to their men in the heartfelt, open manner in which women could always talk to other women. That's never been my desire, however, because I figured out a long time ago that if we could talk to men the same way we talk to each other, as women we would lose one of our most important topics of mutual interest: namely, *men*!

My closest female confidantes hashed out the tumultuous sagas of our love lives together. Selfishly I leaned on them and they leaned on me—because we knew we could. Not one of my sisters was stick furniture—by that I mean, I could actually lean and nothing ever broke. The way that Agatha raised me was to depend on home remedies and avoid hospitals, except for real emergencies. Agatha was biased against the idea of psychological therapy and airing personal strife. As is common in many households, Ma's approach was that penance and pain were synonymous with God: and that was the only therapist anyone needed; if you had to go see anyone with M.D. after their name that meant you were a little special.

⁓

This was a heavy cross to bear for my sisters and me, given that we were already navigating the schizophrenic complexities of dealing with foster care. In adulthood, after conducting a successful search, simply by using the white pages, I reunited all five of my siblings, leasing a Victorian house on Peaks Island in Maine for a weekend. This forum gave each of us the opportunity to courageously show up, look each other squarely in the eye, and break bread, now with our own children playing in the backdrop. Sharing one mother, each of us of different paternity, we could finally determine in this intimate setting whether our relationships would flourish or not. The result: you have to be prepared for an unfavorable response; not everyone wants to face the excruciating pain of learning about one's familial reality. We continued to live very different and separate lives, forever connected by that extraordinary weekend, assembled by the transcendental will of one woman, Dorothy, our mother, a mother of Maine.

⁓

How was it possible that the woman today, now pulling guns and slamming grown men against cement walls, was the same fragile blond-haired child that lay limp in Agatha's arms as she ran to the nearest neighbor, a third of a mile away for a ride to the hospital? My sister, near suffocation, was allergic to goldenrod. In response to the chaos and uncertainty of foster care, Lori had amazed me when she became a policewoman and then a forensic photographer. That was the force of Lori's will, a coping mechanism so singular that she followed one methodical, procedural focused line—from which there would be no veering and no adaptation. She followed her training too well, in fact, because that arrest actually injured her and caused her to be moved to a desk job in the forensics lab as a photographer. Nonetheless, her bravery in the line of duty made me proud, especially because I knew what Lori had to overcome. With that same cool unflappable singular focus, she married and became a mother to four daughters, with the only remaining allergy being her inability to accept any deviations from the set order of things.

Lori, now married for more than two decades, had her own way of dealing in the realm of emotional intimacy. Understanding her helped me know myself better. My sister also helped prepare me to encounter the many individuals, male and female, who were so much like her in not being able to deviate one millimeter from a set plan.

Miraculously, the loving affirmation that I'd always wanted and had never received from Lori came in an indirect form on one occasion when she took me to visit the crime lab where she worked. There was a real sense of pride as she introduced me around to her colleagues, who welcomed me as if she had talked about me more than she'd let on. I, too, felt incredibly prideful to see her in her element.

As the visit was coming to conclusion, I happened to notice bolts of cotton high on a shelf. They reminded me of my years in ballet when I used to pad my blistered toes against the friction of my pointe shoes. I turned to Lori and said excitedly, "That's what I used as cushioning to stand on pointe." Lori, rolling her eyes, as if to say, *Vicki, Still my weird, artsy-fartsy sister,* corrected me, saying, "That's just plain old cotton we use for bullet testing."

She had made her point. In earlier times I might have been affected by her remark, but over the years I had learned to acknowledge that the differences in our relationship were perfect.

What was perfect with both Lori and Sheree was that we had attained a level of fierce independence, honesty, and a no-frills reality in our sisterhood. We didn't have to pretend, or take each other to lunch, give one another gifts, remember birthdays, or talk frequently to make us feel like we were sisters. We knew it in the way Agatha sucked marrow out of a bone. No fat, no gristle, just a bone-to-bone relationship. We didn't have to prove anything to anybody and certainly not to one another. We didn't even need to have the approval of our respective choices in men, either.

Of the three of us, Sheree got the shortest end of the stick, most of all because early on she was pegged as the troubled one and had that beaten into her by Raymond Armstead. To this day I am haunted by the reverberation of the slat and plastered walls at our farmhouse in Maine, as Sheree was thrown against them. Her crime was coming home past curfew or sassing Ma. When I cowered in the kitchen and looked at Agatha, I realized that she knew she'd created a monster by enlisting him to dole out punishment, which she always regretted. Not once did I hear Sheree cry. I never stopped feeling guilty for not doing more to stop that abuse, not that Sheree ever blamed me.

It didn't surprise me that my sister struggled in relationships; we both did, often staying in abusive situations simply because the fear of being alone was too great. Once, when I received a phone call from Sheree describing a problem she was having with her second husband, I realized her situation was more serious than I thought. I offered to cover the expenses of a divorce. She told me to mind my own business, that she would handle it. I knew then that my oldest sister, the warrior of Puerto Rican and English descent, had been unquestionably scarred by the abuse she had endured as a child and into her teenage years. I realized that no matter if you came from the same womb, all aren't given the same innate fortitude to break a cycle. How can you break something that feels familiar, that you believe is all you deserve? Like many of us, it was important to Sheree to be Mrs. Somebody and she didn't always have the ability to say, "Enough is enough and too much is foolish." Meanwhile, the fact that she had already traveled parts of the world as a military wife, raising a son in the process, was extraordinary—a measure of her refusal to be a casualty of abuse and chaos that she had endured.

What were the chances that at this climactic moment in my life, in the anticipation of falling in love, I would meet a man who not only had no intention of falling in love, but would love only one woman, one muse—his trumpet. Silence. Hear the purity of that solo trumpet note bending up into the cosmos, then back down to earth. Powerful, lonely, sensual, manly, soulful, mysterious, angry, wise. Explosive, tender. Hearing Wynton's incomparable virtuosity as he played Hummel's Concerto for Trumpet in E Major blending into Satchmo's "Do You Know What It Means to Miss New Orleans?" colliding with "Big Train," which Wynton composed in honor of our son, Jasper Armstrong.

Falling in love was not in Wynton's plans, in spite of a secretive romance that ensued. With a son and three thousand miles between us, I tried to accept life on his terms. No photographs, and on the rare occasion that we would be seen publicly there would be no displays of affection.

As Pablo Picasso was quoted as saying, "Women are either goddesses or doormats," and I somehow managed to become both in order to maintain any semblance of a relationship. Both with dominant personalities, we had come a long way since our first date, meeting at the Lincoln Center Fountain—he in Nike gym attire, and me in my best dress.

To be in his life you had to accept life on his terms, which I didn't always do. It wasn't long before it became crystal clear to me that this was an all-or-nothing deal in Wynton's favor. I thought I could convince myself to accept this situation—boarding planes, trains, and automobiles, meeting at various destinations. Off and on for five years, my last stop would be Kansas.

Wynton and I emerged from a thorny period, both of us agreeing to compromise, he becoming a paragon of fatherhood in raising Jasper.

"Son, you stole my face," Wynton would often affectionately say to Jasper, his spitting image. The duo often spent quality and quantity time together, touring South America and Europe and RVing across the United States. On one of the occasions that Wynton gave a lecture-demonstration at Jasper's school, Wynton told the student body, "There is tolerance and then there is embracing." Looking right at me he asked, "Do you know the difference?"

As the lesson from all my sisters continued to prove, no relationships were perfect.

If it seemed that I managed to survive my first attempt to love fearlessly and fully, don't pin any awards on me just yet. Unable to face that I was exhausted from overworking, I tried to banish any unpleasant feelings by self-medicating in a variety of ways, and depending on my own prescription of champagne, sage, and rosary beads.

I had just run a marathon, completing two shows, the equivalent of fourteen consecutive years. Instead of feeling celebratory, I felt threadbare and utterly spent. Rallying for me was a cherished friend running her own long-distance race.

I met Lizette McBride in the early 1990s. She stepped into my point of view like a model strutting down a Parisian runway—radiant, graceful, perfectly coiffed, with the most meticulous manicure and pedicure I'd ever seen. Her looks happened to be familiar in Hollywood settings but unlike some of the women who turn themselves into brittle beings offering hollow hugs punctuated with stone breasts, Lizette was the antithesis of that.

Her story had some overlaps to mine, which I learned gradually as I watched her overhaul her life, not once but several times. A self-help Zen master with lightning wit, book smarts, and a sociology major from Lehman College in the Bronx, Lizette was originally from Atlanta, Georgia, and had been raised by a single mother. Family gatherings included raging fights, lots of alcohol consumption, and the drama of TVs sent flying out of living room windows.

Not too long after we met, at the threshold of rebuilding her life

as a single woman, she opened up a nail salon in Beverly Hills, a phenomenal success not only because she was a terrific nail technician
but additionally because of the wisdom, humor, empathy, and insight
she imparted. I told Lizette that she should be charging everyone
double.

Over my nails and her take on my love life, I admitted that I admired that she had gone to college, one of my few regrets.

Lizette was proud that she had opted for higher education instead of
the modeling career that had been offered to her when she went to New
York. Why hadn't she been tempted to model? Because, she laughed, "I
didn't want to eat a French fry and a cigarette for lunch every day."

Her next significant transformation was announced a short while
later when I arrived at the salon and before I could say, "Hey, Lizette!"
and give her a warm hug, she headed me off at the pass saying, "I need
to ask you not to call me Lizette anymore."

"What do you mean? I love your name, it's one of the most beautiful names in the world!"

She said, "If you value our friendship, you will call me Madisonn."

This was not going to be easy. I already had a block against remembering names, and Lizette had rolled off my tongue so melodically for
some time. M's were difficult for me as I was sometimes caught off
guard by a childhood stutter. Nonetheless, after several months of
practice, I adapted to the musicality of Madisonn McBride.

Besides teaching me how inherently we all have the ability to transform our own lives and names if we so choose, Madisonn delivered to
my listening ears the *Reader's Digest* abbreviated version of the volumes and volumes of books on self-help and philosophy that she read
by the truckloads. She was my very own in-house Deepak Chopra,
motivational consultant. It was illuminating to understand why she
chose to divorce her husband, because, as she said, trust had been broken and trust was the foundation for all relationships. "You can't build a
house from the second floor up." The other reason she chose divorce
rather than a reconciliation was her sense that she had lost herself in her

husband. "I went from loving him to worshiping him. I was no longer me." The lesson learned: "Overwatering a plant can kill it."

Madisonn eventually gave up her salon to become a feng shui consultant and to have the time to raise her niece. No matter where she was in her journey of working on herself, she remained devoted spectacularly to exploration, to soul searching and never being satisfied with a pat answer. As Madisonn put it, "You get what you vibrate."

Along the road to that realization were some profound ruts. Overwhelming sadness altered her body during a mourning period that followed the end of her marriage, despite her efforts to sidestep negativity. Watching Madisonn rapidly gain as much as a hundred pounds, I asked her point-blank, "What are you doing?" As her sister, I couldn't pretend that this wasn't happening, that no matter how many fabulous Prada wraps she wore, this was now a health issue.

Instead of being defensive, Madisonn allowed me to work with her, to try to find a release. We went to boot camp together, talked for hours about ex-husbands, significant others, known and unknown fathers we still loved. She came to my workshops, I went to hers. We learned about the second chakra near a woman's root center and breathed away vulnerabilities that were said to cause fibroids. We talked about the importance of anger and shouting, not holding in the pain, so that we might do everything in our power to keep our breasts. We discussed the false protective shield that extra weight provides. We cried, we laughed, and cried some more.

Madisonn gave me the rare gift of allowing me to be there for her, as she had been there for me when I was in my darkest hour. I was able to witness the pivotal moment in her liberation.

Her epiphany was that there could be no physical change, no matter how many spin classes or boot camp hours she put herself through, without the commitment of a psychological shift. It came to her one day while we were working out when she said, out of the blue, "I'll never steal second if my foot stays on first."

That was the start. From there, Madisonn slowly reclaimed her power, slowly losing the weight, which she finally understood was her way of trying to care for herself instead of everyone else. Like relationships, there are no perfect solutions for weight loss, just hard work.

Yet too many women work too hard taking care of everyone but themselves, only to try and give themselves that nurturing and love through quick fixes that are ultimately destructive. Madisonn gained a fondness for saying, "Truth sometimes has no nourishment," but that we all needed to hear it from our closest friends—the sisters who carried her through her divorce and weight crises. Similarly, when I felt myself slipping down into an episode of depression that I allowed myself to acknowledge, my support system held me closer and I knew I wasn't alone.

Madisonn's take-home lesson for avoiding those pitfalls was summed up in a pithy quote she put on her fridge, which read, "Busters, losers and the extremely wounded, please stay away . . . I'm a goddess not a nurse."

ELEVEN

Dolores Marsalis &
LaTanya Richardson Jackson

We now approach what is without question the hardest passage of my life to revisit, but so necessary for tribute to be fully paid to everyone who raised me over the years—especially two extraordinary women, Dolores Marsalis and LaTanya Richardson Jackson, who rose to the call at this juncture and intervened as angels when my soul lay at its lowest.

Dolores and her New Orleans home had welcomed me open-armed during the seventh month of my pregnancy with Jasper, who would become her sixth grandchild.

Exuding formidable strength and wisdom, the remarkably youthful-looking Dolores Ferdinand Marsalis reminded me in many ways of Agatha Armstead, with her abundance of maternal warmth, a similarly determined gait, and an ability to do many things exceedingly well all at the same time. Dolores graduated from Grambling State University where she flourished in home economics and journalism, writing for the school paper.

After marrying Ellis, she became a volunteer in social work and a substitute teacher. She returned to college after raising her six children, attending Virginia Commonwealth University, working on her master's in social work.

Her culinary gifts were amazing. Everything was farm fresh, from the crawfish to the vegetables, even the seasonings. The étouffée was made to perfection—Dolores cooked with love and I could taste every bit of it. She had that Wooten-esque flair about her, reminding me of those remarkable women.

Though she was reminiscent of many of the women who were part of the lineage of women who raised me, Dolores Marsalis was very much one of a kind, with a signature brand of honesty that I respected. Speaking her mind bluntly, whether it was about politics, art, or religion, she did not hold back her opinion. If you asked her a question, she would give you an answer and not always the one you wanted to hear.

Those were only some of the qualities she employed to retain her confidence and power as a woman surrounded by such strong, sometimes demanding, distinctive men—her husband, Ellis, and their six sons.

While Ellis, one of New Orleans's most revered jazz pianists and teachers, would be given credit for instilling music fundamentals into the Marsalis boys, Delores was undoubtedly the reason they were so prolific. She did more in one day than some people do in a month. If she wasn't spearheading support appeals for the New Orleans College for the Arts, she was working on a fund-raiser with the Sisters of Charity-Sisters of the Holy Family, the second community of African American religious Catholic women in the United States, founded by Henriette Delille, taking her vows in 1851. Dolores went on to tell me how many black nuns were not allowed in the church or to receive communion, pre-civil rights; instead, they would stand outside the church to hear the service.

Family trumped all. Celebrity was the least important of attainments in a household that reflected how much everyone counted in her sphere. Presented in photography and keepsakes everywhere I looked was a chronicle of the past, of this exceptional woman and her family. Everyone was represented equally in her collections, regardless of whether Wynton and Branford may have earned more public name recognition. Several lifetimes of sheet music were a reminder of the years of music lessons that were a Marsalis mainstay. Rites of passage were celebrated with everything from Boy Scout badges to a Grammy award that sat next to photographs of her grandchildren. Stories abounded over hearty meals prepared at the drop of a hat for bands rolling into town, giggin' and showing up late for Dolores's gumbo.

On my first visit, as I was ushered into her kitchen, Dolores's mother, Leona Learson, a Creole beauty in her nineties, nodded in welcome, and Dolores's fifth son, Mboya, greeted me with a quick smile. Dolores never complained about caring for her aging mother or the demands of raising a severely autistic adult son. Her attitude was that rising to the call of caring for loved ones was a blessing.

When the question arose about which bedroom was for guests, Dolores asserted, "Your bags are already in the master bedroom, you'll sleep more comfortably in there."

Before I could argue that I couldn't possibly take her bedroom, she gave me a look that was everything I needed to hear. There was no arguing with this powerhouse. The rush of emotion that I felt being treated as a member of the family was only exceeded by the surprise that awaited me in the bedroom. It was the sweetest baby crib, adorned with every conceivable infant-friendly accoutrement, made up and waiting for her future grandson's arrival.

It must have occurred to Dolores that there was no maternal grandmother to welcome my children into the world and why her gift meant so much. Though I again tried to tell her that she was much too generous, Dolores stopped me to say, "I have done this for every one of my daughters-in-law and I consider you to be the same."

How could I not adore her from that moment on? The first eighteen years of my life I had come with that word *foster* attached to me like a shadow, a qualification that described my legal status and restricted my relationships to others. I was a divorcée with one child and another on the way, with no plans of marrying. Yet Dolores Marsalis, staunch Catholic that she was, was not going to dismiss or diminish my worth based on legal standing.

As night fell, I readied myself for bed. Through an ajar door that opened to a dimly lit hallway, I saw Dolores leading her son Mboya, on demi-pointe, toward his bedroom. She tucked him into bed, as she had every night for the past twenty-seven years, and moments later I heard her toss a "Good night, sugar, everything's going to be fine" over her shoulder, which made its familiar way to me as well.

As time and other visits went on, I learned that Dolores and I had more in common than first suspected, at times making us feel like sisters and kindred spirits. We talked about the pressures of wearing different hats, about family, about the rewards of activism on behalf of causes we championed, and about the men who were and weren't in our lives. Born and bred right there in New Orleans, Dolores was a little girl who grew up fatherless.

We both acknowledged that the pain of the fatherless void was not a figment of imagination. Despite not having a father figure, she had found and held on to love in a marriage that would last fifty years and counting.

"The secret? Give and take," she said. Being flexible and having forgiveness weren't easy and could require colossal strength.

As if a part of me knew that I was readying to go through another rite of passage toward a fuller emancipation, I kept that advice close to my heart. What stayed with me like a grounding wire, most importantly, was the vibration and steadiness of her voice, a reminder that "Everything was going to be fine."

As I entered my forties, on the whole I felt plain, grateful for work, for motherhood, sisterhood, for sanity to have a means of serving through my own charity and in collaboration with others. But in the summer of my forty-second year, an overly active sympathy nerve started twitching, not with hyperhidrosis but with a sense of power-lessness at preventing the hurt that was out there.

Passing thousands of cars every day on the freeway, with every slow roll soon followed by an unwelcome stop, I invariably caught an image of someone in my rearview mirror or my periphery and sensed danger. In each instance, I wondered who was hidden in the back of that car, what child was being left behind or taken against his or her will. I couldn't stop thinking of unprotected children, seeing them buried in dirt holes, tied up, stolen as sex slaves, or stuffed into youth correctional facilities, beings forgotten. To escape a child predator, for any child, would be to run for the rest of his or her life toward safety.

I never stopped thinking about those children and never stopped wanting to do more. My own children and my role as their mother continued to stabilize me, as did the work of my charity, which had grown phenomenally with the support of national sponsors, major me-dia campaigns, and leading philanthropists who championed for foster care and adoption. But the ever-growing pandemic of foster care made me feel like I wasn't doing enough. It shouldn't have surprised me that the more influential I became as a national spokesperson for foster care and adoption, the more opposition I earned from entrenched non-profits who did things differently and who obviously saw me as an in-truder on their political turf.

There was no more apparent display of this sentiment than when I received a call from my RFCPP office informing me that I was not needed for National Adoption Day in Washington, D.C., on Sep-tember 10, 2001. This made absolutely no sense as my travel ar-rangements had already been discussed before I had left for travel abroad.

Upon my return, I received another call, this time by way of a folded piece of paper I found with no name on it. I called the unfamiliar number and a young adoptee living in New Hampshire answered the phone. She said excitedly, "Do you remember me? We met on a talk show in New York." Indeed I did remember her. She wanted to make sure that I would be in the capital for the festivities as she would be singing. I assured her that wild horses couldn't keep me away. Immediately following, I began to wonder who these people were who didn't want me there and why. Upon further inquiry I was told that the nonprofit in charge chose its own celebrity. I was aghast and replied, "I am not driven by celebrity; this is my life." The next thing that was said trumped the first: "But, Vicki, you were never adopted."

Was that to say that if you didn't get adopted, you didn't count? Was that to say that the same children these society ladies were professing pride for would one day be punished for exceeding preconceived expectations, the way they attempted to exclude me? This was beyond comprehension. If only I could describe the looks of consternation on their faces when I showed up on the steps of the Capitol. Undeterred, I sat on the dais in a diminutive chair not matching the others and was forbidden to speak by the celebrity of the day, a politician's wife. Was my truth that threatening? Was it my pearls that Agatha taught me to wear or was it my hat and dress? Was it the diction I used that threw you? That I didn't look down at the ground when I spoke to you but looked directly in your eyes? Did you find my sheer will insubordinate, standing up to you and being counted with or without your approval? I couldn't begin to answer these questions. All I could do was forgive and hope they could forgive themselves.

I showed up on the Capitol steps the same way I showed up at Dorothy's funeral when I was not invited, with purpose. I honestly didn't care what others thought. Showing up was what you do because it's who you are and all you are. The same way I showed up at ballet class in Cambridge after being jumped and beaten up in the 'hood. The same as showing up in my own way by standing on my toes in a barn in my red Keds, one hand on a broken-down organ, the other holding a grain pail. That's what the women who raised me taught me to do . . . show up. That wealth cannot deny a person's truth.

The next morning I awoke to a national tragedy. On September 11, 2001, I was ordered into a hotel ballroom, where we were advised of the situation and presented options for travel. With all flights suspended I opted for Amtrak back to California. All that could be offered were the staff's quarters. I took it!

As I looked out across a beleaguered America I strung a flag I bought at Union Station across my bunk in a show of solidarity. I felt the same common bond I felt during the blizzard of 1978 in New York City. The phenomenon of strangers, kinder in crisis, helping one another. I wondered about those icy society ladies on that day; what were they doing?

In the months that followed, I soldiered on in my world, as mother, actress, and activist, but none of my old attempts at making everything fine seemed to work.

The controlled creative chaos of my overly busy life fell into chaos. I wanted off the ride. I was tired of being my own daddy. Tired of having to be the provider and strong leader. Tired of not having a mother.

I simply stopped. The phone rang. I was immobile. The weight of everything had caught up with me. I could not lift my head. For hours I lay in bed listening to my heartbeat and the pulsing truth of unnourished needs.

In that moment, it would have been effortless to morph into Dorothy; after all, I was an extension of her. Everyone would understand. All I had to do was declare my willingness to step over that fine line into her fragmented world.

In stillness, I repeated my childhood mantra: *I must never have six different children by six different men; I must never reveal Dorothy's secret.* Days went by, and I decided that the job of trying to cure my mother posthumously simply was not an option. I was dying in the process. I called for help.

In a quiet convent setting, I began healing for the first time in my life, under the guidance of a nun who preferred to work anonymously. I lived and worked in her home, tending the garden and myself at the same time.

In the weeks that followed, I thought often of a comment that had been made to me some years earlier by LaTanya Richardson Jackson, then a very close friend who evolved into much more—enlightened mentor, earth mother, and soul sister all in one, who would be there for me in my toughest, darkest days still to come.

"You know what, Vicki," she had said to me, in a voice that resonated with depth, wit, and downright brilliance, not to mention the Atlanta, Georgia, accent she'd never quite lost, "you work like a dark-skinned girl."

What she meant, I understood. In my most vulnerable, contorted state of mind, as I slogged it out in the trenches, while layer upon layer of self-applied bandages were ripped off like linoleum being stripped from an old floor, the knowledge that I had always worked hard was intact, such that remembering LaTanya's vote of confidence in me lifted an enormous weight off me.

LaTanya had seemingly appeared in a divine assignment in my garden in 1995, a stunning rose among many other beauties, radiantly shining above the rest. She herself was a hardworking woman, only one of the reasons that her husband, actor Samuel L. Jackson, was smitten with her when they first met while both were starting out in their respective acting careers. Standing in my backyard at an afternoon charity gathering, LaTanya so clearly owned her own skin, her femininity, her power, her razor-sharp intelligence, and rapt interest in supporting a cause that was obviously close to my heart.

For all the years that I had been in Hollywood and had established one community that was connected to my work and another community that was connected to activism, what I had yet to find was that family connection, that true belonging that I sought above all else. LaTanya, without being told, understood that, and in the ensuing years would frequently invite me and my children to be part of her family celebrations and holiday gatherings. At so many junctures, her generosity was medicinal.

My first Thanksgiving at LaTanya Jackson's glorious table, impeccably set with Wedgewood china and Waterford crystal, Towle silver, upon a Belgian lace tablecloth, was a concert of laughter and passionate, intellectual conversation—complete with her aunt Edna's cranberry Jell-O mold. This was the music of my soul, weaving together traditions from all the women who had raised me, with echoes of former foster mothers' Thanksgiving tables: Agatha's roast turkey, Esther's crystal and china, Rosa's collard greens, Sylvia's linens. The swirl of many cultures and many faiths rose up inside me, filling me with grace and a feeling of being at home, safe and loved with a daughter and son at my side who felt as I did.

Mysteriously, even though we had both been in New York at the same time, our paths had never crossed. LaTanya had graduated from Atlanta's Spelman College, the historically black all-women's school, with a B.A. in theater, before going on to earn a master's in drama from NYU. In the same years that I was beginning my scholarship at ABT, she was discovered by the visionary Joseph Papp, whose Public Theatre and New York Shakespeare Festival revolutionized world drama. Starring in several productions for Papp, LaTanya became the toast of the town when she starred in the Broadway run of Ntozake Shange's landmark *For Colored Girls Who Have Considered Suicide When the Rainbow Is Enuf.*

From there she was off to the races, performing with such companies as the Negro Ensemble Theater and the Manhattan Theatre Club during a fantastically fertile period for African American playwrights and drama in which she was a leading light. After marrying Sam in an Atlanta wedding ceremony attended by more than five hundred well-wishers, she made the inevitable leap to Hollywood, where initially it seemed that LaTanya would be offered the lion's share of work while Sam was slowly making a name for himself. In time, those positions changed, although she would continue to be revered in many circles as an actor's actor, working very consistently on the stage, in film, and in television with the slight luxury of being able to pick and choose projects, and even to try her hand at directing and producing.

Sacrifice for the betterment of family was a dominant theme in a long-running conversation that LaTanya and I held about where our goals and ambitions stopped and where those of loved ones began. I learned everything that I could about parenting from how she and Samuel raised their amazing daughter, Zōe, who would later become a Vassar graduate.

Though LaTanya and I had different realities and different priorities, we loved pampering ourselves just a little—in excursions that indulged our shared love for art, antiques, fashion, and travel—as we discussed juggling all the balls in the air we both had. If I thought that I was good at turning over every stone to find that diamond in the rough, LaTanya made me look like an amateur. She proved to have the eye of an eagle.

LaTanya paid her own form of homage to the women who raised her, most notably what had been taught by her grandmother—the sacred knowledge of roots in all the meanings of that word, how to tend a garden, how to grow, become resilient, and share the bounty of success with others. As an activist and philanthropist, serving as a trustee for Spelman College and on numerous boards for organizations in the arts, including Artists for a New South Africa, and many children's groups, which included my charity, LaTanya would continue to inspire and challenge me not to become bogged down in intraorganizational politics but to be about the work itself.

Returning to such undertakings was still not in my realm of acceptance as the hardest phase of life drew to a close. In the stillness and serenity of the cloistered setting, I had come to feel safe and clear. I had taken that foot off first and wanted to believe that I could steal second. The shift in my thinking was the solid knowledge that I was not my birth mother. But I could love her and grieve for her. I could find compassion for Dorothy without blaming myself for not being a better daughter, without having to be the keeper of her memory anymore. The truth, at least as I grasped it theoretically, was that what happened to her wasn't and isn't my truth. But forgiveness of self would require much more work. How to cut myself some slack?

Some days I was ready to return, other days I couldn't imagine leaving that place, asking myself—where was that fearless person willing to risk all to love and be loved when deciding to have hyperhidrosis surgery? Where was that nine-year-old girl who got on a bus alone, with no guarantees whatsoever? Not here.

It was LaTanya who came to visit me at the convent, spiritually tuned in to my despair, determined not to allow me to be left alone in the dark. With the light she brought, the dark disappeared. Her voice soothed a weak heart.

You measure up, LaTanya insisted. *You count.*

Taking my callused feet in her cocoa butter hands, she massaged love into those frayed nerve endings of toes that I didn't think would ever dance again, let alone walk out the door to go home.

A woman whose word is her life, LaTanya promised me something, placing a cloak of protection around me by letting me know that I could rest at her house for as long as I chose. That she would feed me and look after me. Because sometimes sisters need to be mothers.

"What do you mean?"

"What I mean is that you will walk out of here, and you don't have to do it alone, anymore. I am going to adopt you." She looked at me intently and waited to make sure that I knew what she had just said.

Of course, I did.

This symbolic adoption when I was forty-three years old was the ultimate gift that anyone had ever given to me.

Worth every second of the wait, it couldn't have come any earlier or I would have missed out on all the women who raised me, all of whom, living and not, sent me waves of hope and strength to follow their lead and to now become one of them.

TWELVE

VICKI LYNN BEVAN SAWYER COLLINS ROWELL

Without conscious decision, I began writing *The Women Who Raised Me* in diaries and on notepads in pubs and on planes dating back to 1975. It was during that time of self-discovery that I began documenting my life and those who had influenced it. The art of correspondence has always been a lifeline for me, and it continues to be today. For the price of a postage stamp, my grandmothers, mothers, aunts, mentors, fosterers, grande dames, and sisters always found me; their steadfast voices carried and delivered through letters. My nomadic life always made my entry in their neat and organized telephone books a mess of scratched out addresses, but they never gave up searching for me or believing that I was worth finding. Each letter contains its own brand of wisdom and guidance, love and faith, history, honesty, and sometimes sorrow. I preserved every letter and every envelope that I could; each woman's penmanship permanently imprinted on my memory. I took their letters with me wherever I moved, like necessary articles of clothing. The words, scribed by my life teachers, were words I attempted to live by; in that way, I returned to the women, some posthumously, whenever I needed advice or simply wanted to remember joy.

At long last, I acquired my first home at the age of thirty-seven. I always believed it was possible, even if it was a photograph that I kept in my wallet for inspiration. During the year that I formerly began writing my memoir, I embarked on another long term goal—transforming my house into a homestead, eight years spent making it something that was authentically me, yet possessing all the influences of *The Women Who Raised Me*.

This required everything I was ever taught. The process also meant that I had to return to the root of my being and in doing so, pass it on to my loving children, Maya and Jasper. Many months into construction, I realized that we could no longer live in our house. I moved my family into a one-room bed-and-breakfast space that had just enough room for my two children and our leopard gecko lizard, Yellow. It was there that I taught my children about minimalism, that space, no matter how small, was big enough. That room became a gift, and maintaining it with integrity, their responsibility. I promised them that the rewards, born out of our adventure and patience would be great. Eights months later, we emerged victorious, and moved back into our 1923 home with profound gratitude.

I began the laborious and emotional task of unpacking boxes that had been sealed for many years along with forgotten memories and the energy of treasured belongings. Yet, I was excited, because for the first time, I had a place to put on display, my life and the people who breathed selflessly into it. This cathartic process gave me the vision I needed for my book. It crystallized the simple truth I had already been taught by so many mentors, that when we unearth, look just beneath the surface, "bend at the hip," go the extra mile, get on our hands and knees to give thanks and praise, we will discover our naked dreams waiting to be realized.

One of the most difficult parts of writing this book was having to go deep and remember each and every one of the women and our relationships. To say it was an emotional experience would be an understatement. Sharing what had sustained me for so many years was yet another hurdle I had to overcome. The best part about writing my story was also what made it as difficult—the visits, the letters, the photographs, the articles of clothing still holding a scent. With the support of many women and some very special men, I was able to responsibly take the necessary steps to honestly write this book. I passionately believe that what I shared with these women could inspire others to adopt, foster, or mentor themselves, and gently challenge all students everywhere to reach out to their perspective and beloved teachers and thank them for recognizing and fostering the tiniest of flames we all are born with.

As I organized my "ephemera," I found that my memory of scenarios was very accurate and much better than I had thought. I rediscovered many treasures throughout my research, and I recommend this search for anyone wanting to write a life story. Physical history conjures up memories and instigates, assists, and inspires thought.

Some of my most favorite mementos include an early American cut crystal vase Agatha loved and used for special occasions; she believed that her prized possessions should be used and not left on a shelf to be admired. I found an array of books over the years at garage sales and used book stores across America and even one in Capri, Italy, titled, *John Sargent* by The Hon. Evan Charteris, K.C., published in 1927. Other books include, *Days with Ulanova: A Unique Pictorial Portrait of the Great Russian Ballerina* signed by Albert E. Kahn, published in 1962; *Pictorial History of Television* by Daniel Blum; *Lil Gal* by poet Paul Laurence Dunbar, illustrated by Leigh Richmond Miner of the Hampton Institute Camera Club in 1904; and a 1927 publication of *The Complete Poems of Paul Laurence Dunbar,* two of my favorite poetry books. Yes, the Internet is a peerless reference bank, but I love using a good old-fashioned dictionary. So, I turned to my 1967 *Funk & Wagnalls Dictionary,* my *Yankee Dictionary* by Charles F. Haywood, and my *Technical Manual and Dictionary of Classical Ballet* by Gail Grant. In total, I relied on more than forty reference books, and research trips to Maine, Massachusetts, and New York. Other treasures include my coin collection, Booker T. Washington's coin being one of my favorites, and a 1929 silver dollar my brother David mounted in my 1929 Ford which I still drive. I cherish the Eleanor Roosevelt antislavery envelope I received from a woman who thought I would appreciate it. A perfect stranger. A perfect act of giving and mentoring. Lastly, two Coalport cups and saucers, elite-platinum pattern, that I received as a gift from a former employer in New York City nearly three decades ago. I make a point of drinking out of one of those cups every morning, so never to forget working for $100 a month.

I grew up loving photography, realizing the power of photojournalism. Through Agatha's tutelage, I was introduced to a way of seeing my life differently—an adventure—a miracle rather than an obstacle. I came to understand that I could see my world with one eye open while the other was shut. I chose not to wait, instead empowered myself, took responsibility, documented my own living history. There it was, blurry at first then coming into focus—my life. I took pictures and still do of everything; culinary design, faces, landscapes, architecture, hands, feet, pictures of pictures—nothing was or is exempt—resulting in a robust personal archive spanning more than thirty years of images. The landscape of Mother Earth is my church. Everything is worth photographing. I was taught that I didn't need a Hassleblad to snap off a shot. A Polaroid, a disposable camera, or whatever you have is all you need. Just take the picture. The perfect photograph in my opinion embodies lighting, imagination, timing, and passion—poetry frozen in an image—the light and darkness of life. The honesty. The composition need not be staged but shot in real time. Some of my favorite photographers include James VanDerZee, Sheila Metzner, Ansel Adams, Jacques Henri Lartigue, Howard Bingham, Carol Friedman, and Gordon Parks.

I appreciate my special relationship with the Hollywood press core. So many of you have shown up over the years to support foster and adopted children when perhaps glossy events were going on simultaneously across town.

A special thank you:

Dear Arnold Turner,
We have traveled thousands and thousands of miles together over the years, advocating in support of fine arts, foster care, and adoption.

Never once did you complain, always focused on what we knew we had to do—getting the shot and getting the word out through photography. Whether it was on Capitol Hill with the Congressional Coalition on Adoption Institute or in New York City with Americans for the Arts and Aretha Franklin or The House of Blues Foundation Room in Los Angeles for the Rowell Foster Children's Positive Plan Annual Christmas Party or even a simple gathering in my home, it was never too small for your calendar. You have always remained connected to all that matters. Thank you from the bottom of my heart.

Knowing that some of my mothers and mentors were frail and elderly, I, with the assistance of Richard Armstead, began amassing interviews and photographs in the early 1980s. In 1990 I enlisted the photographic expertise of respected photographer, Robert Hale. At the dawn of the new millennium, we began an ambitious East Coast shoot tour. Many of the portraits featured in *The Women Who Raised Me* were beautifully shot by Robert Hale who resides in France and New York City.

I have long relied on my library of new and used books and always found fascinating histories, quotes, and snippets from magazine articles, not all of which I could fit into this book. *The Ladies of the White House, or In The Home of the Presidents,* written by Laura C. Holloway, published in Philadelphia by Bradley and Company in 1881, tells a harrowing story of the fourteenth First Lady, Mrs. Jane Abigail Pierce, wife of President Franklin Pierce. I was struck by her strength and resilience after losing her thirteen-year-old son in a tragic Boston & Maine Railroad train wreck. Early on, I included Mrs. Pierce in my contemporary gallery of strong women who influenced me, who endured in the face of the tremendous loss of a son, Agatha, Kay, Barbara, Sylvia, Francine, Gayle, and Little Joanie.

Another treasure is a book titled *The Mothers of Maine,* published by the Thurston Print in 1895, that tells the stories of so many strong pioneering women of the fourteenth state in the Union. One of my most coveted treasures of all is my archive of more than 500 cards and letters from the women who raised me. One that stands out for me is from Agatha.

June 18, 1981

Hi Vicki,

It was so nice hearing from you, where are you? It sounded so far away. Were you visiting a farm? . . . They always say buy a woodlot next to your house so that you will have plenty of logs if you have a fireplace. That's all Auntie Kay used for heating last winter . . . I see you remember gardening. You talk about your radishes that look like 'zip in distress,' you should see Peter's okra. The stems look like stings . . . I wish them well. I really miss the garden . . . You should have felt the heat here last week. It was so hot you could hardly breathe. The humidity was terribly high. For contrast, Aunt Ruth says it was cold on the Cape . . . I was very happy you heard from your brothers. Lori was pleased too. Your mother got your Aunt Lillian to write me which she did. I heard from your mother this morning. She says you and Sheree want to pay her a visit. Forget it. Her sister Lillian will not allow it (quote): Lil doesn't want the girls coming here to her apartment. Says it will only cause talk all over again like in years past (unquote). Your mother feels sad. Says if she could travel she would come to see you. She said after David got in touch with you, he called her after 22 yrs. She was so happy to see him. I wish there was some way you all could get together for a family reunion. Your mother must be terribly lonely.

I sent you scapulars blest by Fr. Crowley. I bought those. We all wear ours all the time as the Virgin Mary suggests. I hope you finish your book. I hope your play is doing well. Write and tell me all about it . . .

Your loving Mother

oooxxx

I come away from writing about my life experience with infinite gratitude and renewed strength—grateful for everything that was realized and denied. Rising above crushing disappointments and holding on to hope and the ambition to succeed against all odds.

Take caution before writing about your journey and be fortified in every way, mentally, physically, and spiritually so that you may best navigate a most emotional and arduous undertaking, requiring a true reconciliation with the past and a dependable support team.

A single idea was fostered and each mother took the baton passing it on to the next. In addition to all of the women mentioned in my book, there are many others including my first grade teacher, Mrs. Race, my third grade teacher, Mrs. Chambers, and Mrs. Edith Sanders, who took me to the Table Talk Pie factory weekly to get fresh miniature pies. All of these women made an indelible impression upon me: my first big sister at St. Patrick's, Miriam Toppin-Banks, and the dancer/actor brigade in New York City who slugged it out with me, Merle Holloman, Colleen O'Callaghan, Megan Murphy-Matheson, Jennifer Douglas, Susan Jaffe, Kimberly Von Brandenstein Stone, Lisa Headley, Joselyn Lorenz, LaChanze, Kiki Shepard, and Julie Satterfield-Auerbach. The whole team at *Seventeen* magazine that kept me employed in the seventies. Inez Liben, Mae Questel, Stacey Muller, Mrs. Gloria Smart, and Karen Broduer who gave me conversation, a cup of coffee, and a shoulder to rest on, thank you.

To my Los Angeles sisters, Madisonn McBride, Brenda Epperson-Moore, Lisa Quercioli, and Nancy Martinez-Morrison—thank you for always, always having my back. Dr. Tracey Jayne Fein, M.D., who brought my first born into the world and my childhood friend, Dr. Laura Riley Henderson, M.D., who proved that the power of studying classical ballet goes way beyond a simple plié.

This book would not have been possible if it were not for the remarkable patience and good humor of my children, Maya and Jasper, and their fathers, Tom and Wynton. I love you all. To my personal assistant, sister, and spiritual guide, Manuela Menz Hesslup, thank you for the hours of loving support you showed to my children and me and for all of the heartfelt prayers you showered upon us. Never was there a moment I couldn't lean into your strength to finish this memoir.

Not overnight, but soon, I returned to a life whole—not perfect, but victorious in having done the work—thanks to the gentle intercession of my sisters, work I previously had no idea how to approach. At forty-three, I was truly emancipated and began living my powerful life—free in the best sense of the word.

Often, multiple creative undertakings as well as personal ones oc-
cupy the space and time of so many of the women I know. We have
to pause and breathe and remember that we are powerful works in
progress—and that we are enough just the way we are.

In the deluge of memories through which I have been rummaging
in my basement and other places to tell my story, one common observation best describes all of the women who raised me—none of them
wasted time or energy. Each tackled the day before them as though it
were their last. Every vestige of everything was utilized—even the
marrow in a bone. Agatha always said, "It's the most important part."

Whatever the circumstances of my life, I own them completely and
have lived through them to tell you my story.

To those suffering from addictions, mental and physical illnesses,
all foster youth, foster adults, orphans, those who have been adopted
and God's older children—the elderly:

> In every child who is born under no matter what circumstances
> and of no matter what parents, the potentiality of the human race
> is born again, and in him, too, once more, and each of us, our ter-
> rific responsibility toward human life: toward the utmost idea of
> goodness . . .
>
> —James Agee

I was born with no prenatal care and in quarantine because my mother,
Dorothy, was so ill and filthy. How we all get here is an absolute
miracle and what we do with that miracle as individuals in our brief
lifetime is a universal privilege. I love my mother because in spite of
her inner struggle she gave me the ultimate gift—life!

> ". . . Nature in casual bounty to women sends into the world as
> patient listeners."
>
> —Douglas Jerrold
> *Mother of Maine,* 1895

GRATITUDES

For my friend, mentor, teacher and sister, Mim Eichler Rivas, I hold a special place of gratitude. I thank you on behalf of all of the women who raised me for taking me under your steady wing and by my hand, for putting the pen between my uncertain fingers and patiently encouraging me to fly and to trust my own writing, a gift of a lifetime. There is no better teacher or more generous soul. I thank you—we all thank you.

I would like to thank my literary agent, Elizabeth Kaplan, for believing in me and taking the time to teach, listen, and deliver my truth into the best hands of my editor, Henry Ferris at HarperCollins/William Morrow.

Dear Henry,
Thank you for all of your patience and enthusiasm over The Women Who Raised Me. *Thank you for teaching me as we went along, lifting me when I was exhausted. Thank you for designing such a beautiful cover (bet you didn't know that blue was the color for National Foster Care Month). It has been a rare and remarkable experience for me and I am honored that you made it so special.*

Love,
Vicki

Thank you Salvation Army, Morgan Memorials. Bobby from Boston and every mom and pop antique shop across the nation for supporting the resale of used furniture clothing and books. If it were not for your commitment to community and literacy, I never could have afforded myself the luxury of a desk and chair in my youth and an extended education.

I would like to pay special tribute to William J. Bell. When I arrived in Los Angeles in 1990, uncertain, with an infant daughter, one man made all the difference. I will forever remember Bill Bell for his loving kindness and generosity. Bill Bell and his wife, Lee Phillip-Bell, supported my work on and off Stage 41 and 43 at CBS Television City, sponsoring productions of The Rowell Foster Children's Positive Plan on more than one occasion to ensure its success. I thank his sister Mary and will always remember the story he shared with me about his beloved mother, Gertrude "Trudy" Bell, and her commitment to adoption. Thank you Dick Van Dyke, Fred Silverman, Dean Hargrove, and Perry Simon, and Viacom for writing scripts that authentically reflected the challenges that foster children face and giving me my first theatrical writing assignment, allowing me to join the Writers Guild of America. Thank you Viacom and Paul Mason for hiring older emancipated foster youth as production assistants on the production of *Diagnosis Murder*, and lastly for giving me the opportunity to work with so many legendary actors, one of whom was the late Steve Allen. We talked and exchanged music information. Later, Mr. Allen sent me a complete set of his musical compositions. Another treasure.

In closing I wish to extend special thanks to where it all began, in a barn in Maine. Thank you National Endowment for the Arts and The Ford Foundation for making this dream of mine possible with the support of Esther Brooks. The scholarship support went a long way! American Ballet Theatre School, American Ballet Theatre II, Ballet Hispanico, Arthur Mitchell, and School of American Ballet, thank you for the education of a lifetime! Julliard—thank you for introducing me to a man who became a friend, the incomparable Anthony Tudor. Thank you Americans for the Arts for keeping America on pointe, reminding a nation that Louis Armstrong was not the first man on the moon. Thank you the United States Conference of Mayors and your commitment to children and art, believing that Art Saves Lives. Thank you Lebanon Historical Society, Wilson's Publishing in Sanford, Maine. Thank you Veronica Nichols for all of your assistance.

Thank you Margie Cortez for helping me keep all the balls in the air, for being a no-matter-what friend, and a corporate thinker. You are one of the best people I have ever met in my life.

The Women Who Raised Me is a quilt and each woman gave me a piece of herself to sew together, to make me whole.

RESOURCES

The Alliance for Children's Rights—*protecting the rights and future of abused and impoverished children throughout Los Angeles County.*
www.kids-alliance.org

3333 Wilshire Boulevard, Suite 550
Los Angeles, CA 90010-4111
Phone: 213-368-6010
Fax: 213-368-6016

American Ballet Theatre—*dedicated, passionate people who come together to make sure that commitment to the best in dance and movement is upheld and available to all who seek it out.*
www.abt.org

Kevin McKenzie, artistic director
Rachel S. Moore, executive director
890 Broadway
New York, NY 10003
Phone: 212-477-3030
Fax: 212-254-5938

American Ballet Theatre Scholarship Fund—John Banta

AMERICANS FOR THE ARTS—*dedicated to representing and serving local communities and creating opportunities for every American to participate in and appreciate all forms of the arts.*
www.artsusa.org

Robert L. Lynch, president and CEO
1000 Vermont Avenue, NW
6th Floor
Washington, D.C. 20005
Phone: 202-371-2830
Fax: 202-371-0424

THE ANNIE E. CASEY FOUNDATION—*to foster public policies, human service reforms, and community supports that more effectively meet the needs of today's vulnerable children and families.*
www.aecf.org

Douglas Nelson, president
701 St. Paul Street
Baltimore, MD 21202
info@aecf.org
Phone: 410-547-6600

CASEY FAMILY SERVICES—*the direct service agency of the Annie E. Casey Foundation.*
www.caseyfamilyservices.org

Raymond L. Torres, executive director
Lee Mullane, communications director
127 Church Street
New Haven, CT 06510
info@caseyfamilyservices.org
Phone: 203-401-6900

ANTI SELF-DESTRUCTION INC.—*to assist youth in making the transition from adolescence to adulthood.*
www.antiselfdestruction.org

821 Centinela Avenue, Suite #8
Inglewood, CA 90302
adinc7@earthlink.net
Phone/Fax: 310-672-6694

CALIFORNIA YOUTH CONNECTION—*promotes the participation of foster youth in policy development and legislative change to improve the foster care system.*
www.calyouthconn.org

CYC Statewide Office
604 Mission Street, 9th Floor
San Francisco, CA 94105
Toll free: 800-397-8236
Phone: 415-442-5060
Fax: 415-442-0720

CYC Southern Regional Office
The Pacific Center
523 West 6th Street, # 365
Los Angeles, CA 90014
Phone: 213-489-0720
Fax: 213-489-0620

CYC Northern Regional Office
1650 Oregon Street
Redding, CA 96001
Phone: 530-243-8450
Fax: 530-243-8650

CASEY FAMILY PROGRAMS—*to provide and improve—and ultimately to prevent the need for—foster care*
www.casey.org

William C. Bell, president and CEO
1300 Dexter Avenue North, Floor 3
Seattle, WA 98109-3542
contactus@casey.org
Phone: 206-282-7300

CHILD WELFARE LEAGUE OF AMERICA—*an association of nearly 800 public and private nonprofit agencies that assist more than 3.5 million abused and neglected children and their families each year with a range of services.*
www.cwla.org

Headquarters
Shay Bilchik, president and CEO
440 First Street, NW, Third Floor
Washington, D.C. 20001-2085
Phone: 202-638-2952
Fax: 202-638-4004

CHILDREN'S LAW CENTER OF LOS ANGELES—*created over a decade ago to serve as appointed counsel for children who have been abused, neglected, or abandoned.*
www.clcla.org

201 Centre Plaza Drive, Suite 10
Monterey Park, CA 91754-2178
Phone: 323-980-1700
Fax: 323-980-1708

CONGRESSIONAL COALITION ON ADOPTION INSTITUTE (CCAI)—*dedicated to raising awareness about the tens of thousands of orphans and foster children in the United States and the millions of orphans around the world in need of permanent, safe, and loving homes through adoption; and to eliminating the barriers that hinder these children from realizing their basic right of a family.*
www.ccainstitute.org

Deanna Carlson Stacy, executive director
6723 Whittier Ave, Suite 406
McLean, VA 22101
info@ccainstitute.org
Phone: 703-288-9700
Fax: 703-288-0999

THE DAVID AND MARGARET HOME—*a refuge for children in need.*
www.dmhome.org

1350 Third Street
La Verne, CA 91750
Information@DMHome.Org
Phone: 909-596-5921
Fax: 909-596-3954

DCFS—LOS ANGELES COUNTY DEPARTMENT OF CHILDREN AND FAMILY
SERVICES—*with community partners, provides a comprehensive child protection system of prevention, preservation, and permanency to ensure that children grow up safe, physically and emotionally healthy, educated, and in permanent homes.*
http://dcfs.co.la.ca.us

Patricia S. Ploehn, LCSW, executive director
425 Shatto Place
Los Angeles, CA 90020
Headquarters' receptionist: 213-351-5507
Public info line: 213-351-5602

EVAN B. DONALDSON ADOPTION INSTITUTE—*to provide leadership that improves adoption laws, policies, and practices—through sound research, education, and advocacy—in order to better the lives of everyone touched by adoption.*
www.adoptioninstitute.org

Adam Pertman, executive director
56 Hartford Street
Newton, MA 02461
info@adoptioninstitute.org
Phone: 617-332-8944
Fax: 775-796-6592

FOSTER CARE ALUMNI OF AMERICA—*the only national organization that provides opportunities for alumni of foster care to join together and to use their experiences and power to effect positive change.*
www.fostercarealumni.org

Nathan Monell, executive director
118 South Royal Street
2nd Floor

Alexandria, VA 22314
admin@fostercarealumni.org
Phone: 703-299-6767

FREDDIE MAC FOUNDATION—*creating hope and opportunity for children and their families.*
www.freddiemacfoundation.org

Maxine Baker, president and CEO
Renette Oklewicz, manager Foster Care Programs
8250 Jones Branch Drive
Mailstop A40
McLean, VA 22102
Freddiemac_foundation@freddiemac.com
Phone: 703-918-8888
Fax: 703-918-8895

GINA ALEXANDER PHILANTHROPY PROJECT (GAPP)
www.ginaalexander.com/philanthropy.htm

Gina Alexander, executive director
P.O. Box 1919
Burbank, CA 91507-1919
gina@ginaalexander.com
Phone: 818-843-2562
Fax: 818-843-7311

HARLEM DOWLING-WEST SIDE CENTER—*a multiservice agency providing out-of-home foster care, adoption, therapeutic placement, supportive housing for youth aging out of foster care, and other support services.*
www.harlemdowling.org

Administrative Offices
2090 Adam Clayton Powell Jr., Blvd.
New York, NY 10027
Phone: 212-749-3656
Fax: 212-678-1094

Harvard School of Public Health—Center for Health Communication—*researching and analyzing the contributions of mass communication to behavior change and policy by preparing future health leaders to utilize communication strategies, and by strengthening communication between journalists and health professionals.*
www.hsph.harvard.edu/chc/

Center for Health Communication
Harvard School of Public Health
677 Huntington Avenue
Boston, MA 02115
chc@hsph.harvard.edu
Phone: 617-432-1038
Fax: 617-731-8184

Who Mentored You—*thank them, and pass it on . . . mentor a child!*
www.WhoMentoredYou.org

Heart Gallery—*there are more than sixty throughout the United States; they feature photographs of children waiting to be adopted.*
www.heartgallerynj.com
www.bayareaheartgallery.com
www.freddiemacfoundation.org/heartgallery/
www.heartgallerynyc.org

Hope Worldwide—*bringing hope and changing lives.*
www.hopeww.org

Robert Gempel, president and CEO
353 West Lancaster Avenue, Suite 200
Wayne, PA 19087
hope_worldwide@hopeww.org
Phone: 610-254-8800
Fax: 610-254-8989

HOLY NAME—SISTERS OF CHARITY—Dolores Marsalis

INSTITUTE FOR BLACK PARENTING—*resources for foster care and adoption.*
www.instituteforblackparenting.org

> Cynthia M. Willard, LCSW, assistant executive director
> 11222 So. La Cienega Blvd., Suite 233
> Inglewood, CA 90304
> Toll-free: 877-367-8858
> Phone: 310-693-9959
> Fax: 310-693-9979

JENESSE CENTER—*domestic violence intervention program in South Central Los Angeles.*
www.jenesse.org

> Karen Earl, executive director
> PO Box 8476
> Los Angeles, CA 90008
> 24-Hour Hotline: 1-800-479-7328
> Phone: 323-299-9496
> Fax: 323-299-0699

JIM CASEY YOUTH OPPORTUNITIES INITIATIVE—*helping youth in foster care make successful transitions to adulthood.*
www.jimcaseyyouth.org

> Gary J. Stangler, executive director
> 222 South Central, Suite 305
> St. Louis, MO 63105
> info@jimcaseyyouth.org
> Phone: 314-863-7000
> Fax: 314-863-7003

KINGSLEY HOUSE IN NEW ORLEANS—*serving the children and families of New Orleans through times of dramatic change.*
www.kingsleyhouse.org

Keith Leiderman, executive director
1600 Constance St.
New Orleans, LA 70130
khinfo@kingsleyhouse.org
Phone: 504-523-6221
Fax: 504-523-4450

MENTOR/NATIONAL MENTORING PARTNERSHIP—*working to expand the world of quality mentoring.*
www.mentoring.org

1600 Duke Street, Suite 300
Alexandria, VA 22314
Phone: 703-224-2200

MENTOR LA—*improving schools and empowering neighborhoods in some of the most disenfranchised communities in Los Angeles.*
www.mentorla.org

837 Traction Avenue, Suite 403
Los Angeles, CA 90013
Phone: 213-455-1325

NATIONAL ADOPTION DAY—*a collective national effort to raise awareness of the 114,000 children in foster care waiting to find permanent, loving families.*
www.nationaladoptionday.org

NATIONAL CASA ASSOCIATION—COURT APPOINTED SPECIAL ADVOCATES FOR CHILDREN
www.nationalcasa.org

100 W. Harrison
North Tower, Suite 500
Seattle, WA 98119
Phone: 800-628-3233

NATIONAL FOSTER CARE MONTH—*May, National Foster Care Month, will serve as a platform for connecting more of these vulnerable children to concerned, nurturing adults who, no matter how much time they have to give, can do something that will "Change a Lifetime" for a young person in foster care.*
www.fostercaremonth.org

NATIONAL FOSTER PARENT ASSOCIATION
www.nfpainc.org

Karen Jorgensen, MA executive director
7512 Stanich Lane, #6
Gig Harbor, WA 98335
Phone: 253-853-4000 or 800-557-5238
Fax: 253-853-4001

NEW HAMPSHIRE CHILD AND FAMILY SERVICES—*dedicated to advancing the well-being of children by providing an array of social services to strengthen family life and by promoting community commitment to the needs of children.*
www.cfsnh.org

Manchester Office
Statewide Headquarters
99 Hanover St.
Manchester, NH 03105
info@cfsnh.org
Phone: 800-640-6486 or 603-518-4000
Fax: 603-668-6260

NEW JERSEY MENTAL HEALTH INSTITUTE—*to promote quality mental health services through training, technical assistance, research, policy development, and anti-stigma and anti-discrimination campaigns.*
www.njmhi.org

The Neuman Building
3575 Quakerbridge Road
Suite 102
Mercerville, NJ 08619

Phone: 609-838-5488
Fax: 609-838-5480

ST. ANNE'S—*one of Southern California's most highly regarded social service agencies confronting the issues of teen pregnancy and parenting.*
www.stannes.org

155 N. Occidental Boulevard
Los Angeles, CA 90026
stannes@stannes.org
Phone: 213-381-2931

SAVE AFRICA'S CHILDREN—*an African-American founded organization, providing direct support to children affected by HIV/AIDS, poverty, and war throughout subsaharan Africa.*
www.saveafricaschildren.com

Post Office Box 8386
Los Angeles, CA 90008
info@saveafricaschildren.org
Toll-free: 866-313-2722
Local L.A. area: 323-733-1048
Fax: 323-735-1141

SAVE THE CHILDREN—*making positive lasting change in the lives of children in need in the U.S. and around the world.*
www.savethechildren.org

United States Headquarters
54 Wilton Road
Westport, CT 06880
twebster@savechildren.org
Phone: 203-221-4030 (8:00AM–5:00PM EDT)
800-728-3843 (8:00AM–5:00PM EDT)

Washington, D.C.
2000 M Street NW

Suite 500
Washington, D.C. 20036
Phone: 202-293-4170 (8:00AM–5:00PM EDT)

SUPREME COURT, STATE OF ARIZONA, CHILDREN AND FAMILY ISSUES
www.supreme.state.az.us/nav2/childfam.htm

ARIZONA CASA PROGRAM
www.azcasa.org

Bonnie Marcus, program manager
dedavis@courts.az.gov
Phone: 602-452-3407

UNITED CARE—*foster family agency and group homes.*
www.unitedcareinc.org

Pamela Norris-Woods, MSC, administrator
Foster Family Agency
3699 Crenshaw Blvd.
Los Angeles, CA 90016
Phone: 323-508-0200
Fax: 323-296-2440
Toll-free: 888-905-KIDS

VOLUNTEERMATCH—*connecting good people with good causes.*
www.volunteermatch.org

385 Grove Street
San Francisco, CA 94102
support@volunteermatch.org
Phone: 415-241-6868
Fax: 415-241-6869

WORKPLACE HOLLYWOOD—*assisting candidates with employment in the entertainment industry.*
www.workplacehollywood.org

Jaleesa Hazzard, executive director
1201 W. 5th Street, Suite T-550
Los Angeles, CA 90017
Phone: 213-250-9921 ext. 101
Fax: 213-250-9092

For information about hyperhidrosis visit www.hyperhidrosis.org.